Topics in Mathematics for the Twelfth Grade
Based on teaching practices in Waldorf schools

Topics in Mathematics for the Twelfth Grade

Based on teaching practices in Waldorf schools

Differential and Integral Calculus

Peter Baum, Uwe Hansen, Detlef Hardorp, Walter Hutter,
Klaus Labudde, Rolf Rosbigalle, Stephan Sigler
Editor: Robert Neumann

Published by the Lesson Plan Initiative of the Pedagogical Research Center in Kassel
in cooperation with
Waldorf Publications and the Research Institute for Waldorf Education
Printed with the support of the Waldorf Curriculum Fund

www.lehrerseminar-forschung.de
www.waldorfbuch.de
www.waldorfpublications.org

Impressum

All portions of this book are protected by copyright. All rights reserved, in particular the rights to translate the material, and the rights to any form of reproduction or even partial reproduction in any way. The translation has not been revised by the authors.

© Bildungswerk Beruf und Umwelt

1. Edition (Version 2.0)
Reprinted 1-10-2016
Typesetting: Robert Neumann, Freiburg
Printed by Waldorf Publications

Contents

Part 1 Teaching Methodology   **10**

Teaching Mathematics: Some Basic Ideas
    (ROLF ROSBIGALLE) 10

Experiential connection, judgement and concept in the mathematics lesson
    (STEPHAN SIGLER) 19

The higher Senses
    (KLAUS LABUDDE) 28

Part 2 The Infinitesimal Calculus   **32**

The Mathematical as Bridge to the Spiritual
    (UWE HANSEN) 32

Teaching th Concept of Infinity
    (PETER BAUM) 46

The meaning of the infinitesimal calculus
    (WALTER HUTTER) 71

Thinking in processes and threshold experiences in 12th Grade mathematics
    (DETLEF HARDORP) 89

Developing the concept of number from the 1st to the 12th grade
    (KLAUS LABUDDE) 108

Part 3 Teaching know how   **115**

Introducing the Derivative
    (UWE HANSEN) 115

The differential quotient as a numerical phenomenon
    (WALTER HUTTER) 131

Discussing extreme values
    (UWE HANSEN) 163

The integral as an expression of "$\infty \cdot 0$"
    (WALTER HUTTER) 167

A note about integration
    (UWE HANSEN) 187

Preface

The *Zentralabitur*, the centrally set school-leaving and university entrance exam introduced all but nationwide in Germany, confronts the upper High School of Waldorf Schools there with new challenges. For one thing there is the question of whether all individual focus of the setting of the exams as regards content must as a result fall victim to the sheer size of the usually very extensive syllabus. For another, a trend in the central exams towards questions oriented to applications and mathematical modelling has caught on which needs to be judged with pedagogic sophistication. These articles will nevertheless suggest in-depth treatment of corresponding themes at first *without* regard to any exams, so that one can gage the themes' educational value and find ways of making them accessible to the pupils.

This volume, with the differential and integral calculi as its main theme, is the first of a series of three on teaching mathematics to the 12th Grade which continues in volume two with a detailed commentary on the Main Lesson blocks and concludes with a third volume on geometry. All volumes are the result of many years work of a group of experienced colleagues who have met within the framework of the Pedagogical Research Center in Kassel some four times a year and discussed and debated critically the individual contributions that appear so that varied points of view could flow together in the articles. Ultimately however each author him- or herself is responsible for his or her article. The series follows the Curriculum Initiative's publications for the Ninth, Tenth and Eleventh Grades.

The articles on the differential and integral calculi in the present volume are complemented by more general thoughts on the methodology of teaching math, on the one hand dealing with the philosophical backgrounds of the topic areas, on the other with practical methodology and teaching guidance.

Rudolf Steiner does not make it easy for the Waldorf teacher in that he called for the differential coefficient to be developed purely numerically. This he did in the Teachers' Conference of 30 April 1924[1]:

> I do not consider that it is advantageous for mathematical education in general for differential and integral calculus to be linked to geometry, but to be linked to quotients. I would start from the calculus of differences, that is from
>
> $$\frac{\Delta y}{\Delta x},$$
>
> regarding this as a quotient and, merely through the dividend and divisor becoming smaller and smaller, purely out of number, I would proceed to develop the differential coefficient. I would not start from this continuity relationship, from that you get no

---
[1] R. Steiner (1975): *Konferenzen mit den Lehrern der Freien Waldorfschule in Stuttgart* [*Conferences with the teachers of the Free Waldorf School in Stuttgart*], Dornach, p. 154.

concept of the differential coefficient; I would not start from the differential but from the differential coefficient. If you start from series, then you should only go over to geometry finally with the tangent problem, i.e. pass from the secant to the tangent. And when the differential coefficient is properly grasped purely numerically, purely as calculation, only then pass on to the geometrical domain so that the pupil comes to understand that the geometrical is only an illustration of the numerical. You then get integrals as the reverse process. Doing it this way you can start *not* from the calculus as a fixing of geometry, but from geometry as an illustration of the calculus.

One aspect of this suggestion is undoubtedly that infinite processes should be considered and thought through *without* the support of a pictorial image. This is all about a pure and appropriate method of contemplation that does not borrow from another domain – geometry – but has got to become clear entirely out of itself. This goes strongly against the current trend of thought that *visualizes* every arithmetic or algebraic phenomenon almost without exception, and often tries to grant this visualization the character of an explanation. On the other hand it is pleasing to see in the latest pedagogic literature once again viewpoints that do *not* introduce the differential coefficient as the gradient of a tangent, on the grounds that the latter is not an intrinsic part of the concept.[2]

If we follow Steiner's suggestion, questions of epistemology and mathematical philosophy about limit processes and the "infinitely small" associated with Leibnitz and Newton arise immediately. These are questions which have characterized debate of the last 300 years down to questions about for example Cantor's set theory and the infinitesimals of non-standard analysis. Even to such questions the teacher needs to a certain degree to arrive at his or her own point of view, if he wants to produce an atmosphere in the classroom permitting the construction of appropriate and living concepts! In this respect the articles are intended on the one hand as a direct help for the teacher, but on the other to encourage his own research activity.

S. Sigler

---

[2] See for example Danckwerts, R., Vogel, D. (2006): *Analysis verständlich unterrichten* [*Teaching analysis intelligibly*], München, p. 45 ff.

Preface to the English Edition

The 12th Grade is, with few exceptions, the final year of the Waldorf school, and represents a culmination of what has been learned in the preceding years. The 12th grade curriculum is accordingly demanding. Teaching the differential calculus especially presents challenges for a teacher who chooses not to follow the traditional, ostensibly intuitive, approach based on the slope of the tangent line. Other ways to approach this important theme appear in several of the included articles. We hope that this volume can offer fresh encouragement to all teachers. Special thanks go to the translators, Paul Courtney and Charles Gunn; to Bob Dell'Oliver for proofreading, and to those who funded the translation, the Pädagogische Forschungsstelle in Kassel and the Association of Waldorf Schools of North America.

Here we want to acknowledge the special role played by David Mitchell († 2012) of AWSNA in the creation of these translations, it always having been a concern of his to make the available literature in German accessible also to English-speaking colleagues.

Robert Neumann, October 2015.

Teaching Mathematics: Some Basic Ideas

Facts, suggestions and hints from practical experience

ROLF ROSBIGALLE

Introduction

Methods of teaching have been under scrutiny ever since there have been schools. A great variety of possibilities has been tried and tested over the years. With abundance came an agony of choice. Every few decades a different teaching method would be favored, or even proclaimed as the solution to the problem. It is important to be conscious of the fact that not each and every one of these methods is suitable for developing competency. To put it positively: In education a method has to be found that is able truly to develop just this competency. This method is independent of fashion and is only conceived through a thorough study of the human being in his/her learning environment.

Added to this is the didactic working-through of topics, i.e. the preparation of the subject matter in a manner that is intelligible – even if of no interest (!) – to the pupil.

Another area, polar opposite to yet closely intertwined in the process of learning has to do with human interaction, quite independently of the subject matter. This interaction determines the success and long-term outcome of learning, as well as the ability of the young person to go through life without shame, emotional hurt or stigma.

These prerequisites for learning seem obvious. There would be no need for structured teacher training if applying them were as obvious.

1 Doing mathematics

When dealing with the schooling of mathematics *per se* – not just in the high school but starting already in the upper middle school – it is important to practice all kinds of mathematics, if possible without individual pupils' difficulties of, say, calculation hindering their understanding of what is essential. We start with the idea that every human being, even the less talented one, enjoys mathematics by nature if one encourages him in the right way and does not spoil his/her enthusiasm.

Let us take note, with G. Polya[1], of one or two things. We assure ourselves of the validity of our mathematical knowledge by way of so-called *demonstrative reasoning*. Mathematical proof verifies an asserted fact as *certain, indisputable, conclusive*.

---
[1] Georg Polya: *Mathematics and plausible reasoning*, Vol. 1, Princeton University Press 1990, pages v to vii

Yet to arrive at mathematical knowledge it is necessary to work with the creative element that is always coming into being in us, that element that lets ideas rise up in us, allowing us to make factual suppositions. These hypotheses we underpin by means of *plausible reasoning*. This is *risky, disputable, provisional*.

There is no infallible method of learning this plausible reasoning; it is a practical skill and an art, and like all such is learned through imitation and practice[2].

It may be surmised from the following account that the method of giving the main lesson in blocks is the right vessel, or *a* right vessel, for the schooling of what mathematics really is.

2 Lesson structure and method

This elaboration of plausible suppositions should become the means for teacher and pupil to strive towards an understanding of the basics of, say, the infinitesimal calculus, as thematized in this book, for example. What was said above suggests the use of the *genetic method of learning*[3], as it enables the pupil to work independently at creating this understanding.

The *basic steps in the process* may be described as follows:

- We have a *phenomenon*
- its *characterization* throws up questions
- in which a *problem* becomes apparent and can be described
- we *search and discover* facts around the problem in an imaginative way
- which leads to hypotheses
- which have to be tested, discarded, or inwardly understood in turn
- these *plausible hypotheses* may in turn
- be investigated through methods of reasoning which lead to irrefutable certainty.

Fundamentally speaking, *in acquiring something new, we always follow the path "from the problem to the system,"* from the individual to the general. This casts light on the question of the right form for teaching mathematics – and not just for the 12th grade.

---

[2] Polya, see above, page v: "the inductive evidence of the physicist, the circumstantial evidence of the lawyer, the documentary evidence of the historian, the statistical evidence of the economist belong to plausible reasoning."

[3] See also various presentations by Martin Wagenschein, e.g. the book *Verstehen lehren* [*Teaching understanding*], Weinheim und Basel 1997.

The genetic method of learning [*die erkenntnisgenetischen Methode*] is genetic in the sense of being concerned with how understanding or insight *originates*. — *Translator*

For economy in teaching working from concrete examples is always necessary. A subject or complex of subjects is chosen and worked on deeply but succinctly, making possible the unfolding of characteristic thought forms and their applications, and the successful transferring of the learning content to many other subjects or complexes of subjects.

How this is achieved in practice may briefly be described as follows:

a) According to the steps mentioned above we begin with Step One by entering into the "thing," directly into the *phenomenon*, without much explanation, just by doing and adjusting to the doing, thus taking hold of the whole human being. This may be achieved by a suitably introduced task, which enables the pupil to enter into intensive activity, appeals to his sense of discovery and lets him *himself* come up against the mathematical problem.

b) During the phase of *characterization* and the recalling of the experiences in Phase a) plus where necessary the adding of hypotheses, a certain rounding-off of all their experiences and actions happens, without going into discussion of the connecting thoughts.

c) Phases of communal *observation and fact-finding*, which correspond in the main to the further steps mentioned above, must be gone through in outer and inner silence, as well as with a willingness to listen to one another, otherwise depth is not achievable. The teacher must initiate the prerequisite conditions for this to happen. And *because the awakening of spiritual forces in a community is achieved most effectively through conversation*, the conduct of the conversation is to be such that all contributions towards problem-solving are taken into account and made available to the community, all the steps being documented in a suitable medium at the end of the process. The teacher must learn this exacting art of guiding the discussion[4].

Such a *genetic learning process* (steps (a) to (c) above) gives the group of learners the feeling of having learned the topics by themselves in communal striving, and each one is able to notice and understand his/her fellow human beings with their abilities and idiosyncrasies. All talents are recognized and valued in this way: the person finding problem-solving easy is able to join in; the one full of ideas meets with attentiveness to them; the one not so endowed encounters the communal striving to do justice to his incomprehension – which is usually shared by others, and often calls attention to something that the teacher (and also the gifted pupil) had not even taken into account in his or her deliberations, and so on. Everyone who is part of the process is enriched individually and socially.

So the general character of such a phase is: "What did he/she *mean* by this? Ah, that's interesting! What is correct in his/her comments? Which of the thoughts elucidated can help us further? Which ones do we want to follow further? But we must take *this* thought into account as well! Yes, we shall definitely have to come back to this one again ..."

---

[4] This guiding of the discussion is sometimes called "Socratic". But the concept is referred to among educationists and in the literature in many quite different ways and does not seem apposite to me, so I avoid it here.

Such a phase schools the will to concentrate enormously, the motivation "to see our common train of thought through to a successful end." Indeed, the pupils develop the necessary patience in this sometimes arduous process for the reason that they experience that they themselves are allowed to arrive at a mutual solution, that they have time to understand and that the path is always followed through to a satisfactory end. It is of course not always easy for the moderator to keep the process of discovery within a time frame that is not too strenuous; with increasing experience it is possible to improve the timing. In order to keep the teaching from becoming unhealthy, and thus inefficient, one should not "overstep the mark." There must be sufficient space in a main lesson for *other phases*, where the aspect of *breadth* can be taken into account:

d) In order to achieve *breadth*, among other things – also as an *exercise in itself* – one could use quiet individual and/or group work, presentations by pupils or teachers (including stories appealing to the feelings!) and various other teaching methods. The differing abilities of the pupils to create such breadth for themselves can be taken into account by using questions and tasks of widely differing content and level and by means of the various scenarios of this part of the learning. Individual study, which has to be learned as well, and is in seeming contradiction to c), may happen in such phases.

3   Rudolf Steiner's recommendations and the genetic method of learning

I recall Rudolf Steiner's recommendation in the 3rd Lecture of *Education for adolescents* (GA 302) about allocating the different phases of learning to two successive days of a main lesson and in so doing taking account the night (in an educational sense), which is described there in the cases of physics and history. We see that the way of teaching arranged in the above described sequence fits into the framework Steiner gave for the main lesson. Steiner expresses it elsewhere by the sequence "*conclusion-judgment-concept*" in which we can, in a grossly simplified way, classify Phase a) under the heading "conclusion", Phase b) and the following night under "judgment", Phase c) under "concept" (the intellectual working-through subsequent to the rhythmic component in the following main lesson)[5].

Implementing Steiner's recommendation mentioned above is highly effective and, together with the "rhythmic component" (Section 6) and other pedagogic measures, can be regarded as the real pedagogic strength at least of the main lesson blocks.

By now it should be clear that what I mean by the genetic method of learning can be realized ideally; the Waldorf main lesson, provides *a* if not *the* proper vessel for this method. Such a method can never bring its strengths to bear in the way of teaching controlled by the time-constraint of the 45 minute lesson, or the gap of several days in the thought-process. Martin Wagenschein coined

---
[5] R. Steiner, *Education for adolescents*, GA 302, Lecture 3, 14.6.1921. For "conclusion, judgment, concept" see also R. Steiner, *Study of man*, GA 293, Lecture 9, 30.8.1919. A detailed account relating to conclusion-judgment-concept especially in relation to math education is to be found in Stephan Sigler's article in this book. See also my article in *Topics in math for the 11th grade*, Kassel 1999.

the phrase *"taking root and consolidation"* [*Einwurzelung und Verdichtung*]. The first of these can be found in Phases a) and b), the second in Phase c)[6].

4 Documentation of the group work

Looking back to what was said above, by the end of Phase c) we should thus have proper documentation in some medium of what has been achieved at each stage as communal knowledge. This can happen during this phase if the teacher outlines in retrospect on the blackboard the individual steps in thought, possibly partly summarized – including the verbal contributions of the pupils. Looking at it together may make further improvement possible. The teacher should learn to develop the task of "scribe" to perfection – not adding anything that has not been spoken about or understood! He organizes the blackboard in his imagination in such a way that the subsequent well-organized write-up is coherently ordered, with the necessary emphases. This way he continuously corrects imperfections and thus arrives at a rounded presentation of the communal cognitive path, which in turn helps the pupil to a comprehended internalization of it.

This blackboard picture – arrived at by working together – is not now copied "automatically" by everyone, as may make sense in the lower and middle school, but in the high school one pupil takes on the task (voluntarily!) of printing it out, with each pupil receiving a (colored) copy. He generally gets his reward for doing this responsible and carefully executed task and is relieved of other duties if he wishes.

Such a way of working has proved to be successful and is willingly accepted by the pupils. It is highly efficient because it has the great advantage that the testing and strengthening of the learning outcome can be gone into directly in the following *phase of quiet work*. For this there are diverse tasks, from those of a more repetitive, polishing or copying type to problems that lead on further, which can also help cater to special talents and whose solutions may result in individual contributions of the pupils concerned.

5 Creating breadth *as well as* efficiency

Quite apart from what was said in Section 2(d) it is beneficial to create breadth in another way. One does not have to finish topic after topic in successive main lessons in a comprehensive linear arrangement; it may be much more interesting and more effective for the process of learning to connect separate topics in such a way that they are seen as overlapping and mutually fructifying. If what seems disparate is chosen suitably then the resulting tension, Wagenschein's "productive unease", is resolved most beautifully when, for example during the course of the investigation, topics turn out to be different aspects of the same problem. Also revisions, extensions, brief glances at peripheral areas and connections to other subjects may successfully be included. In this way abundance and diversity are created at the same time with economy.

---

[6] See also Peter Buck, *Einwurzelung und Verdichtung*, Dürnau 1997

6 The "rhythmic component"

As far as I know, Rudolf Steiner never gave an explicit indication of this facet of teaching, nor did he describe it directly; it seems that once thought out it developed and was found useful in practice.

There is of course a beginning and an end to every lesson: a focusing on the task, as well as a leaving off and moving on. This process needs to be managed creatively.

Steiner calls the art of education a balancing out of the young person's physical nature and spiritual being. He sees the process of education as one of incarnation and the incorporation of the 'I' into the human organization. He examines the therapeutic effects of subjects and methods. In doing so he takes into special consideration "achieving the anchoring of the 'I' in the human organization" and "not allowing the 'I' to become absorbed too strongly into the rest of the organization"[7]. These indications provide some insights *for the beginning of the lessons* (as well as their end, and for the duration and arrangement of the lesson's developmental stages):

In order to achieve an "anchoring of the 'I' in the human organization", which brings about an ability to focus on the task in hand, we can profit by using, e.g., speech exercises, recitation, mental arithmetic and/or imaginative exercises. The last two activities arise naturally in teaching mathematics and can easily be contrived to adapt almost imperceptibly into the thinking component, either in reviewing what was done the previous day or even in something new. This proves to be the most efficient move in many instances!

Speech exercises and recitation, too, done beforehand or even exclusively, have a similar effect, and weld the group into a cohesive whole. It has been found that age-specific material for recitation affects the developmental situation of the group, and might even be able to be linked to the subject matter taken up during the course of a main lesson. We have a wide range of possibilities here, which could be expounded upon, but would go beyond the scope of this essay.

I have been testing method this by teaching both with and without the rhythmic component and found that conditions for subsequent learning are incomparably better with a suitable rhythmical part. The pupils corroborated this finding – "although time is lost doing it". Actually one doesn't lose time, one *gains constructive learning time!*

7 Essential remark about the choice of method

From the above it may become apparent that the genetic method of learning cannot really be bettered – by its advantages for working on new topics and their thought-forms in a class group – as it allows the pupil's own discoveries to emerge creatively rather than merely be re-created. Insight, literally, into the being of mathematics is created. The main lesson is the perfect vessel for this method, as it is described above.

---

[7] R. Steiner, *Meditatively acquired knowledge of man and social understanding through spiritual scientific knowledge*, Stuttgart, 15, 16, 21, 22 Sept. 1920, and Dornach, 4 Oct. 1919, GA 302a, Wynstones Press, Gloucester, UK, 1982

If it's a question almost exclusively of weekly lessons, the method cannot be employed as effectively: it greatly impedes perception of what mathematics is essentially about. Independent seeking and discovering is not possible, as quick formulaic methods are called for to give the necessary mathematical know-how, possibly demanded by the teacher prematurely – before the dawning of actual understanding. In this way the lessons may deteriorate, either into working with the few remaining interested studends, or into automatic drill.

It is well known that for most people the latter way is ineffective as a vehicle for the understanding of mathematics, thus making the subject into a "bugbear" at school, attended by well-known psychological blocking. This endemic failing in math teaching is compensated for by the use of extra lessons, private tuition and coaching, which merely confirm the negative image.

Yet if, as suggested above, the gist of a *new topic* is learned by the genetic method in the way described (best of all during the main lesson blocks), then the necessary mathematical skills, as well as amplifications in the widest sense, can be worked on with a variety of other methods and ways of teaching. Mention may be made in this context of what was described in Section 2(d), e.g., the phases of quiet work[8], as well as in the continuous practice sessions additional to the main lesson blocks.

8   The 12th grade pupil and mathematical schooling

The year of the 12th grade has proved a suitable age to make precise the concept of infinity. At this age the young human being may be guided, and indeed is often inclined, to enter a sort of "meta-plane" in order to observe some process, even the process of training him-/herself in various ways of thinking. Mathematics' educational aspects (and indeed self-educational aspects) focus increasingly on observation of thinking. Here are some key thoughts embracing all subjects:

1. Everything is connected to everything else.

2. All things need to be looked at individually from as many different points of view as possible[9].

Further to (a): How does one find out what is connected with what, i.e. what methods do we have at our disposal to do justice to the different areas of life and thought? What methods are there and which are suitable for what?

Further to (b): There are many possible paths. Every individual has to search for his/her own way and has to learn to find it as well. Not all paths are found to be useful. See (a).

---

[8] What is described here forms the basis of my articles in this *Topics in mathematics* series and can be referred to in detail there.

[9] See e.g. W. Rauthe: "Stufen der Urteilskraft [Stages in developing the power of judgment]" in *Zur Menschenkunde der Oberstufe* [*Study of the human being in the High School*], Stuttgart 1981 (for the 12th Grade the individualized power of judgment)

An exciting field of experience is opened up for the young person by here offering a means of developing manifold *skills* the importance of which goes far beyond schooling and becomes part of education through life. As an overview of mathematical competence in a stricter sense, the following[10] may be useful:

Competency of method at the end of the 12th grade

- Conscious use of heuristic methods (ability to use different approaches with acumen)
- Thinking in processes, observation of these
- Fluency with concepts by effort of will*
- Moving freely in thought-forms (not based on outer sense perception)
- Verbal description of processes
- Mathematical formalization

*Not just combining well-established concepts, but thinking new thoughts in original ways.

Competency of mathematical content at the end of the 12th grade

- Comprehension of the infinitely small and the infinitely large, consideration of limiting values
- Formalization of the concept of function
- Graphical representation of algebraic expressions
- Applying various analytical methods to geometrical objects
- Imagining geometrical forms in transformation (families of curves, geometrical metamorphoses)
- Duality in geometric thinking
- Handling the concept of mapping in various geometries

Of course other competencies, such as social skills and "self-competence," should also be mentioned; this should be obvious from what was said in Section 2.

---

[10] In the framework of a work-group of the team working on the future of graduation exams, Peter Baum, Uwe Dombrowski, Karl-Friedrich Georg, Detlef Hardorp and Rolf Rosbigalle developed a characterization of mathematical competence, which is incorporated in an overall competence project of the *Bund der Freien Waldorfschulen* [*Association of Waldorf schools*]. What follows is taken from this competence specification and restricted to the 12th Grade. The overall project is published in W. M. Götte, P. Loebell, K.-M. Maurer *Bildungsplan. Entwicklungsaufgaben und Kompetenzen. Zum Bildungsplan der Waldorfschule*, Stuttgart 2009.

9   Mathematics as spiritual schooling

The inner forces that enable us to deal with everyday life and direct it in a meaningful way are all well known to us. They are natural abilities of the soul of which we make constant use in everyday life. To develop these further seems to be desirable in face of the tasks everyone has to face today.

Perusing this article with this in mind, we notice something which becomes particularly obvious in Section 2. In a sense, all those soul-spiritual abilities which are the object of "subsidiary" or "moral" exercises are skills which are practiced intensively and developed as a matter of course in such a way of teaching[11].

For example, to really understand what he or she means, I have to take in without prejudice the comments, and what I perceive, of someone with whom I'm involved in some capacity, and to assimilate them positively: I have to control my thoughts and thus reach some sort of understanding; I have to learn to handle with equanimity the fact that something still needs clarifying before we can move on in our deliberations; and I have to learn to steer the whole process with my will, even if something quite personal gets in the way, and so on. Other desirable qualities can be added to this, such as patience, endurance, the ability to be observant, attentiveness, concentration, etc. Also the exercise of *reviewing in reverse*, introduced consciously by the teacher at the beginning of the thinking part, belongs here ("How did we come up with this?" ... "What thought led us to it?" ... "What thought led us to *that* thought?"... and "Where did it all start?") Such qualities are of inestimable value in a time of enormous challenges of soul and spirit[12].

10   Conclusion

By way of conclusion it may be mentioned that teaching mathematics in the way described here has, in practice, stood the test of time extraordinarily. Going about it in this way isn't easy, and a teacher must summon up considerable stamina and persevere before such teaching "runs smoothly". After a short time, however, he/she will be rewarded by the response of even those young people who had been struggling with the subject matter and are now experiencing that mathematics can be fun, and that even a deeply rooted satisfaction of spirit and soul may come from it.

It is well-established that the way of teaching described even enables a student to achieve commendable exam results, which should be obvious from the description.

For all these reasons I would encourage people to take up these suggestions.

---

[11] See for example R. Steiner, *Guidance in esoteric training*, GA 42/245, I. General requirements (Subsidiary exercises); see also Frans Carlgren, *Der anthroposophische Erkenntnisweg* [*The anthroposophical path of knowledge*], Stuttgart 1995

[12] In his extremely enlightening articles, the Swiss mathematician Louis Locher-Ernst stresses these very qualities which are developed in the activity of mathematizing and which he understands in the sense of the title of his collection *Mathematik als Vorschule der Geisteskenntnis* [*Mathematics as a preparatory training for spiritual cognition*], Dornach 1973. To prevent misunderstanding I should add that this is obviously not to imply than other school subjects and activities cannot develop some of the skills mentioned here.

Experiential connection, judgement and concept[1] in the mathematics lesson

Can the principle of "Schluss" (experiential connection), "Urteil" (judgement/assessment) and "Begriff" (concept) also be applied to mathematics lessons.[2]

STEPHAN SIGLER

The question asked is whether the three-fold nature of the lesson described by Rudolf Steiner is also valid in high school mathematics education?

The teaching structure described by R. Steiner that follows a sequence of experiential connection, judgement and concept proves itself valid in high school mathematics education. This is the main thrust of this article. Direct experience leads to a "Schluss", the following reassuring assessment, the lateral expansion during the night and then the deepening of thought processes around the concept. Thus the learners embark on an experiential path that will lead and inspire them to create their own biography.

On June 14, 1921, when the oldest class of the new Waldorf School had entered Class 10, Rudolf Steiner gave a series of lectures, the so-called "Ergänzungskurs" cycle. The third lecture was entitled "Menschenerkenntnis und Unterrichtsgestaltung" (The study of man and the creative structuring of the teaching process). He had given only a little instruction concerning special teaching methods for the main lesson in senior Waldorf classes.

A year later a conference took place where Steiner brought to the teachers' attention that they were not coming to grips with their classes, especially the higher grades. He felt that "something had grown above their heads"[3]. As problems, he referred specifically to fragmented classes lacking homogeneity, a lack of will on the part of the learners to be self-reliant and to work independently. He also felt that there was clearly a sense of alienation or a disturbed relation between the learner and the learning material. His main criticism was that the teachers pontificated too much, thus alienating the pupils from the material. In class there was too much lecturing and not enough instruction or guidance and the pupils were not receiving real answers to their questions. He said that not enough attention had been paid to his lectures the year before[4]. He encouraged the teachers to apply more seriously the methods he had referred to in those lectures when he had also briefly outlined their application in class, albeit using only the examples of Physics and History. Mathematics was not mentioned.

---

[1] «Schluss, Urteil und Begriff»
[2] Translated and developed (2008) by Catrin Pagani, Derek Gripper and Stephanie Rupp from "Soll auch der Mathematikunterricht nach Schluss, Urteil und Begriff gegliedert werden?" by Stephan Sigler (2007), JUPITER, Vol. (2), ISSN 1661-8750 Verlag am Goetheanum, Dornach/Switzerland.
[3] vgl. Steiner, R. (1975): Konferenzen mit den Lehrern der Freien Waldorfschule, Bd 2, S. 94f, GA 300b, Dornach
[4] ebd., S. 95

The experimental connection

The essential substance of the 1921 lectures is a teaching method that ensures an appropriate adaptation of the material to be conveyed to the life processes of young people, both "spirit-soul" (mental/spiritual) and "physical-material" (corporeal/physical). In a holistic sense, this focus is fundamental and is the usual way of teaching in Waldorf schools; maybe not so much in the upper classes where the focus often becomes the actual, measurable result of the teaching process as one already has the school-leaving qualifications in mind. This is in a sense regrettable as the pressure to produce a good final result "creates" a tendency to proceed with a purely "outcome-based" view in mind, at the expense of this holistic approach. This is often to the detriment of the 'outcome' in real terms. Steiner explains the sequence of processes that take place in the course of perception:

A new world-experience presents itself to the learner through the eye, the ear and his/her awareness or intellect. This new part of the outer physical world is witnessed, but only in a way that, at the first stage, remains outside the learner's own physical reality. There is usually no indication from the teacher of the material being put into any kind of context, as well as no explanation about how this new information links up or follows from anything previously learned. The teacher has not at this stage motivated the learner and no sense about which aspect of the new information should be noted or even what purpose can be achieved by knowing the new facts. Why in fact should this knowledge be relevant at all? This process embarks with a certain 'raw' immediacy and the physical reality of the new world experience reveals itself in sharp contours, an almost rough process. The learner is confronted directly by an onslaught of physical facts. It is the teacher who guides or facilitates the process of this first encounter. Steiner explains that when the teacher introduces a new topic, the material is "performed" before the learner, e.g., the telling of a story or the playing of a piece of music. This means that the teacher is relating to the external reality of the child as has been described. The child has not yet achieved a relation of spirit to the material and this must certainly follow if real learning is to take place.

In anthroposophic terms the astral body and the ego – the "inner life" – are guided and defined; even dominated, by the physical and ethereal body and therefore partake in everything. Steiner refers to the practice of Eurythmy as an example of this process. At first there is resistance against what is implemented through a person's own physical being. Eventually the astral body and the ego adapt to these eurythmic movements. Steiner talks of a motion, a manifestation of the will, that acts on or is imposed on the astral body and the ego. It is important to see that it is something wilful that is the impulse and not something coming from an intellectual concept.

Process 1: Experimental connection "Schluss"

This direct, physical confrontation with the learning material, which is neither led by theory nor an intellectual reception, is called "Schluss" or "experiential connection". The situation in the class should be quiet and concentrated, with sufficient time available for this learning experience. The learner's whole being needs to participate if he/she is to experience the reality of this encounter.

The question is how mathematics corresponds to the external physical facts of the world. What actually happens during a certain calculation has to reveal itself to the learner independently. This requires time and a concentrated mindset; unnecessary talking or explaining should be avoided by the teacher. The matter speaks for itself, as all elements can be clearly observed. In the context of mathematics education let us assume that the learners are given the task of converting all the unit fractions from $\frac{1}{2}$ to $\frac{1}{32}$ into decimal fractions. During such an exercise the learner has to enter the special realm of numbers and their sense of this faculty has to become active. Diving into this number space and the subsequent divisions evoke many already known ideas, concepts and connections. The navigation of tables from 1 to 10 and the division algorithm will be required. For example, the calculation for 1 reveals a sequence of digits that eventually repeats 7 itself. This realization might have to be struggled for by unnecessary repetition if the learner has slipped too deeply into the activity of the calculation. The learner will, sooner or later, come to the required result, i.e., that the division chain repeats itself. The moment of realization of this repetition depends on the alertness of the learner as well as on his/her memory. This realization will most likely require a small moment of detachment from the action. It is at these moments of detachment that punctuate the immersion into subjective activity when something relevant takes place. The AHA experience! The learner wakes up! This moment has a special significance in the process of learning, because while calculating the learner is busy, is connected with the particular topic, lives through it and doesn't question the meaning or the sense of the operation taking place. It means that on the one hand the learner is in a sleep-like state as he/she is completely involved with his/her operation, on the other hand the learner steps out of this process during 'moments of waking up' in which he/she sees the results of the calculations as something clear and distinct.

$$\frac{1}{7} = 0,142857142857142857$$

In practice:

$$
\begin{array}{l}
1:7 = 0,142857... \\
\underline{0} \\
10 \\
\underline{-7} \\
30 \\
\underline{-28} \\
20 \\
\underline{-14} \\
60 \\
\underline{-56} \\
40 \\
\underline{-35} \\
50 \\
\underline{-49} \\
1
\end{array}
$$

This result appears as an image in which the whole process of calculating is merged together. By noticing the periodicity, calculation steps which haven't even been executed yet can be anticipated. A process which was initially one of the will configures itself to shape a clear and conscious image. It has solidified into form as if lifted out of the formless flowing forces. The underlying emotional experience of evidence takes place and the "Schluss" becomes conscious and articulated.

The above process involves all areas of human activity. Calculation and perception refer to the "Willensmensch", the oscillation between the internal process of calculating (sleep-like) and the confrontation with the results of the calculation referring to the sphere of feeling. After the process of calculating has come to an end, there appears a representative image. The "Schluss" enters the sphere of awareness and can be verbalized.

In the course of these particular calculations a question arises concerning the different characteristics of the results; namely finite, purely periodic, mixed periodic or infinite. Mostly, the learners do not differentiate between these characteristics beyond noting that some are comfortably easy and some are more complex. For example, fractions like $\frac{1}{5}$ or $\frac{1}{3}$ are much easier to convert to decimals. The numbers and their qualities are perceived in a feeling or aesthetic sense, which is a preliminary stage to the factual contours taking shape.

$$\frac{1}{2} = 0,5 \qquad \frac{1}{3} = 0,\overline{3}$$

$$\frac{1}{4} = 0,25 \qquad \frac{1}{5} = 0,2$$

$$\frac{1}{6} = 0,1\overline{6} \qquad \frac{1}{7} = 0,\overline{142857}$$

$$\frac{1}{8} = 0,125 \qquad \frac{1}{9} = 0,\overline{1}$$

$$\frac{1}{10} = 0,1 \qquad \frac{1}{11} = 0,\overline{09}$$

$$\frac{1}{12} = 0,08\overline{3} \qquad \frac{1}{13} = 0,\overline{076923}$$

$$\frac{1}{14} = 0,0\overline{714285} \qquad \frac{1}{15} = 0,0\overline{6}$$

$$\frac{1}{16} = 0,0625 \qquad \frac{1}{17} = 0,\overline{0588235294117647}$$

$$\frac{1}{18} = 0,0\overline{5} \qquad \frac{1}{19} = 0,\overline{052631578947368421}$$

$$\frac{1}{20} = 0,05 \qquad \frac{1}{21} = 0,\overline{047619}$$

$\frac{1}{22} = 0,0\overline{45}$ 	 $\frac{1}{23} = 0,\overline{0434782608695652173913}$

$\frac{1}{24} = 0,041\overline{6}$ 	 $\frac{1}{25} = 0,04$

$\frac{1}{26} = 0,0\overline{384615}$ 	 $\frac{1}{27} = 0,\overline{037}$

$\frac{1}{28} = 0,03\overline{571428}$ 	 $\frac{1}{29} = 0,\overline{0344827586206896551724137931}$

$\frac{1}{30} = 0,0\overline{3}$ 	 $\frac{1}{31} = 0,\overline{032258064516129}$

$\frac{1}{32} = 0,03125$

Table 1: The decimal expansion of the unit fractions from $\frac{1}{2}$ to $\frac{1}{32}$.

This example reveals something about the characteristics of mathematical experience:

1. The mathematical space has to be created by the learner.

2. If the learner isn't capable of this he/she won't be able to execute the mathematical operation.

3. This means that mathematics is the only discipline in which the object of analysis has to be created by the learner himself or herself.

4. In all other disciplines perception paves the way to the learning material.

5. With learning mathematics, the wilfulness of perception remains in a sleep-like state; it is unconscious.

6. In mathematics the learner must make a wilful effort to create something which can then turn into experience.

To effect the "Schluss" as described by Steiner and to ensure the quality of the experience, it is important that the teacher sets the task without elaboration, without an introduction which might anticipate certain results, i.e., the three types of decimal fractions. The learner should achieve the results and experience this independently. Any contextualizing prevents the learner from meeting the subject matter innocently and in an unbiased manner. The teacher should as far as possible avoid watering down the encounter, depriving the learner of a direct experience and the chance to develop his/her own assessment. The learner could easily be demotivated if this advice is not taken; the will to incarnation and the desire to stand firmly in the world would be disturbed by the introduction of intellectual categories. The important thing is that the learner discovers the nature of the subject by him/herself, for him/herself. The contact that takes place should be with an immediate reality and without scientific concepts or the arbitrary comments of a teacher, which could obscure or prevent the "Schluss" experience.

Steiner described a similar process for physics lessons where an experiment should be executed without preliminary explanations. The teacher shouldn't speak in order to not disturb the perception of the learners. Thus the learners can establish a physical relation to the performed experiment.

Process 2: "judgement"

At this stage, a characterization of the phenomena should take place. The class should make some assessment and recapitulate its experience with some distance from the actuality. A certain order could be established. In our example the fractions could be divided into 'friendly' and 'unfriendly', this process could result in the realization that the prime factors into which the denominator can be factorized are responsible for the type of decimal fraction. Out of a multitude of aspects a unity evolves that the learner can emotionally relate to. As a relationship with the facts starts to form, everything starts to feel more comfortable. The results are discussed and commented on; the difficulties pointed out. Maybe there is even some humor to be discovered. There is, anyway, an opportunity to recognize the differing nature of the results and the discussion can penetrate to the correct conclusion or judgement; namely, that the prime numbers appearing in the denominator are responsible.

Only now has one acquired an understanding of the content; the facts revealed by an act of will come together in a complete image. At this point the learner can begin to 'own' the material and the relationship becomes animated and alive, without the learner being immediately compelled to question it intellectually. What should not happen at this stage is a questioning where the learners start to challenge the new-found image. The results, principles and relations to other phenomena should not be scrutinized. Such a procedure would make the learning process weak and somehow shallow.

One would have to conclude that the "Schluss" was not a well-formed experience and was emotionally unsatisfying. The learners should go home that day with a feeling of excitement and awe at having discovered something new and amazing.

The night:

According to Steiner, the astral body and ego are detached from the physical and the etheriC body during the night. The activities of the previous day are relived in a broader archetypal sense. The astral body and the ego rework the experience they had, especially during the mathematics lesson, on this expanded, more spiritual scale. What has been experienced is infused with spirit and the essential substance of it is absorbed and integrated. This is what becomes available to the learner during the night and is present as part of him/her the next day. This essential substance is to be understood not as a sharply defined concept but as a moving and fluid spiritual faculty. This means that the learner comes to school the next day with a certain mental flexibility. The physical and etheric bodies also store the experience of the calculations of the day before. Steiner calls this

"Fotografieren/photographing". The interaction of these two spheres effects a lively and creative approach to the subject. In this correspondence lies, according to Steiner, a particularly effective healing potential.

In a properly guided class one should be able to identify a manifestation of life and spirit infused energy. Much depends on whether a teacher can observe this, as this would be a true criterion for good teaching.

Process 3: Concept "Begriff"

The next day a deepening and lateral expansion of thoughts takes place. During this next main lesson, this expansion and mental intensification regarding the topic should take place and a concept of the learned material should be developed. The question in our example could be: "Why don't the numbers 0, 3, 6 and 9 appear in the decimal fraction development of $\frac{1}{7}$?" In this context the learner has to analyze the division algorithm and acquire a wider perspective. One notices that certain remainders produce particular numbers.

Remainder	1	3	2	6	4	5
Repeating digit	1	4	2	8	5	7

The next question could be "Which number is in the 73rd decimal place?" Here one penetrates the subject and starts to apply the knowledge that has been gained. Another question could refer to the periodicity of the fraction and the differing lengths of the periodic results. One could also question whether one can be sure that each fraction will produce either a repetition of the sequence or a finite result. Do fractions exist that produce infinite results? It is important to avoid leading questions which could result in yes/no answers or merely repetitive questions. Questions should inspire a genuine inquiry. Questions like: "How long can the longest period be?" tend to prevent, rather than further this aim. The teacher should create a light, maybe even humorous learning situation. There should be a free atmosphere in class which evokes mental activity.

In an emotional sense the learners are clearly aware that a divisional chain has to either end or start to repeat itself eventually. Does it? If so, why? In the case of $\frac{1}{7}$ only 6 remainders are possible, all 7 being smaller than 7, the denominator, and each remainder has a specific resulting digit. When all six possible remainders have appeared, the calculation comes to an end or the sequence starts to repeat itself. So in fact the result for $\frac{1}{7}$ has the longest possible sequence that can emerge from 7. When looking at all the results in Table 1 one notices which results do in fact have the longest possible sequence, namely $\frac{1}{17}$ and $\frac{1}{19}$, whereas $\frac{1}{3}$ only has a sequence of 6 digits out of a possible 12 digits.

Realization

The learner in this way achieves an insight into rational numbers through his/her own activity; no theory was necessary to explain the phenomenon. The phenomenon of divisional chains has become transparent because everything could be openly examined. This is significant in the process of teaching. It goes without saying that a learner who was unable to execute the mathematical operation in the first lesson would not be able to benefit from the instruction as a whole. The aim, of course, would be to get the whole class to participate.

On the second day, two things are experienced. Firstly the subject is solidified and integrated with previously explored concepts. It becomes applicable and transferable to other areas. Secondly, the connections widen and lead to new areas that can be explored. Questions like "Why do maximum sequence lengths appear with certain denominators?" or "What is the deepest reason for the length of sequences?" can inspire and outline the content of subsequent lessons. In summary, the "Concept" (Begriff) part of the second lesson has combined the manifestation and generalization of the mathematical experience of the day before, opening up perspectives on new questions and further investigations.

Conclusion and consequences

A didactic sequence starts with the "Schluss" (experiential connection) at around 9 o'clock, in the middle of the main lesson. Here the direct 'physical' experience is the focus of attention. Strictly speaking the described learning curve will only have an effect in a biographical sense if the "Schluss" experience was genuine. If this does not take place the learner will not comprehend what follows, as there will be nothing to assess or come to a conclusion about. The learner has to be given the opportunity to encounter the world itself and not just the concepts or images of it. The "Schluss" as a direct, wilful approach to the learning material and to the world prevents the learner attaining preformed concepts deriving from the forces of the past, even prenatal, stages. Only thereafter can guidance of certain differentiating thought processes by the teacher take place.

In the "Schluss" and the "Begriff" section of the lessons, the whole class, both stronger and weaker learners, can participate in the learning experience. There is great benefit from this communal aspect. In a purely "outcomes-based" system of teaching the quick and strong performers are always going to be favored at the expense of the others, who risk dropping off into a void and being demoralized, possibly even giving up. In contrast, the teaching method described here encourages a strong coherence in the class, which is cultivated through common direct experience and witnessing of the world. This communal energy can be a motivating factor that contains the seeds for future efforts to be made.

Mathematics, in particular, is often imagined as something cast in stone, rigid and smoothly polished, researched and proven by the experts, like a building which isn't easy to enter. The teaching method described above opens up a door to the creative nature of mathematics and even allows for a sense of "partaking in the forming process". The didactic method of "Schluss, Begriff und Urteil" facilitates a creative approach in which the actual structure of mathematical approaches can be relived. This method doesn't aim at cognitive realizations, but is a way to include the whole person with all his/her abilities in the learning process. The moment of the "experiential connection" connects the learner's wilful approach to the topic with the then-occurring mental analysis.

This process evades a static definition, can stay alive, open, expandable and receptive, and therefore has a corresponding effect on the spirit. This in turn will inspire the learner to learn and to apply this living creative energy in the shaping of his/her own life-path. It will motivate the learner to penetrate his/her own deep, dark spiritual compulsions with the light of consciousness, to give them form and thereby to stand firmly in the world. Will and emotion are transferred into a sphere of awareness. We should note, however, that the teacher is the first to take the step of an "experiential connection" to the world. The teacher needs to cultivate this relationship in a correct and impeccable way.

The higher Senses

The significance of the senses of ego, thought and speech in the High School math lesson

KLAUS LABUDDE

In this article an attempt is made to show a connection between some typical teaching experiences and the three senses of ego, thought and speech. What the author has in mind are experiences which could bring the career beginner and the relatively inexperienced teacher into difficulties. To recognize these as soon as they appear, and then to try to handle them, I consider to be an urgent task if getting to grips with being a teacher is to be successful. It is in this sense that what is brought forward here is meant, as a suggestion and aid to overcome these difficulties.

It is useful to know the essential features of what Rudolf Steiner has to say about the senses. A compendium of Steiner's original texts can be found in the paperback *Zur Sinneslehre* in the series *Rudolf Steiner, Themen aus dem Gesamtwerk*, edited by Chr. Lindenberg, Verlag Freies Geistesleben. Further literature is also referred to there[1]. And special mention may be made of this publisher's latest book, E.M. Kranich's *Der innere Mensch und sein Leib*, particularly the Chapter entitled "Die Sinne des Menschen".

That the theme dealt with here is also significant for teaching other subjects should be clear. The thought-sense seems to me to have a special relevance for mathematics instruction.

Why should we consider the question about the connection between teaching mathematics in the High School and those senses serving for perception of another human being? What caused this question? We shall pursue this first with some experiences that may be familiar to the reader, experiences I've had in my own teaching, as well as when I sat in on classes with colleagues or trainee teachers.

In these experiences one would be intending to introduce the class to a new subject by means of a complete and well-rounded picture, or to demonstrate some important proof. Perhaps not even to strive for a mathematically perfect construction, but rather to draw the students' attention to a particular kind of mathematical thinking. Thus a typical situation in teaching in which only the teacher is speaking. Impossible as a permanent institution, justifiable in appropriate doses, probably sometimes necessary even.

Occasionally it could happen that the teacher talked and talked, at first without noticing that he'd stopped reaching the students with what he wanted to convey to them. The teacher was more conscious of the material than of the students. He'd lost contact with them, at the same time leaving them to their own devices. In this situation many students simply switch off, sink into passivity. Others direct their interest to other things or chat with their neighbors, generally not

---

[1] See also: R. Steiner, *Man as a being of sense and perception*, Steiner Book Centre, N. Vancouver, 1981; R. Steiner, *The boundaries of natural science*, Anthroposophic Press, 1983, Lecture VIII given on 3 Oct. 1920.

about the theme the teacher is addressing. Again, others become restless and create disciplinary problems.

What is happening here? Or, better put perhaps, what is lacking when teaching leads to such a situation? What lacks, in my opinion, is the perception of the teacher. That he is seeing and hearing too little of what is going on among the students is surely worth mentioning, even if it's obvious. Again and again I've had the impression though, that that doesn't really get to the heart of the problem. With increasing experience I've tended more and more to see the main source of the "evil" in the lack of perception of the egos of the students. Constant exercise in the area of perception can work as a "precautionary measure", in the sense of not getting into the situation described in the first place. Ego perception as the becoming aware of the fact that the person I'm face-to-face with is an independent, self-conscious being just as I am – going through this process once is sufficient to *know* this fact from then on. But if ego-perception is to be beneficial to what happens every day in the classroom, it needs continued attention. Knowing alone is not enough here. This perception must be experienced again and again if it's to be effective.

How, quite concretely, does one practice ego-perception? How exactly is it done? It is difficult to find the right words to answer this question. This could be because it may be equally difficult to determine an organ for this sense. Some things related as I understand it to the realm of ego-perception were revealed to me and may be outlined here.

Suppose I confront another human being. I sense that if I want to understand what my vis-á-vis, as a being endowed with an ego, allows to appear to me, first and foremost I must look into his or her eyes. Other activities must however be added if I want to win further impressions, particularly if I want not only to perceive that the other is an I-being. My need to perceive does indeed go further. After all I want to gain the most comprehensive impression of just this "I" in particular. Thus I must include senses other than merely that of sight to help the perceptive activity. It seems that sense-perception with just a single sense is simply not possible, or hardly so. In our case it is clearly the other higher senses that are also involved in this complex process; but even one or other of the middle group of senses – generally not as explicitly as the higher senses – may contribute. On the other hand the example of the blind Jaques Lusseyran shows that in perceiving the ego the collaboration of the sense of sight, which we perhaps take for granted, is not absolutely necessary.

It follows from what has been described that the teacher grasps every opportunity in his day to day work to practice ego-perception vis-á-vis his students. Lesson periods alone are not really enough for that, since just then one is so occupied with the class as a whole that there is probably insufficient time for attending to each individual. Every encounter however brief, for example before the lesson commences, in breaks or on special occasions (school events, excursions, etc.) is suitable for this. I think it important to obtain the most comprehensive picture possible of the student's individuality. Thus I pay attention to how he or she speaks when describing something, when expressing thoughts, or how he moves, and so on. A wide field is opened up here for ratification in this sense.

Another experience one can often have in the teaching particularly of mathematics arises when the teacher puts a question to the class. Not so much a question appealing to knowledge as one which challenges thought. It can occur that a student – let's call him Ethan – gives an answer which doesn't on first hearing mean much to his schoolmates, perhaps not even to his teacher. Awkward wording possibly makes for keeping both the way Ethan is thinking and his thought-content hidden. All of a sudden it dawns on someone listening to him that there is something in his answer. This listener has not only heard words but has perceived a thought, perhaps after Ethan has tried once more with different words to express what he wanted to say. If this doesn't succeed in encompassing the answer and for that reason the teacher doesn't take any notice of his words or even dismisses them as inapplicable, the result can be that a student does not volunteer to speak any more, possibly for a long time. Damage is done, which can cost much effort and patience to repair.

A similar situation sometimes occurs if for example a particularly able student makes an eloquent spoken contribution, perhaps in the form of a project. The teacher doesn't have much trouble following, but what about his schoolmates? After initially listening with interest, many begin to look questioningly at the teacher. "What does he really want to tell us?" are their unspoken words. They hear their classmate speak but cannot perceive his thoughts.

Such experiences suggest that one has a faculty which serves to comprehend the thought-content of a fellow human being directly when they express the thought in a suitable form, in the classroom generally through the spoken word.

Steiner's call on the teacher to give time and attention to the latent questions of the student can, I believe, also be seen in relation to this. Not being able to understand a thought hopefully triggers off a question albeit, particularly in mathematics classes, sometimes an unexpressed question, for whatever reason. A latent question therefore. Here the teacher's thought-sense is required.

To describe the role played by the speech-sense in the math class is harder than in the case of the I – or thought-sense. While the sense of hearing mediates what finally comes through the ear as sound waves, the speech-sense allows us to understand the spoken word as such and because of that to distinguish between noise and tones, that is to say spoken sounds. What role does this sense play? Two contrasting experiences are related to it. More often than not High School instructors teaching the so-called academic subjects are eloquent. They find it easy to speak about themes within their field. So it can happen in teaching that one isn't fully conscious of one's speech. Not, please note, of the *content* of what's spoken (which is also important of course), but of speech as such. When one then "wakes up" the feeling can arise that *it is not I who has spoken, but the speech has spoken out of me*. What is happening here may well be understood as the speech-sense — which is "sleeping" in the speech — suddenly waking up and becoming active once more. If this awakening doesn't happen, sooner or later the students will very probably react in their own way.

The other experience often came to me when I consciously intensified my attentiveness to my own speech. As a result it became possible to keep the student's attention, or to regain it once it had slipped. The *way* I speak has an effect on how the students respond, how they go along with me. In this respect the teacher's conscious acknowledgment of the speech sense for the perception of one's own speech is a means by which one can bring an influence to bear on the course which the lesson takes.

Here I see the main task of the school speech therapist for his work with individual teachers. Under his guidance they should learn to bring their speech into action in support of their teaching and therewith to help the students' development.

There are in my experience two specially important difficulties with which many a beginning teacher has chiefly to struggle. First to get to know their students through the work in the teacher's specialism, and second to convey to them a sure feeling that they've understood what the teacher wants to impart to them, so well in fact that they can even do something with what's been learnt.

Whether and how often these difficulties arise depends essentially, I'm certain, on whether the teacher is in a position to activate the ego- and thought-senses in the skilled task of being aware of the students, and to set in motion the speech-sense for the perception – and thus improvement – of his own speech.

Looking back we note that we were concerned almost exclusively with the three senses as tools for the *teacher* in his pedagogic work. This raises the question about developing these senses in young people. Doesn't this happen more or less automatically by mutuality in the teacher's efforts to sharpen his own senses? If so, everything undertaken in this area has the function of an example. Or does teaching about the senses, at least in its main features, have a place in "life skills" which many Waldorf schools offer as a subject?

Thus two ways of proceeding may be suggested, which can be seen as extremes between which there are certainly many practicable middle paths. The point of these remarks as I see it has been to pinpoint the responsibility which exists here, one which is particularly important just in our time.

The Mathematical as Bridge to the Spiritual

UWE HANSEN

In his early lecture "Mathematics and Okkultism" from 1904, Rudolf Steiner gives a characterization of the mathematical which can serve the teacher in the 12th grade as a guide and foundation for his teaching – not only in regard to methodology and choice of themes, but also for how to form concepts in an appropriate way.

Steiner refers at first to Plato and says:[1]

> Plato regarded mathematical contemplation as a means to learn about life in the sense-free world of ideas. For the constructs of mathematics hover on the boundary between the sense-perceptible and a purely spiritual world .... When I think mathematically, I think about the sense-perceptible, but I simultaneously think outside of it .... That is the essential aspect of mathematical contemplation, that a single sense-perceptible figure leads beyond itself, that it can be for me only an analogy for an encompassing spiritual actuality. And thereby the possibility is still open that I bring the spiritual to sense perception. Via the mathematical form, I can get to know supersensible realities .... Learn through mathematics to free yourself from the senses, then you can hope to rise to a sense-free traffic with ideas. Plato wanted to impress this on his students. (GA 35, S. 8-9)

In a notebook entry from Steiner (Commentary to GA 114/5, S. 40-41) one finds entries which draw together the ideas of this essay:

> Mathematics is the inner lawfulness of space. There, at the furthest limits where spiritual and physical meet, there this limit is lawful in a mathematical way. They (the mathematical truths) are the first really spiritual nutriment of the human being. – These mathematical truths are independent from position and time; by them one finds in the simplest form, that one instance serves as an analogy for infinitely many.

In the lecture cited above, Steiner then elaborates further (S. 11):

> Mathematical knowledge has made significant progress in the modern era. During this time it has completed an important step into the super-sensible. This occurred with the analysis of the infinite, which we owe to Newton and Liebniz.

This is followed by references to the differential:

---

[1] The translations of all citations in this article have been made by the translator, the citations thus refer to the german editions.

> The differential retains all the properties that make calculation possible, but it isn't any longer subject to sense-perceptible observation. Sense perception is first brought to disappear in the differential, and then we have the new, sense-free foundation for our calculations. That which is accessible through the senses is calculated from that which is no longer present for the senses .... With the infinitesimal calculus we stand at an important boundary: We are led out of the sense-perceptible, and yet we remain so much within reality that we calculate that which can't be seen. And having thus calculated, the visible then reveals itself as the result of the calculation from out of the invisible.
>
> That is, we calculate the sense-perceptible out of the super-sensible, the formed out of the unformed. The sense-perceptible is traced back to the point of the super-sensible.

One realizes the significance of these statements

> ... in this way, that one makes clear to oneself through self-knowledge how one conducts oneself in his spiritual activity, when, beginning with the infinitely small, one conquers the finite by means of infinitesimal calculus. One is continuously confronted thereby with the momentary appearance of something sense-perceptible from out of something which is no longer sense-perceptible.

These passages show how much Steiner considered the mathematical as mediator, as bridge between the sense-perceptible and that which is not sense-perceptible. Already as a nine-year old Steiner had experienced this "bridge function" of mathematics through his study of a geometry text. In his autobiography "The Course of my Life", he wrote about his experiences:

> That one could live in the construction of purely inwardly-observed forms, without impressions from the external senses, provided me with the highest satisfaction. I found therein consolation for the mood that had arisen in me due to unanswered questions. To be able to comprehend something purely through the spirit, that brought me inward happiness .... In regard to geometry, I said to myself, here one can know something which only the soul itself through its own power experiences. I found in this feeling the justification to speak about the spiritual world, which I experienced in the same way as the sensual one.

This mediating aspect of the mathematical is restricted when one too soon draws upon what is visible, that is, something spatial. Thus, Rudolf Steiner recommended (conference from 30.4.1921) that the differential quotient be developed from numerical relations, and to employ all that is visual, the geometric – including for example the slope of the tangent line – only as a demonstration of what has already been learned. The visible should be developed out of the invisible, out of the reality of one's own will activity. What has become is developed out of what is becoming. It is also revealing that Steiner proposed that the differential should not be introduced in isolation, but rather to study the formation of the differential out of the coming-into-being of a ratio (conference from 30.4.1921).

As an illustration we observe the simple example of squaring. Let ε be an arbitrary, non-zero number. If one increases 1 by ε, the square of 1 changes by

$$D = (1+\varepsilon)^2 - 1^2 = \varepsilon(2+\varepsilon)$$

The smaller the change in ε, the less the difference is between $2+\varepsilon$ and 2; that is, the more exactly the square changes, doubled as strongly as ε. The number 2 appears here as "limiting factor."

In the lecture of March 18, 1921 (GA 324), Steiner distinguished the mathematical as "something which lives totally within ... the act of constructing in the soul, which is thus experienced in sustained activity and in observation of one's own activity."

The treatment of the differential quotient – as well as the example above – bears out this feature of the mathematical. That is, the differential quotient does not begin with the quality of a mental picture, it is only led to a visible presence through the observation of one's own activity.

Let's look a little closer at one's own activity in the formation of the differential quotient described above. One compares the change of D with the change of ε. Insofar as one carries out this vanishing process for D and for ε in an arbitrary way, and in such a way, that one always observes these two activities in proportion to each other, one is musically active. The musical can be so characterized that one experiences its basic elements, melody, harmony, and rhythm – even though unconsciously – as proportional relationships. Thus, the determination of the differential quotient – the experienced proportion is in fact a quotient – is therefore a musical event, a musical activity.

The musical experience is weakened – the understanding is correspondingly shallower – when one goes more in the direction of geometry. One can also recognize the "2" that arose in the given example by the enlargment of a square with side length 1; if the side length is increased by a sufficiently small ε, the area on the right and upper sides grows (the other two sides are fixed to the coordinate axes), so that the overall area grows twice so strongly as a single side of the square.

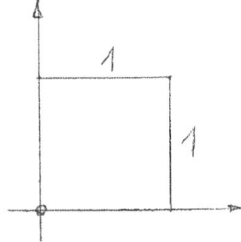

Also in this explanation the factor 2 is only understandable through inner activity; one compares the increase of the edge length with the increase 2ε of the area. When the magnitude ε and therefore the area increase 2ε have a non-zero value – and therefore belong to the sphere of mental pictures – then the factor is not exactly 2. That means that the factor 2 only appears when the process has not become a picture, but rather remains in the realm of the will. With the differential quotient we are dealing with a concept which cannot be grasped through a mental picture, which cannot be understood through something spatial. Also, at this point the characterization of the differential by Steiner is understandable; something unformed is brought into form. One can also say that here one has to do with creation of form out of something not yet born.

The will element, the musical element, withdraws even more if, instead of the increase of the area of a square, one observes the slope of the parabola $y = x^2$ at the position $x = 1$.

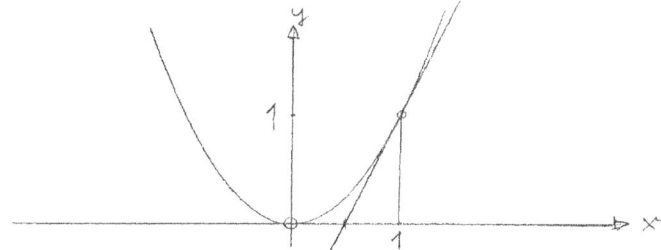

At the position 1 the tangent to the parabola has a slope of 2; if a points moves along the curve to the right and up, it moves twice as fast in the vertical direction as to the right. In that which can be viewed, the process-oriented, and hence the musical, is much less present than in the approach based purely on number.

In the given examples the differential quotient appeared as "limiting factor". One can apply its role as a factor to explain the Fundamental Theorem of differential and integral calculus.

If $F(x) = \int_a^x f(t)dt$, then $dF(x) = f(x) \cdot dx$ or $\frac{dF(x)}{dx} = f(x)$

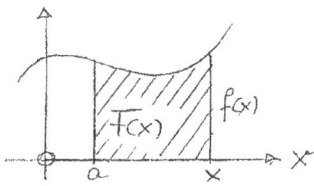

This middle equation asserts that in order to obtain the increase of the area $dF(x)$, one has to multiply the increase in x (as it approaches 0) with the function value $f(x)$.

The Chain Rule is also made immediately comprehensible. Let $y = f(x)$ and $z = g(y)$, and suppose y at the value $y_0 = f(x_0)$ changes twice as fast as x at the value x_0, and z at the value

$z_0 = g(y_0)$ changes 3 times as fast as y at the value y_0, then z changes at the value z_0 $2 \cdot 3 = 6$ times as fast as x at the value x_0.

R. Steiner pointed out that at the time of the change of teeth, the etheric life forces free themselves partially from building up the body and thus are available to the child as formative forces for thinking and imagination. However this sculpting activity is mixed at this point with an unconscious musical impulse: So says Steiner:

> ... and that is the essential with respect to the child as he comes into the school; that one knows one has to do with an unconscious musician in the child. And one has to work against the urge that it wants to handle its own organization, like a new violin behaves under the influence of a violin player, so that it ends up leading its own organization into the peaks and the valleys of the waves. (GA 303, 3rd lecture)

In the same lecture Steiner recommends that one has to take account of the inner needs of the organization of the child:

> The child is in this direction predisposed to rhythm, to beat, to the sensitive awareness of all that harmonizes.

Steiner then points out that additive, counting arithmetic is not consistent with the inner organizing forces of the child, that the child has no inner understanding of an external repetition of unity when learning numbers. The musical-rhythmic in the child's constitution has the need to comprehend numbers as organic differentiations of unity. That means, when introducing numbers and arithmetic operations, one should take the whole as the point of departure, and one should introduce summands, etc., through subdivision, through the inner structuring of numbers.

These references show that one is musically active when one divides the whole into its parts. We have already remarked, that doing mathematics consists of observing one's own activity, through the bringing-into-picture of one's own will activity. This bringing-into-picture is a process of the soul, which has as foundation one's own life forces. Steiner describes that the astral body in fact creates the pictures, but these are only perceptible when the etheric body, by resisting, reflects back the activity of the astral body (lecture from 19.8.1922, GA 129). Only through this reflection does this picture become conscious knowledge.

These connections are expanded upon through remarks in a lecture from 23.4.1921 (GA 204):

> All of arithmetic is in us, and it has been born in us by our astral body, so that it actually comes out of our astral body, and our 10 fingers are just the impression of this astral and the etheric. And both of these only make use of these external fingers, while we, when we calculate, bring to expression that which, through the astral body, brings about inspiration from numbers in the etheric body, and then count through the etheric body, which makes it possible that we can think at all. [: check meaning]

A little later one reads:

> When he [the human being of previous cultural epochs] looked at that which his astral body directed into the etheric body, he had to say: the astral body numbers, but numbers in way differentiated from the etheric body. It forms the etheric body by a number activity. The number lies between the astral body and the etheric body, and the number is alive, something that works within us.

In connection with other remarks regarding the astral body and the etheric body – the astral body is a musician, the etheric body is a sculptor – one can characterize the mathematical as the encounter within us of the musical and the sculptural.

This description of the mathematical can also be a help in evaluating concept formation and the choice of themes in the high school. The student always has to have the possibility to engage his sculptural-musical formative forces.

For example, group theory shows a musical impulse of the mathematical. It can justifiably be seen as the study of various subdivisions of one (see the article: "Group theory – an subdivision of unity" in the second volume for the 12th class).

This encounter of musical and sculptural activity also shows itself there, where algebraic and geometric elements work together, for example, in analytic geometry. This connection between geometry and algebra, however, did not only lead to analytic geometry. All of modern mathematics has received great impulses from this connection, impulses which also show essential elements of the mathematical. One may not however overlook the fact that the inner activity of the mathematician can become lamed through an over-arching abstraction, through extended formalism. Through the avoidance of the element of time and the intensive turning toward the spatial element, one faces the danger of losing the essential nature of the mathematical.

Thus, one notices today a strong need to represent everything numerical upon a line, or more generally upon a surface, even though the numerical is something whose nature is not spatial. The tendency to build up all of mathematics set-theoretically arises from the need to create an overview through generalizing, to observe everything as if from a "greater distance." That which is studied is presumed to be something which stands outside and opposite from the observer.

In a lecture Steiner, characterized this situation with the following words:

> The modern human being has more and more cultivated this orientation towards the spatial ... cultivated in relation to his external worldview, but also cultivated in relation to all his thinking, and we are actually today experiencing – as it were – a zenith of this spatial form of thinking. Just consider how difficult it is for a contemporary human being to follow an explanation or argument purely temporally. People are quite glad when one can at least get assistance from space, so one draws something on the board. With "making comprehensible" one means actually "making spatial"

> – that is what the modern human being strives for with respect to all explanation. The temporal, into which it flows, has become something discomforting for him .... But on the other hand we are striving, with what we call anthroposophical spiritual science, to come out from the spatial .... We strive however out of this spatial .... We strive into the temporal and also into the super-temporal, into that which leads actually out of the sense-perceptible. (Lecture from 17.12.22, GA 219)

In connection with the theme of this article, the following remarks are particularly important:

> Our contemporary spiritual culture is, in conceptual thinking, not yet advanced beyond the mathematical. For the spiritual researcher it is sometimes grotesque how little people have advanced beyond the mental picture .... In relation to mathematical things the human being of contemporary culture can rise up to concepts. For example one proves through inner constructions that the sum of the angles of a triangle is equal to 180 degrees .... Goethe created the Ur-plant, the Ur-animal, in this way .... The Ur-plant and the Ur-animal are such inner spiritual constructions. (Lecture from 20.10.1908, GA 108).

And in a lecture from 13.11.1908, GA 108, one reads:

> The complete net of concepts that the human being has, from number concept and so on up to the concepts that Goethe constructed – which however in our western culture lies still completely at its beginning – you can imagine as a blackboard that forms the limit between the sensible and the super-sensible world. Between these two spheres, the world of concepts forms the boundary.

Here one can ask the question whether this characterization of mathematical concepts also holds for the concepts of modern mathematics, in particular for set theory as created by George Cantor, whose foundation is provided by this modern mathematics. Cantor made this definition:

> By a "set" we understand a collection M of determined, distinct objects in our observation or thinking (called the "elements" of M) into a whole. (Georg Cantor "Collected Works", edited by E. Zermelo, S. 282)

This definition later came to be seen as the cause of the set-theoretical antinomies. On the one hand there lies a complete freedom in the choice of what objects are to be collected; on the other hand it is presumed that one is dealing with a ready-made whole that, somehow, is given. Out of arbitrary parts one supposes that something whole can arise.

It is therefore not surprising that contradictions quickly appeared that have led to the foundational crisis of mathematics. Bertrand Russell wrote in the year 1902 to Gottlob Frege that the set of all sets that do not contain themselves as elements hides a contradiction within itself, even though this set corresponds to the definition given by Cantor. Frege answered: "Your discovery of the contradiction utterly surprised me; I almost want to say disturbed, because thereby the ground on which I thought to construct arithmetic began to tremble and shake."

If the set M_a of all sets, which do not contain themselves as an element, actually exists, then both the assumption that M_a contains itself, as well as the opposite assumption, lead to a contradiction: if it doesn't contain itself, then it must by its definition nevertheless contain itself; if it contains itself, then it may not contain itself, since it only contain sets which do not contain themselves.

In this example the basic question of set theory once more reveals itself: "Can I really think of every multiplicity as a unity? Is every collection of elements which are conceptually determined also a unity which is conceptually determined? Do the elements determine the set?"

Also, Paul Finsler, in his inaugural lecture (1926): "Are there contradictions in mathematics?" concerned himself with the set of all sets which do not contain themselves. In general a set does not contain itself as an element (for example the set of the first 25 prime numbers is not a prime number). Finsler showed – what Russell had proved – that this set could not exist and asked the question: "How is it possible that there are things which cannot be collected together into a set?"

Finsler answered:

> If one really thinks that the set of all sets which do not contain themselves, as given, then on can imagine, that one can also collect all these into a whole to form a set. To that one must retort: That is not true! One cannot imagine that. One imagines something or other, but not that, which fits this situation. For if one can imagine it, then one has to be able to say whether this collection itself includes itself or not, whether one imagines this set as one, which contains itself, or as one which does not, and one cannot say this. No, something logically contradictory one can really never imagine, this set exists just as little as the biggest number, which also doesn't exist.

These statements are very insightful. Finsler emphasizes that one cannot bring objects together into a unity while simultaneously observing this activity as a completed mental picture; therefore also cannot say which properties this set has.

Also the concept of "set of all sets" is an empty concept. It is not possible to think of all collections as a finished whole: if I collect together all already given collections, then this activity of my collecting, which I carry out in the present, cannot be given, since I carry it out just now. That which one produces just now by thinking, one cannot think of as already thought. That which is becoming cannot be considered as what has become; one's own "giving" is not "given."

Similarly, all such concepts as "the set of all thoughts" (Dedekind) or "the set of everything that can be thought" (Cantor) are empty of content.

In "Truth and Science" (GA 3) Steiner writes:

> However we know immediately that concepts and ideas first enter in the act of cognition and through this into the sphere of the immediately given .... Everything in our picture of the world has this property – that it must be given – if we want to experience it: only by concepts and ideas is the converse also valid; we have to produce them if we want to experience them. Thinking extends therefore beyond the domain of the given.

Out of Cantor's set theory, it follows, that Cantor considers infinite sets as actually given, therefore given in finished form.

It is truly characteristic that the mathematicians and philosophers before Cantor denied the thought of an actual infinite. So for example Aristotle says that infinity exists only in the potential, in the possibility, but not as a finished actuality: It has to constantly remain incomplete. This point of view can be also found by all the scholastics ("infinitum act non datur", Thomas Aquinas), by Pascal, by Kant, and the significant mathematician C. F. Gauss ("... so I protest .. against the usage of a infinity quantity as completed, which is never allowed in mathematics").

In this connection, the remark of C. F. Weizsäckers ("The Unity of Nature" IV. 4, "Possibility and Motion, a note on aristotelian physics", dtv, 1974) is interesting:

> As a matter of fact, the potential interpretation of the infinite avoids the paradoxes which critical spirits have again and again found in the idea of an actual existing infinity .... Whoever has understood that might indeed wonder why the mathematics of the second half of the 19th century nonetheless switched over to the actual notion of infinity, which is so much more difficult to justify – with such success, that one can hardly drive out the superstition from today's mathematic students, that this actual interpretation is the only possibility, it is the theory of the infinity and the continuum .... But the discovery of the paradoxes of set theory destroyed not only Cantor's picture of simple conceptual given-ness of the fundamental set-theoretical concepts, but also Frege's attempt to create a purely logical derivation for these concepts, whose dubious nature he recognized.

Cantor was convinced that the potential infinite logically implied the actual infinite. His reasoning is of fundamental importance and is closely connected with the problematic of modern mathematics. He writes ("Notes on the theory of the transfinite", see "G. Cantor, "Papers on mathematical and philosophical content", edited by E. Zermelo, p. 410 [convert to english or keep the german title]):

> Supposing that there is no doubt that we cannot measure the variable magnitude of the potential infinite, then one can prove the necessity of the actual infinity in the following way: In order that such a magnitude can be evaluated in a mathematical process, strictly speaking, the "domain" of the variable must be known; this "domain"

cannot however be something variable, since then a solid foundation for the process would then be missing; therefore this "domain" is a determined, actually infinite set of values. Thus, every potential infinite, if it is to be applied in a strict mathematical sense, implies the existence of an actual infinite.

Thus, for Cantor the actual infinite is the container within which processes are able to run their course. This makes it clear that Cantor's thinking still lives thoroughly in the world of ideas of the middle of the 19th century. Modern physics had to free itself – through difficult labors – from these ideas: that which is given are the immediate experiences, are the phenomena. To speak about objects, about things, that somehow lie behind these phenomena, is an inadmissable speculation. There is no "thing in itself" behind the appearances.

The stance of Cantor regarding the actual infinite was at first generally rejected, for example, by Leopold Kronecker and the important French mathematician Henri Poincare. Today, however, Cantorian set theory enjoys a general acceptance, even though it contains contradictions that are not easy to penetrate.

These contradictions arise, for example, when one postulates something contradictory: No one would search for the smallest odd number. Paul Finsler gives a more complicated example. He says: If one writes the three numbers 1, 2, and 3 on a blackboard, and then also: "The smallest natural number that isn't given on this board", then one obtains a contradiction; one can conclude that: the number 4 is on the board, as well as that: it is not given on the board."

On the one hand, the number in question is not explicitly mentioned in the statement on the board; on the other hand, the statement (in that it stands on the board) does in fact implicitly refer to the number. One postulates therefore something contradictory: the searched-for number should appear on the board, and it should also not appear on the board.

Other contradictions appear when the contents of a statement refers to who is making the statement. If someone says, "I am lying now," then this statement has no content (like the set of all sets), since it simultaneously asserts: "I speak untruth and I speak truth."

Other contradictions appear when something that takes place in process is converted into space. For example, let B_n be the set of natural numbers m with $n \leqslant m \leqslant 2n$. The limiting value

$$G = \lim_{n \to \infty} B_n$$

is observed. Even thought the set B_n contains $n+1$ numbers, hence the number of these numbers with increasing n becomes arbitrarily large, one is forced to the conclusion that G is the empty set. One can find namely no natural number that could be an element of G. But can this set G exist at all? The contradiction here involves the fact that on the one hand one only recognizes that which is fixed, what can be given; on the other hand, as one lets n grow arbitrarily large, n is handled like a "becoming" magnitude.

The following example is very illuminating. It shows how certain thought habits have established themselves in mathematics today.

Let the quadrilateral ABCD be a square with side length 1, so that its perimeter is equal to 4 side lengths. Let M be the center of the quadrilateral, and A_1, B_1, C_1, D_1 be the centers of the sides of the square.

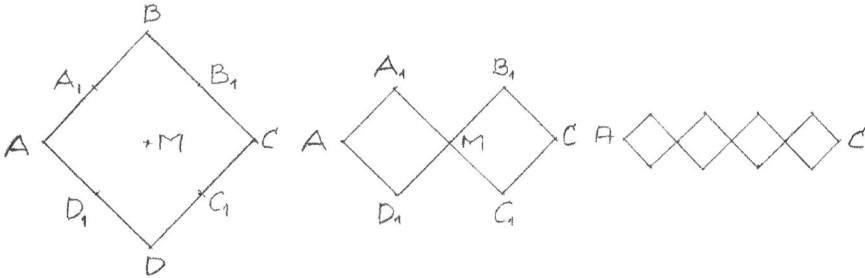

The squares AA_1MD_1 and MB_1CC_1 are then likewise squares, where the total perimeter is once again 4. Each of these new squares is then transformed into two smaller squares, so that a chain of 4 squares arises, having once again the total perimeter of 4. This chain of squares is denoted with K_2. In general let K_n be the chain of squares that contains 2^n squares. In the figure K_0, K_1 und K_2 are shown.

Since one can carry out the process described here indefinitely, the question naturally arises: Does the chain of squares K_n, with increasing n, approach some "limiting line?"

There are two possible answers to this question: Since all the corners of the squares that don't lie on the diagonal AC approach this diagonal arbitrarily close – with each step the distance of the corners above and below to this line is cut in half – one is obliged to consider this diagonal as the limiting line of the chain of squares. This can also – by a corresponding definition of "limiting line" – be proved with familiar concepts of epsilon-neighborhoods:

The segment BM has a length of $0,5 \cdot \sqrt{2}$. This length is denoted with a. Then the distance of the superior and inferior corners of the chain of squares K_n Kn from the diagonal is equal to $\frac{a}{2^n}$. To each positive ε one can find an $n_0(\varepsilon)$, so that $\frac{1}{n_0} \leq \varepsilon$. Hence all the points of K_n with $n \geq n_0$ have a distance from AC that isn't larger than ε. This fact can be seen as a definition of the statement that the limiting value of K_n as $n \to \infty$ consists of all points of the segment AC.

One can also take a different point of view: Since the perimeter of this chain of squares is always 4, it is independent of n, and the diagonal, whose doubled length is different from 4, cannot be the limiting line. From this perspective, there can be no limiting line.

The difference of the two interpretations can be so described: In the latter, the chain of squares is treated as whole (constant perimeter), while the former treats properties of the points of K_n, hence dissolves the whole process "pointwise." This corresponds to the assumption that time is a collection of moments.

When one treats the chain of squares K_n as a finite sequence of segments, then all these segments have a slope of either $+1$ or -1. From this point of view, the segment AC also cannot be a "limiting line", as this has a slope of 0.

This example shows that the question of the existence of a limiting value is dependent upon how one defines the limiting value. It can happen that these definitions do not always capture what an intuitive understanding would like to capture with the concept of a limiting value.

Using indirect proofs one can arrive at an incorrect judgement. This can lead to questionable concepts if the constructed contradiction is directed not against conscious assumptions, but rather against an assumption which one makes without knowing it. The following example is indeed content-wise without value, but it shows the logical structure of such a problematic proof. One claims that the largest natural number is odd. If this number were even, then with $n+2$ one would have a larger even number, which is a contradiction. Hence, the claim "follows." Here one makes the assumption – which is obviously absurd – that there is a largest natural number. In this way it can happen that the existence of certain sets is assumed, for which properties are then attributed based on indirect proofs. In this way concepts arise, which can hardly be attributed to the properties indicated by Steiner.

The following remarks from R. Steiner point out, that the way to the super-sensible in mathematics can only be found through active, willed activity:

> This natural science employs ready-made mathematics. He who will understand the clairovoyant process has to seek it where it is present in the most primitive form: in the forms of the mathematical. (Lecture of 8.4.1922, GA 82.)

Thereby is once more posed the question: is this path to the super-sensible present when everything related to number is made visible by points on a number line? It is not possible, for example, to construct a point – that is, to grasp it conceptually – that represents the transcendental number "Logarithm of 2 in base 3." The concept of this number generates only a nesting of rational intervals that become arbitrarily small, whereby a single interval says nothing regarding the number being represented. Only the sequence of intervals, that is the lawfulness of their coming-into-being, characterizes this number. One is demanding, in effect, that the quality of a number that expresses itself completely in rhythmical, in processual, should be grasped as something spatial.

In this sense, it is also not possible to consider a segment with its infinitely many points as a finished, given object. It's quite impossible to raise into consciousness all intermediate points – rational and irrational – as one traverses a given segment. This contradicts the experience anyone makes who thinks about this.

In his book "Paradoxes of the infinite" (1848, p. 23) B. Bolzano says :

> Indeed, not only is the set of finite parts, out of which all of time and all of space is composed – that is, the set of time- and space-points which exist – infinitely large,

but even the set of time-points (that lie between two time-points α and β, and let these be as close together as you wish, just as the set of space-points, that lie between two space-points, again as close together as you wish) is also infinite.

This atomistic way of thinking is typical for the middle of the 19th century. It no longer is fitting for the time we live in.

C. F. Weizsäcker also justifiably makes reference, in connection with Aristotle's refutation of the paradoxes of Xeno, to the fact that in reality the complete continuum, that is, the undivided segment, the full time interval of a real, completed process, exists.

> The points on a segment, the Nows in the temporal sequence of a experienced motion, don't actually exist if they are not actualized. Hence, a real motion "counts," for example just those points that are singled out through an objective feature, such as a temporary stillstand or a change of direction; of these, however, there are only finitely many. (The Unity of Nature, p. 432, dtv)

A student should leave school with the conviction that mathematics is not anything ready-made or completed, that there is still much to discover. In particular, discussions of trains of thought that lead to contradictory results enliven the instruction. If the teacher also calls into question generally accepted beliefs, then impulses can arise that lead strongly into the future. Furthermore, to examine what is already known from a new point of view awakens the spirit of research in the students.

In the 12th grade, the ability to form responsible judgements should be developed. To penetrate transformations and metamorphoses with thought leads to a thinking which is enlivened by will impulses.

Steiner repeatedly recommended to make all thinking lively, mobile. Through this submersion in a temporal element, one comes as teacher into an artistic process, through which all artistic fields can be taken hold of.

We have shown that the sculptural and the musical meet in the mathematical. While sculpting is a help to grasping the etheric, music-making is a help in grasping the astral, so that both activities support the mathematical. Even more broadly, Steiner says in a lecture from April 10, 1924 (GA 308), that one can only educate the human being if one studies the relationships of his bodily sheathes; in this way one learns the physical body abstract-logically, the etheric body through inner sculptural forms, the astral body through musical sensations, and the ego organization, when one identifies with the genius that is active in words. Thus: "cognition has to ascend from learning to sculpting, to the musical, to speech". In the evening lecture from April 24, 1924, (GA 316) one reads: "The spatial has to disappear into the sculptural, the sculptural into the musical, and the musical into that which can have a sense." These indications of Steiner appear to me to be very important for the mathematics teacher in the high school.

To the theme "Foundational Crisis of Mathematics" the following sources are recommended:

Paul Finsler: „Gibt es Widersprüche in der Mathematik?" abgedruckt in „Aufsätze zur Mengenlehre" herausgegeben von Georg Unger, Wissenschaftliche Buchgesellschaft.

Georg Unger: „Die Rettung des Denkens" Verlag Freies Geistesleben

L. Locher-Ernst: „Von der Gedankenlosigkeit in der Behandlung der Mathematik", Zeitschrift "Elemente der Mathematik" September und Oktober 1961

Ernst Schuberth: „Erziehung in einer Computer-Gesellschaft" Verlag Freies Geistesleben, 1990

Teaching the concept of infinity

PETER BAUM

A motto for the following thoughts might be *Observing our thinking when dealing with the infinite*. The thoughts were prompted by Uwe Hansen's article entitled *Mathematics as a bridge to the spiritual*, where Hansen goes into the concepts of the "actual infinite" and the "potential infinite". This led me, using examples, to look into these concepts and in the process find a way of speaking with students about the infinite in such a way that on the one hand there is agreement about certain basic experiences, particularly that trust in one's own thinking is built, yet on the other hand we are clear about the problems which can be bound up with the idea of the infinite.

First some thoughts about the concept of the limit in the infinitesimal calculus are set out in connection with Uwe Hansen's article. Then follow some thoughts about numbers, counting, the concept of the infinite and infinite sets, as well as the historical context. To conclude there is a short summary of how the infinite can be dealt with in school education, a way which seems meaningful to me.

1 The concept of the limit in the infinitesimal calculus

1.1 Null sequences

Uwe Hansen is mindful of the process we accomplish inwardly when we form a differential quotient. He draws attention to our own will activity appearing in that inner process, and compares it with the action of a musical sound: a differential quotient is the limit of a ratio after all.

His characterization prompts us to observe our own mathematizing activity, which is thought activity as well as will activity. How are the two activities related?

Steiner repeatedly stressed that will activity happens in the unconscious. This is comprehensible in the control of our limbs. We do indeed consciously experience the goals of our action as mental images, say fetching a particular book from the shelf, but not generally the action *as such* of the limbs which conveys the book to the writing table. Or we have a sound image of the particular tone we want to realize on the cello. Yet the movements of the left hand and right arm proceed unconsciously.

How is it with thinking about mathematical things? Is the will activity unconscious here also? Individual things I grasp consciously in my imagination. For example let's consider the thought activity leading to our comprehending that 0 is the limit of the null (or zero-tending) sequence of, say, reciprocals of natural numbers. We can describe the thought-process in the following steps:

1. First I have a picture of the natural numbers 1, 2, 3, ...

2. Then I picture to myself the sequence of reciprocals $\frac{1}{1}, \frac{1}{2}, \frac{1}{3}, \ldots$

3. Next I consciously compare the size of these fractions and ascertain that the bigger n gets, the smaller $\frac{1}{n}$ becomes, in other words that $\frac{1}{n} > \frac{1}{n+1}$.

4. I then come to the crucial insight that the number $\frac{1}{n}$ can be made as small as one wishes, in other words that there is no number $\varepsilon > 0$ such that $\frac{1}{n} > \varepsilon$ for all natural numbers n.

5. This demonstrable fact which I can also establish with other sequences of numbers leads to the idea of the *null sequence*; and I summarize the unique relationship of the number 0 to such a sequence, which no other number can have, in the concept of *limit*.

In a subsequent observation two things stand adjacent in my consciousness. First, the process of traversing the sequence 1, 2, 3, .. of values of n; second and independent of it, traversing the sequence $\frac{1}{1}, \frac{1}{2}, \frac{1}{3},....$ which I can follow for a while but not to the end in my mental image, and connected with it the better and better approximation of the fractions to the number 0 which thus merits being called the limit of the sequence $\frac{1}{n}$. That as "vanishing quantity" (*werdende Null* as Locher-Ernst[1] calls it) this variable $\frac{1}{n}$ never becomes zero [2] is immaterial for the concept of limit.

Is there also a will activity connected with this thought- or mental-imaging-activity? After all, we even spoke about "steps" in thought in imitation of walking with legs and feet, in the execution of which ambulatory motion the action of the will comes – unconsciously to us – into play. Yet of the train of thought itself, through which I can also run repeatedly forward and backward, I'm fully conscious. Here the activities of thinking and of willing appear to coincide.

1.2 The differential quotient

All limits can be reduced to a null sequence: if the sequence a_n has limit a, then the sequence $b_n = a_n - a$ is a null sequence.

Even the differential quotient is a limit, albeit the limit of a quotient in which both numerator and denominator are independently vanishing quantities. The term "differential quotient" comes from Leibniz, who regarded it as the quotient of the differentials dy and dx. In his article *Mathematics and occultism*[3], a record of his lecture given on 21 June 1904 in Amsterdam to a theosophical congress, STEINER describes mathematics as a means of developing spiritual cognition. Here he goes into the differential, subsuming under the concept *Euclidean mathematics* everything that

> can be described and constructed in the field of the finite. What I say in the sense of Euclidean mathematics about a circle or a triangle, or about number relationships is within the finite, can be constructed sense-perceptibly. This is no longer possible with the differential with which Newton and Leibniz taught us to calculate. The differential still has all the properties that make it possible for us to calculate with

---

[1] Louis Locher-Ernst: *Differential- und Integralrechnung*, Basel 1948, Chapter 4
[2] There are vanishing quantities which actually reach zero, repeatedly even, for example the distance of a pendulum from its resting position.
[3] *Mathematik und Okkultismus*, GA 35, pages 7 to 18.

it, *but as such it eludes sense-perception*. In the differential, sense-perception is first made to disappear; then we get a new, sense-free basis for our calculating. The sense-perceptible is calculated from what is no longer sense-perceptible. Thus the differential is something infinitely small as against the finitely sensible.

An indication of how the term differential was used in Steiner's time is found in H.B. Lübsen's book *Einleitung in die Infinitesimal-Rechnung (Differential- und Integral-Rechnung) zum Selbstunterricht* [*The infinitesimal calculus, differential and integral: a teach-yourself introduction*], Leipzig 1874, 5th edition. It was widely read at that time and is found in Steiner's private library. Indeed in Chapter II of his autobiography *The story of my life* Steiner writes:

> Another event deeply influenced my life. The mathematics books which Lübsen had prepared for home study became known to me. I was then able to teach myself analytical geometry, trigonometry, and even the differential and integral calculi long before I learned these in school.

Lübsen like Leibniz takes a start from the problem of finding the tangent to a curve and investigates using the function $y = \frac{x^3}{3} - 2x^2 + 3x + 5$ how the change in y depends on the change in x, by replacing y by $y + \triangle y$ and x by $x + \triangle x$. Lübsen then generalizes this train of thought by looking at a continuous function $y = F(x)$. An increase $\triangle x$ in the abscissa x entails an increase $\triangle y$ in the ordinate y so that $y + \triangle y = F(x + \triangle x)$.

Such a continuous function can be expanded as a power series in $\triangle x$, so that

$$y + \triangle y = F(x) + p \cdot \triangle x + M \cdot (\triangle x)^2 + N \cdot (\triangle x)^3 + \ldots$$
$$\triangle y = p \cdot \triangle x + M \cdot (\triangle x)^2 + N \cdot (\triangle x)^3 + \ldots$$
$$\frac{\triangle y}{\triangle x} = p + M \cdot \triangle x + N \cdot (\triangle x)^2 + \ldots$$

where the coefficients p, M, N are in general functions of x.

The first term p in the last series is obviously the limit of the difference quotient as $\triangle x \to 0$, and is completely determined by the function $F(x)$. This new function p of x we therefore call the *derivative* and following Lagrange we denote it $F'(x)$. Lübsen goes on:

> As Leibniz and Newton foresaw, not just for the tangent problem but also in many different and more important problems, knowledge of the first term $p \cdot \triangle x = F'(x) \cdot \triangle x$ in the total difference of a function is of great importance, as precisely this first term helps to solve these problems. Consequently for brevity an invented word is used to name this first term, it being called the *differential* of the function. And just as one habitually uses the symbol $\triangle y$ to denote the function's whole difference, so following Leibniz one uses the symbol dy to denote the first term $p \cdot \triangle x$ or $F'(x) \cdot \triangle x$

of this difference, which is the differential of the function $y = F(x)$. Thus $dy = p \cdot \triangle x$ or, by replacing $\triangle x$ by dx as well for the sake of symmetry,

$$dy = p \cdot dx.$$

In a footnote he then adds:

> Just as dy is called the differential of y, so dx is called the differential of x. The differential of the function $y = F(x)$, namely the *first* term of the total difference $\triangle y = p \cdot \triangle x + M \cdot (\triangle x)^2 + N \cdot (\triangle x)^3 + ...$ is obviously nothing other than the product of the increment dx of the independently varying quantity x and the derivative p or $F'(x)$ ... and one sees that the size of the differential $dy = p \cdot dx = F'(x) \cdot dx$ remains undetermined until the size of the increment dx is also given. Yet this indeterminacy can remain since we never need to know the absolute magnitudes of the differentials dx, dy but only their ratio, namely the differential quotient $\frac{dy}{dx} = p = F'(x)$ resulting from $dy = p \cdot dx$, which quotient is determined by x alone and coincides with the aforementioned limit, as $\triangle x = 0$, of $\frac{\triangle y}{\triangle x}$, which to begin with we had to denote by the indeterminate form $\frac{0}{0}$.
>
> [...]
>
> Since, that is, the differentials dx, dy even if left indeterminate signify quantities, one can do what would not be possible with the indeterminate limit symbol $\frac{0}{0}$, that is, separate the differentials and carry out arithmetic operations with them, and write for example $dy = p \cdot dx$ instead of $\frac{dy}{dx} = p$, $\frac{dy^2}{dx^2} = p^2$ or $dy^2 = p^2 \cdot dx^2$ instead of $\left(\frac{dy}{dx}\right)^2 = p^2$, etc.

The latter possibility was and is a particular strength of the differential notation. Leibniz gave, for differentiable functions $y(x), z(x), v(x), w(x)$, the following Rules of Differentiation:[4]

1. $da = 0$, if a is constant

2. $d(ax) = a \cdot dx$

3. $y = v \quad \Rightarrow \quad dy = dv$

4. $y = z - v + w \quad \Rightarrow \quad dy = dz - dv + dw$

5. $d(y \cdot z) = z \cdot dy + y \cdot dz$

6. $d\left(\frac{y}{z}\right) = \frac{z \cdot dy - y \cdot dz}{z^2}, \quad z \neq 0$

7. $d(x^n) = n \cdot x^{n-1} \cdot dx, \quad n \in \mathbb{N}$

---

[4] Moritz Cantor *Vorlesungen über Geschichte der Mathematik*, Vol. II, p 193, 2nd edition Leipzig 1901

8. $d\left(\frac{1}{x^n}\right) = d(x^{-n}) = -n \cdot x^{-n-1} \cdot dx = \frac{-n \cdot dx}{x^{n+1}}, \qquad n \in \mathbb{N}$

9. $d\sqrt[b]{x^a} = \frac{a}{b}\sqrt[b]{x^{a-b}} \cdot dx, \qquad a \in \mathbb{N}, \quad b \in \mathbb{N}.$

Leibniz emphasized particularly that Rules (h) and (i) are embraced by Rule (g), when n is a general rational number.

So while the two differences $\triangle x$ and $\triangle y$ and even their quotient $\frac{\triangle y}{\triangle x}$ are vividly present (for $\triangle x \neq 0$), the differentials dx and dy are indeterminate and usually thought of as "infinitely small" quantities. For that reason and because of their indeterminacy, their quotient $\frac{dy}{dx}$ is not calculable from them like a fraction with definite values in numerator and denominator. This seems to me to be the reason for Steiner's words on page 12:

> The differential still has all the properties that make it possible for us to calculate with it, but as such it eludes sense-perception.

This and the succeeding sentences of Steiner's quoted above possibly relate to the expression $\frac{0}{0}$ which indeed eludes sense perception in so far as the differential quotient as limit of the difference quotient is not revealed in it.

2 The natural numbers

2.1 Ordinals and cardinals

Our encounter with the numbers 1, 2, 3, ... in childhood years happens as a rule at two equivalent levels:

1. the level of time, for example in counting or the rhythmic reciting of multiplication tables

2. the level of space, for example using them for numbers of things.

A number appearing as something in a sequence in time with a predecessor and a successor we call an *ordinal number*. A number characterizing an arrangement in space, for example the number of apples in a set of apples we call a *cardinal number*.

2.2 Representing numbers

We first come to know the numbers as words. When a child learns to count he or she takes to heart the sequence in which the words one, two, three, and so on are recited on after the other. Later come the symbols for the numbers, the 10 digits. The next step is using the place value notation, the method of writing the digits next to each other and what this means. Consciousness of what a great invention it is to be able to represent every conceivable natural number with just 10 or 2 or 16 different symbols (digits) is only awoken later when binary and hexadecimal numbers are discussed. Already prior to that the place value notation is quite well understood in that pupils have learnt the correct use of the words one hundred, one thousand, ten thousand, etc. and can correctly classify the size of the number *three hundred thousand seven hundred and fifty four*, say. Only by means of the place value notation can we proceed ever further along the sequence of natural numbers.[5]

3   Concept of the infinite

Sometime or other, like any other word of our language, we come to know the word *infinite*. It describes some process or thing that has no end. The expression "infinitely many" is asserted if a process has no end in time or space. This is the way in which we are confident that the counting process can – thanks to the place value system – be continued, that every every natural number has a successor and – with the exception of the number one – a predecessor, so that there is no greatest natural number. Because by using the decimal, binary or other place value notation, we know how we get from a particular natural number to its successor.

> In the end it is only the certainty that this step from a natural number to its successor can always be made that convinces us that there can be no final (ordinal) number or greatest (cardinal) number, so that infinitely many numbers *can be generated*.

Here "infinitely many numbers" are understood to be a *potential infinity* (late Latin *potentialis*, "according to ability").

The fact can also be phrased:

> In the end it is only the certainty that this step from a natural number to its successor can always be made that convinces us that there is no final (ordinal) number or greatest (cardinal) number, so that infinitely many numbers *exist*.

In this formulation "infinitely many numbers" are thought of as an *actual infinity* (late Latin *actualis*, "active", "effective").

Many mathematicians cannot endorse this conception of the infinity of the natural numbers as an "actual".[6] They deem it inadmissible to consider the totality of the natural numbers as something that exists.

---

[5] Cantor was deeply involved with number systems and generalized the place value notation. In his paper *Über die einfachen Zahlsysteme*, Zeitschr. f. Math. u. Phys. 14 (1869) pages 121-128, he showed amongst other things that every number can be uniquely represented in the form

$$n = \sum_{v=1}^{N} \beta_v \cdot v!$$

where $\beta_v \in \{0, 1, 2, 3, \ldots v-1\}$ (see under http://gdz.sub.uni-goettingen.de)
See also H. Meschkowski: *Probleme des Unendlichen, Werk und Leben Georg Cantors*, Braunschweig 1967

[6] Henri Poincaré: "There is no actual infinity; ..." in *Wissenschaft und Methode*, Darmstadt 1973, p 179
Wolfgang Mückenheim (http://www.math.princeton.edu/~nelson/papers/rome.pdf)

Consequently they do not accept the existence of irrational numbers as "complete" numbers. Because in the decimal system these can only be represented as non-periodic decimals with infinitely many places. And like the natural numbers or any infinite sequence, these do not actually exist as complete wholes. According to this conception one can it's true calculate an irrational e.g. $\sqrt{2}$ to any degree of precision, yet no existence as a fixed quantity can be assigned to it. Personally I cannot subscribe to this view.

Since it sets a higher value on the virtual infinity of a counting process than on the certainty of being able to count indefinitely, does this view not represent a materialistic conception of mathematics?

This conception, allowing only a potential infinity, says:

> You can indeed count indefinitely, but since you will never finish, the totality of the natural numbers as a complete whole cannot exist.

The other conception, allowing even an actual infinity, says:

> Since at every point of the sequence of numbers you can continue counting and know precisely how to do it, it does not matter as far as the existence of all the natural numbers goes how far you've actually counted, in just the same way that the numbers from 10^{63} to 10^{64} and beyond exist, even though you can never actually count that far.

Again, clearly nobody can count or write down all the numbers. Yet to conclude that the totality of natural numbers cannot exist is just as questionable as the opinion that the set of natural numbers from 1 to 10^{63} doesn't exist simply because they can never be counted in reality.

Archimedes calculated the "sand number" 10^{63} to prove that a sphere of the size of that of the fixed stars filled with grains of sand still contained finitely many grains, rather than an infinite number as quite a few people believed at that time. For our point of view it doesn't matter whether or not Archimedes' estimate of the size is correct. For even among finite sets there are always those we would never be able either to count or to picture spatially in our imagination. Is this a reason to deny their existence? Probably not as it would lead to contradictions. The concept "finite" would actually become meaningless.

4   Infinite sets and the concept of the power of a set

If it's clear – for whatever reason – which elements belong to a set, and no contradiction results from the existence of the set, as e.g. in the case of the set of natural numbers, I'd regard disallowing a mathematical existence to such a set as an unacceptable thought restriction. A mathematical object's existence, in my view, arises in the moment a mathematician can conceive of it in such a way that it doesn't lead to a contradiction. That is how we are able think about the various sets of numbers (natural numbers, integers, rationals, irrationals, algebraic numbers, transcendentals, reals, complex numbers) without falling into contradiction.

Cantor used the concept of one-to-one correspondence to enable us to compare and classify infinite sets. By means of the concept of "power" he expanded the concept "number of elements" in finite sets, to infinite sets.

This basic approach shouldn't be withheld from students (see Section 6). It's a particularly important aspect of the infinite that a proper subset of an infinite set can have the same power as the latter (e.g. the set of even numbers as proper subset of the set of natural numbers). When we compare infinite sets, expressions like "equally many" or "more" or "fewer" lose their meaning. To perceive and experience this in one's thinking is an important step. It shows, in an easily comprehensible sphere, that thinking can go beyond supposed limits of knowledge.[7] See also footnote 14 on page 64.

The term "countable" as description of the power of the natural numbers arises as a consequence. Using the diagonal process it can be shown that the set of real numbers – if we assume that it's a given whole – is *not* countable.

An associated proposition is:

For each set $A \neq \emptyset$, the set $T(A)$ of its subsets is of higher power than the set itself.

First we should clarify how different powers (also called cardinal numbers) can be compared and ordered. This works as follows:

Suppose M and N are two sets with cardinal numbers $\overline{M}$ and $\overline{N}$ respectively, which have the following properties:

1. There is no subset of M which is equinumerous to (i.e. has the same power as) N

2. There exists a subset $N_1 \subset N$ such that N_1 is equinumerous to M (written $N_1 \sim M$).

Then $\overline{N}$ is said to be greater than $\overline{M}$, indicated by $\overline{N} > \overline{M}$ or $\overline{M} < \overline{N}$.

Applying this definition to the sets $\mathbb{N}$ of natural numbers and $\mathbb{R}$ of real numbers, we have:

1. $\mathbb{N}$ has no subset with the same power as $\mathbb{R}$.

2. There is a subset $R_1 = \mathbb{N} \subset \mathbb{R}$ such that $R_1 \sim \mathbb{N}$, i.e. that has the same power as $\mathbb{N}$.

---

[7] On 16 and 25 January 1916 Steiner compared the infinite sequence 1, 2, 3, ... with the infinite sequence 2, 4, 6, ..., the second of which contains *both* equally many numbers *and* half as many as the first. From this contradiction he concludes " ... that mental activity is really valid only in the finite. It is insecure and inconclusive as soon as it leaves the finite. Mental activity can do nothing whatsoever with its own inherent laws when it comes out of the finite into the infinite." (16.1.1916, GA 165).

And again "There's no doubt whatsoever that one gets into confusion in ones thinking as soon as one goes over to the infinite [...] Because of this the human being is lead, in a way, to say this to himself about his concepts: I really must not use them for the infinite, for what goes beyond the world of the senses (and the infinite does go beyond the sense-world), I mustn't apply them to the infinite." (25.1.1916, GA 166)

Hence $\overline{\mathbb{N}} < \overline{\mathbb{R}}$.

$\overline{\mathbb{R}}$ is also called the power of the continuum.[8] The concept of the continuum can be dealt with in school only in a naive sense – sets of all the points of a segment, all the lines of a pencil, all the points of a bounded surface, etc. The question of whether there is a set A whose power $\overline{A}$ satisfies the inequality $\overline{\mathbb{N}} < \overline{A} < \overline{\mathbb{R}}$ is still unsolved. The supposition that such a set *does not exist* was made by Cantor and called the "continuum hypothesis". In 1938 Gödel showed that this conjecture cannot be disproved provided the usual Postulates on which set theory is based are free from contradiction. In 1963 Cohen showed that neither can the continuum hypothesis be proved on this assumption. Together these two results mean that the continuum hypothesis is independent of the other Postulates.[9]

5 Historical perspective

5.1 Aristotle

People like to quote Aristotle as a representative of the view that no actual infinity ("infinitum actu non datur") exists. It's worthwhile however to consider the context of this passage.

The context is the Lectures on Physics, usually just called the *Physics*. It comprises eight Books concerned with various aspects of Nature. Book III deals with concepts of 'motion' (or 'process' in other translations) and 'infinity' – but simply from the point of view of being clear about Nature and what can be experienced by the senses. The following paragraph begins the discussion:[10]

> Nature has been defined as a 'principle of motion and change', and it is the subject of our inquiry. We must therefore see that we understand the meaning of *'motion'*; for if it were unknown, the meaning of 'nature' too would be unknown.
>
> When we have determined the nature of motion, our next task will be to attack in the same way the terms which are involved in it. Now motion is supposed to belong to the class of things which are continuous; and the infinite presents itself first in the continuous – that is how it comes about that 'infinite' is often used in definitions of the continuous ('what is infinitely divisible is continuous'). Besides these, place, void, and time are thought to be necessary conditions of motion.
>
> Clearly, then, for these reasons and also because the attributes mentioned are common to, and coextensive with, all the objects of our science, we must first take

---

[8] In Chapter 10, "Continuity", of his book *Space and counterspace* (AWSNA Publications, 2003) LOUIS LOCHER-ERNST naturally uses Cantor's conception. There he shows, in a somewhat different way than Cantor, that the set of points of a square including its boundary has the same power as the set of points of an arbitrary line-segment. He also showed that the the set N, whose elements are the subsets of an arbitrary set M, has a greater power than the set M. LOCHER-ERNST calls the different powers *degrees of infinity*, which are obviously not bounded above.

[9] Cf. Richard Courant and Herbert Robbins, revised by Ian Stewart, *What is mathematics? An elementary approach to ideas and methods*, 2nd edition, Oxford University Press, 1996, p 87

[10] Aristotle *Physica*, trans. R.P. Hardie and R.K. Gaye, Digireads.com Publishing, 2006.
Online at http://classics.mit.edu/Aristotle/physics.html

each of them in hand and discuss it. For the investigation of special attributes comes after that of the common attributes.

To begin then, as we said, with motion.

Aristotle was concerned with producing a concept of nature and not with mathematical investigations, even if later on he deals here and there with mathematics.

Discussion of the infinite begins in Chapter 4:

> 4. The science of nature is concerned with spatial magnitudes and motion and time, and each of these at least is necessarily infinite or finite, even if some things dealt with by the science are not, e.g. a quality or a point – it is not necessary perhaps that such things should be put under either head. Hence it is incumbent on the person who specializes in physics to discuss the infinite and to inquire whether there is such a thing or not, and, if there is, what it is.
>
> The appropriateness to the science of this problem is clearly indicated. All who have touched on this kind of science in a way worth considering have formulated views about the infinite, and indeed, to a man, make it a principle of things.

There follows a historical discussion about the thoughts of natural philosophers about the infinite. After that Aristotle remarks (Chapter 4, p 34):

> But the problem of the infinite is difficult: many contradictions result whether we suppose it to exist or not to exist. If it exists, we have still to ask how it exists; as a substance or as the essential attribute of some entity? Or in neither way, yet none the less is there something which is infinite or some things which are infinitely many?
>
> The problem, however, which specially belongs to the physicist is to investigate whether there is a sensible magnitude which is infinite.

Aristotle now looks into this latter problem. At the beginning of Chapter 5 he states:

> 5. Now it is impossible that the infinite should be a thing which is itself infinite, separable from sensible objects.

Then he remarks (Chapter 5, p 34):

> This discussion, however, involves the more general question whether the infinite can be present in mathematical objects and things which are intelligible and do not have extension, as well as among sensible objects. Our inquiry (as physicists) is limited to its special subject-matter, the objects of sense, and we have to ask whether there is or is not among them a body which is infinite in the direction of increase.

The investigation which follows comes to this conclusion (Chapter 5, p 37):

It is plain from these arguments that there is no body which is actually infinite.

We now, in Chapter 6, have the oft-quoted passage (p 37):

> 6. But on the other hand to suppose that the infinite does not exist in any way leads obviously to many impossible consequences: there will be a beginning and an end of time, a magnitude will not be divisible into magnitudes, number will not be infinite. If, then, in view of the above considerations, neither alternative seems possible, an arbiter must be called in; and clearly there is a sense in which the infinite exists and another in which it does not.
>
> We must keep in mind that the word 'is' means either what potentially is or what fully is. Further, a thing is infinite either by addition or by division.
>
> Now, as we have seen, magnitude is not actually infinite. But by division it is infinite. (There is no difficulty in refuting the theory of indivisible lines.) The alternative then remains that *the infinite has a potential existence*.
>
> But the phrase 'potential existence' is ambiguous. When we speak of the potential existence of a statue we mean that there will be an actual statue. It is not so with the infinite. There will not be an actual infinite. The word 'is' has many senses, and we say that the infinite 'is' in the sense in which we say 'it *is* day' or 'it *is* the games', because one thing after another is always coming into existence. For of these things too the distinction between potential and actual existence holds. We say that there are Olympic games, both in the sense that they may occur and that they are actually occurring.

Clearly Aristotle here is considering infinity within the bounds of the sense-perceptible, not in the supersensible domain of mathematics. He now compares infinity in the direction of decrease (division) with infinity in the direction of increase and finds them in some way identical. On page 38 of Chapter 6 he goes on:

> The infinite, then, exists in no other way, but in this way it does exist, potentially and by reduction. It exists fully in the sense in which we say 'it is day' or 'it is the games'; and potentially as matter exists, not independently as what is finite does.
> [...]
> A quantity is infinite if it is such that we can always take a part outside what has been already taken. On the other hand, what has nothing outside it is complete and whole. For thus we define the whole – that from which nothing is wanting, as a whole man or a whole box.

Finally he also gets to speak of mathematical objects (Chapter 7, p 39):

> It is natural too to suppose that in number there is a limit in the direction of the minimum, and that in the other direction every assigned number is surpassed. In magnitude, on the contrary, every assigned magnitude is surpassed in the direction of smallness, while in the other direction there is no infinite magnitude. The reason is that what is one is indivisible whatever it may be, e.g. a man is one man, not many. Number on the other hand is a plurality of 'ones' and a certain quantity of them. Hence number must stop at the indivisible: for 'two' and 'three' are merely derivative terms, and so with each of the other numbers. But in the direction of largeness it is always possible to think of a larger number: for the number of times a magnitude can be bisected is infinite. Hence this infinite is potential, never actual: the number of parts that can be taken always surpasses any assigned number. But this number is not separable from the process of bisection, and its infinity is not a permanent actuality but consists in a process of coming to be, like time and the number of time.

From this it follows, in my opinion, that Aristotle regarded not only a divisible segment but also a sequence of numbers not as something ideal but as something sensory, only existing in so far as someone is counting. This also becomes clear from the following words of comfort for the mathematician, and he evidently meant the geometer (Chapter 7, p 39):

> Our account does not rob the mathematicians of their science, by disproving the actual existence of the infinite in the direction of increase, in the sense of the untraversable. In point of fact they do not need the infinite and do not use it. They postulate only that the finite straight line may be produced as far as they wish. It is possible to have divided in the same ratio as the largest quantity another magnitude of any size you like. Hence, for the purposes of proof, it will make no difference to them to have such an infinite instead, while its existence will be in the sphere of real magnitudes.

In the last Chapter of Book III too it became clear to me that in these observations Aristotle is thinking about sensorily experiencable Nature and not about a purely spiritual content (Chapter 8, p 40):

> 8. It remains to dispose of the arguments which are supposed to support the view that the infinite exists not only potentially but as a separate thing. Some have no cogency; others can be met by fresh objections that are valid.
> (1) In order that coming to be should not fail, it is not necessary that there should be a sensible body which is actually infinite. The passing away of one thing may be the coming to be of another, the All being limited.
> (2) [...]
> (3) To rely on mere thinking is absurd, for then the excess or defect is not in the thing but in the thought. One might think that one of us is bigger than he is and

> magnify him ad infinitum. But it does not follow that he is bigger than the size we are, just because some one thinks he is, but only because he is the size he is. The thought is an accident.
>
> (a) Time indeed and movement are infinite, and also thinking, in the sense that each part that is taken passes in succession out of existence.
>
> (b) Magnitude is not infinite either in the way of reduction or of magnification in thought.
>
> This concludes my account of the way in which the infinite exists, and of the way in which it does not exist, and of what it is.

Steiner's observations about Aristotle in the lecture of 17.9.1915 (GA164) are also interesting in relation to Aristotle's comments on the infinite. There Steiner takes up Aristotle's proposition that

> There is nothing in intelligence which is not in the senses.

and says of it (page 16 of GA 164):

> This sentence of Aristotle's cannot be interpreted in any materialistic way, because Aristotle is far removed from every world view that's the slightest bit materialistic in its coloring. With Aristotle this sentence does not betray a world view but is to be taken in a knowledge-theoretic sense. In other words Aristotle refused to believe that one could obtain insights about any world *from within*, but asserted that one can only have insights by directing one's senses to the outer world, by receiving sense-impressions and using the faculty of reason to make oneself concepts from them; he does not of course deny that one takes in the spiritual with the sense-impressions. He imagined Nature to be permeated by spirit. Only one cannot, so he believed, approach the spirit if one doesn't look out into Nature.

5.2 Gauss

On 25 May 1831 Schumacher had sent Gauss a proof about the angle sum of a triangle, a proof that managed without parallels but instead allowed a triangle to have infinitely long sides. On 12 July 1831 Gauss writes to Schumacher[11], that a reply to the proof really required "page-long arguments", for which he "currently lacked the necessary serenity of mind" and goes on:

> Nevertheless to give you practical proof of my good will I will set down the following.
>
> The real nub you direct at once to every triangle; only you would essentially be using your very argument, if you applied the business first to the simplest case and established the Proposition:

---

[11] Letter no. 396 on page 268 of the Correspondence: www.sgipt.org/wisms/geswis/mathe/gsb396.htm

> *1) In every triangle in which one side is finite but the second and consequently the third is infinite, the sum of the two angles with the first side = 180°.*

There follows the proof of this Proposition according to Schumacher's idea. Gauss continues:

> As far as your proof to 1) is concerned, I object first and foremost against the use of an infinite quantity as something complete, which is never allowed in mathematics. The infinite is just a way of speaking, in that one is really talking about limits to which certain ratios approach as near as one wants, whilst others are allowed to increase without restriction.

After further remarks of a geometric nature the letter ends:

> But there's nothing contradictory in this, if finite man does not presume to want to regard something infinite as something given and as something that may be encompassed by his customary way of perceiving the world.
> As you see, here the point in question actually touches directly on the metaphysical. But that's enough. As always with the warmest friendship of your C. F. Gauss.

This letter should serve as evidence that even Gauss rejected the actual infinite. Meschkowski too appears to interpret the letter in this way:

> The protest of the "prince of mathematicians" must be based on his view that a reliable mathematical theory of the (actual) infinite is not possible and that every attempt must end in a maze of contradictions[12]

Yet the context of these remarks of Gauss' imply, in my opinion, that Gauss protests purely against allowing a triangle to have infinitely long sides to prove that the angle sum is 180°. This would prove the Parallel Axiom – which was the aim of Schumacher's deliberations. But the fact that in Euclidean geometry one cannot allow infinitely long line-segments in a 'proof' of the Parallel Axiom is not in dispute (as is not permitting a number ∞ in arithmetic) and has nothing to do with a possible existence, or indeed rejection, of the actual infinite. There is a difference between a) regarding infinitely long segments as something given and treating them like finite ones, and b) regarding the sequence of natural numbers a something given. One should study how Gauss' texts deal with the natural number sequence to find out in what sense he understood it.

---

[12] H. Meschkowski *Probleme des Unendlichen. Werk und Leben Georg Cantors* Braunschweig 1967, p 65

5.3 Hilbert

On 4 June 1925 David Hilbert gave a lecture in Münster ON THE INFINITE.[13] He ties up with the contribution of Weierstrass who had created a secure basis for the infinitesimal calculus and the theory of rational numbers by deriving statements about the infinitely great and the infinitely small from relations between finite quantities. But the problem of the infinite has still to be clarified, since the infinite still appears in infinite sequences of numbers and in the real number system understood as a complete totality. Hilbert remarks that many inconsistencies, absurdities and contradictions about the infinite have been formulated, and continues:

> By these remarks I wanted to show only that the definitive clarification of the *nature of the infinite* has become necessary, not merely for the special interests of the sciences, but rather for the *honor of the human understanding* itself.
>
> The infinite has always stirred the *emotions* of mankind more deeply than any other question; the infinite has stimulated and fertilized reason as few other *ideas* have; but also the infinite, more than any other *notion*, is in need of *clarification*.
>
> If we now turn to this task, to the clarification of the nature of the infinite, we must ever so briefly call to mind the contentual significance that attaches to the infinite in reality; first we see what we can learn about this from physics.

After considering matter, the atomic theory and electricity, Hilbert concludes that

> ...the net result is, certainly, that we do not find anywhere in reality a homogeneous continuum that permits of continued division and hence would realize the infinite in the small. The infinite divisibility of a continuum is an operation that is present only in our thoughts; it is merely an idea, which is refuted by our observations of nature and by the experience gained in physics and chemistry.

Without drawing any conclusions from this, Hilbert turns to the possible infinity of space and remarks that in astronomy serious objections have arisen against space being infinite. Euclidean geometry necessarily leads to an assumption of the infinity of space. Though this geometry is free of contradictions, that doesn't imply that it is also valid in *reality*. This could only be decided by experience. Einstein's theory of gravity suggests a finite world and even the results found by astronomy are compatible with elliptic geometry.

> We have now ascertained in two directions, toward the infinitely small and toward the infinitely large, that reality is finite. Yet it could very well be the case that the infinite has a well-justified place in our thinking and plays the role of an indispensable notion.

---

[13] Can be found in *From Frege to Gödel. A sourcebook in mathematical logic, 1879–1931*, Jean van Heijenoort, toExcel, Lincoln NE, 1999, p 370ff. ÜBER DAS UNENDLICHE can be found on the internet at http://gdz.sub.uni-goettingen.de/no_cache/dms/load/img/?IDDOC=26816

Hilbert turns to number theory and notes that even a simple formula, e.g.

$$1^2 + 2^2 + 3^2 + \ldots + n^2 = \frac{1}{6} n(n+1)(2n+1)$$

can contain infinitely many statements.

Another very fruitful conception bearing on the infinite is the introduction of ideal elements in geometry in the form of limit points and limit lines.

In analysis it turned out that many results, though true in the finite, cannot immediately be applied to the infinite.

Then Hilbert comes to speak about set theory:

> But analysis alone does not yet give us the deepest insight into the nature of the infinite. Rather, this is conveyed to us by a discipline that is closer to the general philosophical way of thinking and was destined to place the entire complex of questions concerning the infinite in a new light. This discipline is set theory, whose creator was Georg Cantor. Here, however, we are concerned only with what was truly unique and original in Cantor's theory and constituted its real core, namely, his theory of *transfinite numbers*. This appears to me to be the most admirable flower of the mathematical intellect and in general one of the highest achievements of purely rational human activity. Now what is it all about?
>
> If we wanted to characterize briefly the new conception of the infinite that Cantor introduced, we could no doubt say: in analysis we deal with the infinitely small or the infinitely large only as a limit notion – as something that is becoming, coming to be, being produced – that is, as we say, with the *potential infinite*. But this is not the real infinite itself. That we have when, for example, we consider the totality of the numbers 1, 2, 3, 4, ... itself as a completed entity, or when we regard the points of a line segment as a totality of objects that is actually given and complete. This kind of infinite is called the *actual infinite*.

Hilbert now goes into Cantor's transfinite numbers and the calculus created in a "gigantic" collaboration with Dedekind and Frege.

Then he graphically describes the irruption arising from the paradoxes of set theory, the so-called fundamental crisis of mathematics.

He shows a way of overcoming the crisis:

> Bu there is a completely satisfactory way of escaping the paradoxes without committing treason against our science. The considerations that lead us to discover this way and the goals toward which we want to advance are these:

> (1) We shall carefully investigate those ways of forming notions and those modes of inference that are fruitful; we shall nurse them, support them, and make them usable, wherever there is the slightest promise of success. No one shall be able to drive us from the paradise that Cantor created for us.
>
> (2) It is necessary to make inferences everywhere as reliable as they are in ordinary elementary number theory, which no one questions and in which contradictions and paradoxes arise only through our carelessness.
>
> Obviously we shall be able to reach these goals only if we succeed in completely clarifying *the nature of the infinite*.

In what now follows Hilbert outlines the program of his proof theory. He concludes his lecture like this:

> Finally let us recall our real subject and, as far as the infinite is concerned, draw the balance of all our reflections. The final result then is: nowhere is the infinite realized; it is neither present in nature nor admissible as a foundation in our rational thinking – a remarkable harmony between being and thought. We gain a conviction that runs counter to the earlier endeavors of Frege and Dedekind, the conviction that, if scientific knowledge is to be possible, certain intuitive conceptions [*anschauliche Vorstellungen*] and insights are indispensable; logic alone does not suffice. The right to operate with the infinite can be secured only by means of the finite.
>
> The role that remains to the infinite is, rather, that of an idea – if, in accordance with Kant's words, we understand by an idea a concept of reason that transcends all experience and through which the concrete is completed so as to form a totality – an idea, moreover, in which we may have unhesitating confidence within the framework furnished by the theory that I have sketched and advocated here.

In the onward development of mathematics it has turned out that Hilbert's program is not really feasible. In Chapter 2, Section 4.6 of "What is mathematics?" by Richard Courant and Herbert Robbins (revised by Ian Stewart) which every mathematics teacher should know, it says on page 88:

> Luckily, the existence of mathematics does not depend on a satisfactory answer. The school of "formalists", lead by the great mathematician Hilbert, asserts that in mathematics "existence" simply means "freedom from contradiction". It then becomes necessary to construct a set of postulates from which all of mathematics can be deduced by formal reasoning, and to show that this set of postulates will never lead to a contradiction. Recent results by Gödel and others seems to show that this program, at least as originally conceived by Hilbert, cannot be carried out. Significantly,

Hilbert's theory of the formalized structure of mathematics is essentially based on intuitive procedure. In some way or other, openly or hidden, even under the most uncompromising formalistic, logical or postulational aspect, constructive intuition always remains the vital element in mathematics.

5.4 Overview

The texts of three authors were looked at in relation to the question, Can the natural numbers be understood only as something coming into being, as a potential infinite, or also as something completely existing, as an actual infinite?

With Aristotle it should be borne in mind that in the *Physics lectures* what matters to him is the investigation of manifest Nature. The above-quoted words of Aristotle in Chapter 6: "The alternative then remains that *the infinite has a potential existence*" appears indeed to relate to what is manifest. On the other hand the words of Chapter 7, page 39 are pretty unambiguous:

> Hence this infinite [of the number sequence] is potential, never actual: the number of parts that can be taken always surpasses any assigned number. But this number is not separable from the process of bisection, and its infinity is not a permanent actuality but consists in a process of coming to be, like time and the number of time.

We can conclude from these words that Aristotle simply rejects an actual infinity for the number sequence. Yet the fact that he says "*this* number" suggests that the number sequence can also be understood in a different sense.

The passage in the letter of Gauss seems very clear to me: it relates to the (as a matter of fact inadmissible) reasoning with infinitely long sides of a triangle.

Hilbert is in no doubt in his view that the true infinite is the actual infinite. Because so long as we are considering something that's coming into being, we're seeing something finite.

6 Teaching about infinity

In my experience, provided students can meet the expression "There are infinitely many ..." with intuition that can be reconstructed in thought, it meets with no protests. Thus in a naive sense it's obvious that there are infinitely many natural numbers, points in a line-segment, points in a plane surface, and lines in a plane. From the 9th Grade one can also prove that there are infinitely many prime numbers. We should not withhold this beautiful example of an indirect proof from students. The irrationality of $\sqrt{2}$ can be proved in the 9th Grade as well, perhaps at the same time as Hero's method for finding square roots, which leads after a few steps to results that are more precise than does a calculator.

6.1 Types of numbers

In arithmetic one will go into the various types of numbers and how they're related in the 11th Grade at the latest, and explain how, by successively increasing the number of the arithmetic operations, they are produced from each other; this is a good opportunity to introduce as well the concepts set, element, subset, union, intersection and the associated symbols $\in, \subset, \subseteq, \cup, \cap$:

- By subtracting natural numbers we obtain the negative integers: $\mathbb{N} \Rightarrow \mathbb{Z}$

- By dividing integers we get the rational numbers: $\mathbb{Z} \Rightarrow \mathbb{Q}$. A rational is characterized by the fact that when it's expressed as a simple continued fraction, the continued fraction terminates somewhere, that is, it only has a finite number of partial denominators.

- By extracting roots of positive rationals we obtain the algebraic irrationals: $\mathbb{Q}^+ \Rightarrow \mathbb{A}$. Their simple continued fraction representations are infinite. They're periodic if and only if they represent irrational roots of quadratics.

- By square rooting negative numbers we obtain the imaginary numbers and thence the complex numbers $\mathbb{C}$.

All infinite continued fractions represent irrational numbers, which are either algebraic irrational or transcendental. Rationals and irrationals together constitute what we call real numbers. We have

$$\mathbb{N} \subset \mathbb{Z} \subset \mathbb{Q} \subset \mathbb{R} \subset \mathbb{C}$$

6.2 Correspondence

The positive even numbers $\mathbb{E} = \{2, 4, 6, ...\}$ constitute a proper subset of the natural numbers. Indeed, the fact that there's exactly one odd number before every even number in the sequence of natural numbers suggests that the set of naturals contains exactly twice as many numbers as the set of even numbers.

On the other hand for every natural number, by doubling we can find just one matching even number:

$$\begin{array}{cccc} 1 & 2 & 3 & 4 & ... \\ \updownarrow & \updownarrow & \updownarrow & \updownarrow & \\ 2 & 4 & 6 & 8 & ... \end{array}$$

So we *could* say, There are exactly as many natural numbers as even numbers.

The result of this contradiction is that formulations like "equally many" or "twice as many" become meaningless with infinite sets[14]: Some mathematical concepts set up in the finite are not

---

[14] In my opinion it was exactly this that STEINER wanted to express in his words of 16 and 25.1.1916 (see footnote 7 on page 53).

applicable to the infinite. Steiner, who always fought against erecting limits to knowledge, cannot have meant to deny absolutely to thinking the ability to concern itself cognitively with the infinite, even though the following words seem to suggest this:

> What I've just been saying [about the confusion of one's thinking as soon as one goes over to the infinite] is extraordinarily important. Because people completely ignore the fact that they only have a certain field – the physical plane – in which concepts can be used, and that this must be so for a definite reason.[15]

But if we can assign to each element of the one set exactly element of the other set, and vice versa, we have a possibility of comparing the sets, which in finite sets results in the same no of elements. Infinite sets whose elements can be put into a one-to-one correspondence are called *equinumerous* or *equivalent*. Sets equinumerous with the the set $\mathbb{N}$ of natural numbers are called *countable*, since we can enumerate their elements in a sequence.

Surprisingly the positive rational numbers are also countable, even though a given rational has neither a next greater nor a next smaller rational: between any two fractions there are infinitely many other fractions. Each rational number can be represented as an irreducible fraction $\frac{N}{D}$. This irreducible fraction can be ordered according to the sum $S = N + D$ of the numerator and denominator. For $S = 1$ we just have the number $\frac{0}{1} = 0$, for $S = 2$ the number $\frac{1}{1} = 1$ and for $S = 3$ the numbers $\frac{1}{2}$ and $\frac{2}{1} = 2$, and so on. The finitely many fractions belonging to the same sum S can be ordered by size. In the end we get a sequence of all the positive rationals. We can arrange the negative rationals between the positive ones and then enumerate the lot. Therefore the set of rationals is countable.

Even the algebraic numbers are countable. This is because each algebraic number satisfies an equation of the form

$$0 = a_0 + a_1 x + a_2 x^2 + a_3 x^3 + \ldots + a_n x^n \tag{1}$$

where $n \in \mathbb{N}$, $a_i \in \mathbb{Z}$ and $a_n \neq 0$.

To such an equation we can assign the number $h = n + |a_0| + |a_1| + |a_2| + \ldots + |a_n|$, called the *height* of the equation.

Now there are only finitely many equations with a given height, and since equation (1) has at most n distinct solutions, for each height there are finitely many algebraic numbers, which can likewise be written sequentially.

Are there any sets that are *not* countable?

Georg Cantor showed that the set $\mathbb{R}$ of real numbers is not countable. For the proof we can restrict ourselves to the interval $0 < x < 1$.

The claim is, The real numbers in the interval $0 < x < 1$ are uncountable.

---

[15] Rudolf Steiner, 25.1.1916, GA 166

Proof: Assume that they *are* countable. Then there must be a sequence in which each of these numbers appears somewhere or other:

$$\begin{aligned}
&\text{1st number:} && 0.a_1 a_2 a_3 a_4 a_5 \ldots \\
&\text{2nd number:} && 0.b_1 b_2 b_3 b_4 b_5 \ldots \\
&\text{3rd number:} && 0.c_1 c_2 c_3 c_4 c_5 \ldots \\
&\quad \ldots && \quad \ldots
\end{aligned}$$

We now produce a contradiction by constructing a number in the interval $(0,1)$ that doesn't appear in the sequence:

Let $a=1$ if $a_1 \neq 1$, otherwise let $a=2$;
let $b=1$ if $b_2 \neq 1$, otherwise let $b=2$;
let $c=1$ if $c_3 \neq 1$, otherwise let $c=2$; and so on

Then the number $0.abc\ldots$ we've constructed differs from each of the numbers in the above sequence in at least one decimal place. This contradicts the assumption that all real numbers in the interval $(0,1)$ appear in the sequence. So we have proved the claim.

In this context we can go into the concept of the transcendental number. It is a relatively recent concept: that non-algebraic numbers actually exist was first proved in 1844 by the French mathematician Joseph Liouville (1809 – 1882). They're called transcendental (Latin *transcendere* = climb beyond), since they go beyond the realm of algebraic numbers. That the numbers e and π are irrational, that is to say not representable as a fraction, has been known since Euler (1737) and Lambert (1768). In 1873 Charles Hermite (1822 – 1901) proved the transcendence of e, and in 1882 F. Lindemann achieved the proof of the transcendence of the number π. As a result it became clear that a quadrature of the circle with rule and compass alone is impossible.

Although we only know a relatively small number of transcendental numbers, and although it's often quite difficult to prove the transcendence of a number, it's precisely the set of transcendental numbers that makes the reals uncountable.

The number line

Already in middle school pupils learn that a line segment can be measured by repeatedly marking off a standard length. Assigning numbers to a straight line as on a measuring ruler becomes an obvious idea. From this emerges the correspondence of points of a line to the real numbers. But the realization that something is actually being posited here must first be engendered.

Assigning the reals to the points of a line is based on dual constructions:

- marking off a segment $\overline{AB}$ along a line to produce a sequence of points $P_1, P_2, P_3, P_4, \ldots$ with the property that $\overline{P_n P_{n+1}} = \overline{AB}$

- dividing a segment $\overline{AB}$ into n congruent subsegments, where n is any natural number.

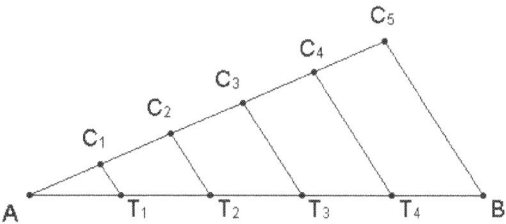

Figure 1: Division of a segment AB

The second construction is briefly described:

> An arbitrary segment is marked off n times on an arbitrary line through A giving rise to the points $C_1, C_2, C_3, ..., C_n$. Parallels to the connecting line $\overline{BC_n}$ are constructed through these points. These intersect the segment $\overline{AB}$ in the required dividing points
>
> $$T_1, T_2, T_3, ..., T_{n-1}.$$

The correspondence of the reals to the points of the oriented line follows from two claims:

1. If p is the number assigned to the point P and q the number assigned to the point Q, then the length of the oriented segment PQ is the number $\overline{PQ} = q - p$.

2. Congruent segments – up to sign – have the same length.

If we now assign to the points A and B the numbers 0 and 1 (the segment $\overline{AB} = 1$ is called the unit segment), then by the two claims and the two constructions to the points P_k are assigned the natural numbers k and to the dividing point T_k the rational number $\frac{k}{n}$ for each n.

By reflecting the half line AB in the point A we get as well the points associated with the negative rationals.

The points constructed in this way – "rational points" – are *everywhere dense*, because there are infinitely many other points between any two of them, just as between any two rationals $a < b$ there are infinitely many rationals x with $a < x < b$.

We might guess that this assigning of the rationals to the points of a line would capture all the points of the line. It turns out that this isn't the case though. If we construct a square $ABCD$ above the unit segment $\overline{AB}$ and draw a circle about A with diagonal AC as radius we obtain two points of intersection X and Y on the line AB which are not assigned to any rational, since by Pythagoras' theorem $\overline{AC}^2 = 2 \cdot \overline{AB}^2 = 2$ and so $\overline{AX} = \overline{AC} = \sqrt{2}$. The number assigned to X is therefore $\sqrt{2}$ which cannot be written as a rational $\frac{p}{q}$, and so is irrational.

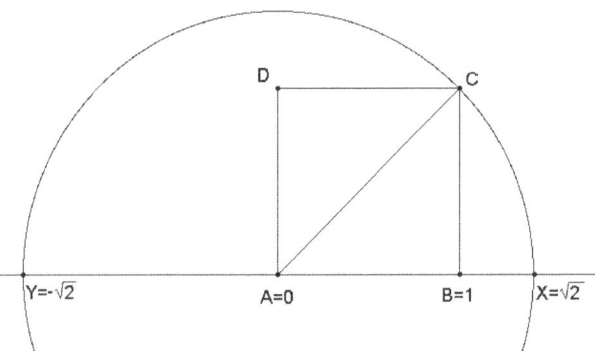

Figure 2: Points assigned to irrational numbers

Here we have a phenomenon which, although it eludes sensory perception and we cannot mentally picture it, we can nevertheless grasp in thought: Notwithstanding that the rational points are everywhere dense, there are any number of gaps between them filled by other points which we must assign to the irrational numbers.

6.3 The well-spring of the continuum

It's actually rather reassuring that mathematics isn't subordinate to any formal system. It's open to the forming of ever new concepts – whose mathematical existence must then be checked. In the process fallacies are of course possible: the history of mathematics is full of them. Even so, thinking is sovereign and ultimately decides about the existence of a mathematical object.

Considering the various possibilities for constructing the real numbers can make one aware of the "candour" as it were – one could also say the uncertainty – of the continuum.

For there are those which are are generated by a particular construction rule, e.g.

- quadratic roots by periodic simple continued fractions,
- or $\pi = \frac{1}{2} \cdot \lim_{n \to \infty} T_n = \frac{1}{2} \cdot \lim_{n \to \infty} S_n$, with $S_0 = 6$ and $T_0 = 4 \cdot \sqrt{3}$ [16] and the alternation between harmonic and geometric means

$$T_{n+1} = \frac{2 \cdot S_n \cdot T_n}{S_n + T_n} \qquad S_{n+1} = \sqrt{S_n \cdot T_{n+1}}$$

- or $e = \sum_{n=0}^{\infty} \frac{1}{n!}$.

---

[16] S_n is the perimeter of a regular $6 \cdot 2^n$-gon inscribed in a circle of radius 1, T_n is the perimeter of the associated regular $6 \cdot 2^n$-gon of tangents circumscribing the circle.

A formation rule can even be based on the positions after the decimal point (place values) of an infinite decimal, e.g. $x = 5.101001000100001\ldots$ Since this rules out a period, x is an irrational number. It's uniquely determined by the rule.

But what happens with decimal fractions whose place values are randomly generated? Can we speak of a well-defined real number in this case? We only know that with each step the interval containing the number is getting smaller. Nevertheless in each of these narrowing intervals there are always infinitely many numbers, and it forever remains an open question, what number will result. So one could justifiably claim that this number doesn't exist since it's created by a physical process which never comes to an end.

The process of forming the natural numbers is completely clear. One can even manage to generate the rational numbers $\frac{Z}{N}$ by way of the sum $S = Z + N$ and be confident that in doing so every rational is captured. Generating all of the *ir*rationals numbers however is not possible in this way. What comes to mind, rather, is the picture that in every interval however small there are infinitely many sources from which ever new irrationals ceaselessly gush. Of course every infinite sequence of digits which has no period represents an irrational and one would have to be able to give a procedure which captures every single infinite non-periodic sequence of digits. Yet this appears impossible. Can we nevertheless assume that the set of reals exists as a whole just like the set of natural numbers?

7 Paradoxes and antinomies

It seems important to me to discuss with the students the phenomena of paradoxes and antinomies, since one can use them to make clear the difference between purely logical thinking and thinking oriented toward reality.

They need to discover that apparently plausible-sounding descriptions of things can be unfounded. In 1918 Bertrand Russell formulated this example of a logical antinomy:

> The barber of Seville is a male inhabitant of Seville and shaves precisely those male inhabitants of Seville who do not shave themselves. Does he shave himself or not?

At first this sounds like a perfectly reasonable situation: a town has male residents who either shave themselves or not. Whoever doesn't shave himself goes to the barber. So the barber shaves those people who don't shave themselves, actually *only* those, since of course the others shave themselves.

So far so good – unless we have to answer the final question.

Let's assume the barber shaves himself, something we can well imagine. In that case he belongs to those male inhabitants of Seville not shaved by the barber, since the latter only shaves those who don't shave themselves. From this it follows that the barber *doesn't* shave himself. This contradicts our assumption, which consequently cannot be correct. Yet if we assume the barber *doesn't* shave himself, this leads to a contradiction too. Because if he doesn't shave himself, he of course belongs to those who are shaved by the barber, so he *does* shave himself.

How do we get out of this predicament? The students should discuss this for a while. Perhaps they themselves will come to the solution of the problem: there *is* no barber like the one characterized.

A second classic example is that of the Cretan Epimenides, who maintained that all Cretans are liars. Did Epimenides speak the truth or did he lie? If he has spoken the truth then his statement applies to himself since he's a Cretan. Yet this means that he has lied – which contradicts our assumption. So the assumption that he has spoken the truth is false.

But if he has lied then at least one Cretan is not a liar. But the Cretan who speaks the truth cannot be Epimenides otherwise our assumption that Epimenides has lied would be contradicted.

By reflecting in this way with the students we show them on the one hand that we can have confidence in our thinking and on the other that, with problems of the infinite, we also come up against limits (see Section 6.3) about whose meaning and consequences each must decide for him- or herself.

The meaning of the infinitesimal calculus[1]

WALTER HUTTER[2]

The infinitesimal calculus has become an established component of our reality, both as a method of calculation and as a way of thinking. We have become so used to using the word *infinity*, that the only way to bring life back into the concept is via conscious reflection on the content and relationships of the thought processes in their historical context. We speak quite glibly, for example, of an "infinite universe". In doing so, we apply a name that appears disconnected from our own experience, and isn't supported by comprehensible, living concepts rooted in well-rounded perceptions.

The following points of view are presented to stimulate a deeper discussion of the archetypal phenomena of the infinitesimal calculus. For the teacher, the text can serve as historical background. Given the opportunity, some details can also be profitably shared in the classroom.

1 Egypt

Interest in numbers is an ancient and distinctive feature of human thought. The Egyptians dealt with counting and related everyday problems in a very practical way. They created no science, least of all a theory of numbers, but they placed arithmetic, study of volumes, and geometry at the service of such concrete tasks as surveying, calculating the pyramids, determining annual harvests, or taxes. They even employed powers of numbers and geometric progressions, but without actually thinking about limiting values.

The infinite and the infinitesimal were not an object of their considerations. The additive character of Egyptian mathematics is evident in the Rhind papyrus (ca. 1650 BC) [Ei77].

> Neither did the ancients provide proofs or explanations; the recipe sufficed for them, but – and this is the point – they showed no interest in a principle. The latter way of thinking was first practiced by the "father of logic", Aristotle. Yet if, for the Egyptians, the results of their mathematical thought are single-valued, their methods were, by contrast, manifold. They discovered a solution in an accumulative way, so to speak "aspect-wise", a peculiarity reminiscent of the different ways of measuring in today's quantum mechanics. [Br90, p. 136]

---

[1] Revised version of the article with the same title appearing in: *Tübinger Berichte zur Funktionalanalysis*, Volume 14, 2004/2005, pp 233 – 251.

[2] The author would like to thank Dr. Klaus Weinrich for valuable suggestions and corrections.

2 Greece

The Egyptian high culture greatly influenced classical antiquity. By reshaping mathematics and taking it further, the Greek cultural epoch paved the way for the age of science. Thinking – at once abstract and hair-splitting – along with proving, became necessities for the Greeks. With his paradoxes, the sophist Zeno of Elea (around 450 BC) introduced new challenges into the world and arrived at an antithesis between a discrete conception of the world and of numbers, versus a continuum capable of ever-further division.

Zeno's first paradox is supposed to show that motion is impossible, the argument being as follows. To cover a given segment, one must first traverse half the segment; but before this half-segment is covered, half of *it* (a quarter of the full segment) must be covered, and so on for ever. But covering infinitely many segments in a finite time is impossible.

His second paradox is the famous story of the race between Achilles and the tortoise. Achilles starts somewhat later than the tortoise. When he reaches the place where the tortoise was when he (Achilles) started, the tortoise has already gone a stretch further. When Achilles reaches this further point, again the tortoise has gone a certain distance further, and so on ad infinitum. For the same reason as above, Achilles never catches up with the tortoise.

The fire of a new thinking was kindled. Aristotle (384–322 BC) offered solutions to the paradoxes.

> He proved that the assumptions of the paradox, that infinitely many things cannot be traversed in finite time, is not admissible in the sense used in the paradox. We have to distinguish between an infinitude of quantity and an infinitude by dint of continued division. [...] Aristotle sought above all to show that finiteness in measurability and infiniteness in divisibility do not exclude each other. ... Aristotle had not overlooked the deficiency of his formal refutation [of Zeno's paradox], in that it did not eliminate the possibility of an obvious contradiction when finite and infinite are brought into relationship with each other. [Sc62, pp. 60, 61]
>
> In a broad sense there are no insoluble problems, but only those which, arising from a vague feeling, are not yet suitably expressed. This was the position in Greek thought of Zeno's paradoxes; for the notions involved were not given the precision of expression necessary for the resolution of the putative difficulties. It is clear that the answers to Zeno's paradoxes involve the notions of continuity, limits, and infinite aggregates – abstractions (all related to that of number) to which the Greeks had not risen and to which they were destined never to rise, although we shall see Plato and Archimedes occasionally straining toward such views. [Bo59, p. 25]

These beginnings of an infinitesimal way of thinking turn up in the method of exhaustion of Eudoxus of Cnidus (ca. 400–347 BC) which he used in squaring the circle [Be66, p. 93], or the area calculations (e.g. quadrature of the parabola) of Archimedes of Syracuse (287–212 BC) [Be66, p. 109].

> Archimedes' *Method of mechanical theorems* (Ephodos) [...] was first brought to light in 1906 in a Greek monastery in Constantinople by Heiberg, whose attention had been drawn to it by a German philologist. Its appearance was a genuine sensation. Here, in a letter to an expert friend, Archimedes for once gives a glimpse into his workshop. He gives a mechanical procedure by means of which he had discovered a variety of his sensational results, which he subsequently furnished with the rigorous, indirect proofs appearing in his scientific writings. Previously one had only been aware of this *Method* through some remarks of Hero of Alexandria's. When the *Method* appeared in 1906, one could see that so-called "indivisibles" were used in it with full clarity, the same indivisibles upon which Cavalieri at the beginning of the 17th century sought to build a systematic infinitesimal calculus. [Wi29, p. 46]

The infinitesimal calculus is based moreover on the idea of *function* and being able to represent functions (relationships between variable quantities) in a coordinate system. The origins of both can be traced back to earliest times even if the concepts, well-known to us, were lacking.

> Here one must keep in mind that the word 'function' was completely unknown to ancient mathematics. It belongs, indeed, to a much later age. But are we for that reason justified in concluding that they had no idea of functional relationship? [Pe74, p. 35]

Already the comprehensive tabulated astronomical observations recorded in antiquity and the chord tables of Hipparchos of Nicaea (around 150 BC) or Claudius Ptolemy (85–165 AD) reveal a thoroughgoing treatment of quantities which determine each other lawfully (see e.g. [Tr03, vol. 2, p. 190]). Furthermore Babylonian tables, originating in the period 2000–300 BC and handed down in large numbers, furnish evidence of a clear understanding of functional relations, alongside highly developed algebraic methods.

> The Babylonians, as far as we know, had no geometric model but rather used certain arithmetical functions whose values at an instant in time described the position of a celestial body with respect to the background of fixed stars as seen from the earth. ... These functions, or tables of values, were intellectual abstractions and not just the results of observations. [RW84, p. 84]

Orientation based on spherical coordinates and perpendicular axes has been well-known from earliest times in astronomy and cartography [RW84, Fu98] and constitutes, along with the treatment of numerical correspondences, a highly sophisticated basis for the development of modern mathematics. What we would call number theory finds a provisional high point in Diophantus of Alexandria (around 250 AD). In a similar way, a dazzling geometry skill shines in the work of Euclid (340–270 BC), in the treatise on conics of Apollonius of Perga (around 200 BC) and in the commentaries of Pappus of Alexandria (around 300 AD) which summarize the knowledge of his time.

3   Transitions

In the fourth century A.D., we find many typical representatives of the forces and impulses working at such a momentous point of time in the evolution of humanity. The significance of this century is at once apparent when we think of the following dates. – In the year 313, religious tolerance is proclaimed by the Emperor Constantine; in 363, with the murder of Julian the Apostate, the last hope of a restoration of ancient thought and outlook is suppressed; Hadrianople is conquered by the Goths in the year 378. In 400, Augustine writes his Confessions, bringing to a culmination, as it were, the inner struggles in the life of soul through which it was the destiny of western European civilisation to pass. [St89, p. 36]

While the Arabs elaborated to full clarity the Greek approach to mathematics, and then subjected it to a rigorous "algebraization" [Ca65, Ju64, Ge84], the Christian occident lived through nearly a millennium of mathematical stagnation without new discoveries [Ju64, Ge90]. The Christian world-view detached itself from the culture of antiquity. While the Greek sage had still felt a spiritual nature within himself, and as a partly earthly and partly divine creature, in the Middle Ages the question came more and more to the fore, "Does anything *eternal* exist in the human being at all?" The novelty in this, was that one began to think about reason.

Christianity came to the conviction that God has disclosed wisdom to the human being through revelation, and that an image of divine revelation comes to it through its faculty of knowledge. The wisdom of the Mysteries is a hot-house plant, revealed to a few individuals who are ripe for it; Christian wisdom is a mystery revealed as knowledge to *none*, but as a content of faith to *all*. The viewpoint of the Mysteries lived on in Christianity, but in an altered form. All people, not only particular individuals, were to share in the truth, but it was intended that at a certain point man should admit his inability to penetrate farther by means of knowledge, and should then rise further by faith. Christianity brought the content of the evolving Mysteries out of the obscurity of the temple into the clear light of day. [St25, p. 150]

Life in the Middle Ages was determined by humble outer living conditions, by the monasteries established early on in this period, by the feudal system characterized by serfdom, and by the suppression of the powerful Greek and Roman cultures. Against this background, faith and the limits of knowledge show that they belong together in a centuries-long process of emancipation of the understanding from "it thinks in me" to "I think": the Middle Ages can be seen as the reorientation of an intellectuality freeing itself from its bondage within in the world process, the progressive liberation of reason from the outer world, as the defining quality of an epoch of transition from world-consciousness to self-consciousness.

Among the forerunners of early modern science are Robert Grosseteste (1175–1253) who presses forward to a geometric modelling of optical phenomena, and Roger Bacon (1214–1292), who further shows the usefulness of mathematics for knowledge of nature and advances the process of separating the secular sciences from theology. At the threshold of the 15th century a newly freed power appeared which had already started begun to announce itself in the 13th century, as a result of the opening to science: no later than 1401 Brunelleschi discovered *perspective,* which, in a broader sense, became a symbol for all inner activity: the *overview* in the natural sciences and humanities, rather than discussion about separate aspects to be found in the world, now moves to center stage. From now on the "perspective" rather than the "aspective" [Br90] gave direction to the ripening intellectual powers, which turned gradually from the theologically-tinged observation of the world of the Middle Ages, towards the outer world of natural phenomena.

4 New impulse

Figure 3: Nicole Oresme, painted by the author

A particularly noteworthy personality of the 14th century was the mathematician and philosopher Nicole Oresme (1323–1382), bishop of Lisieux from 1377. Like Leonardo of Pisa (ca. 1170–1240), Jordanus Nemorarius (around 1200) or Thomas Bradwardine (1290–1349), Oresme took the heritage of antiquity and developed it further. For example, in his mathematical works, taking the classical theory of proportion as his starting point, he introduced fractional exponents. He also concerned himself with numerical series, and posed the question of their limits [Or66, Wi14]. Oresme was at the same time a thinker in the medieval tradition and made a thorough study of Aristotle, preparing French translations of his works. In essence he decided in favor of the concept of motion as Aristotle had shaped it. According to Oresme, the so-called *impetus* of a moving body is the inner basis of the movement. To move means to conduct oneself differently in relation to space, which is thought of as unmoving. Oresme came to an independent conception of the possibility of manifold movement, thereby overcoming the Aristotelian view [Bo34, Cl59, Di56, St69].

Abbildung 4: René Descartes, copper engraving around 1820

Oresme found himself at the threshold of the analytic geometry of Descartes and Fermat, the dynamics of Galileo and the geometry of indivisibles of Cavalieri. At the center of Oresme's teaching was the idea of the *variable extension of forms* and their graphical representation. This outstanding representative of scholastic science arrived at this picture through his attempts to grasp the natural philosophy of antiquity and that of his time from a new standpoint [Ju64, p. 412].

This is a relatively important theoretical moment: people begin to perceive natural laws as functional dependences, and interactions between mathematical thinking and kinematic conceptions emerge [DP94, p. 230].

Since Oresme's time, research has been conducted based on this new point of view. [3] Johannes Kepler (1571–1630), René Descartes[4] (1596–1650), Bonaventura Cavalieri (1598–1647), Pierre de Fermat (1601–1665), John Wallis (1616–1702) and Isaac Barrow[5] (1630–1677) are only some of the names of those who developed analysis before Leibniz and Newton (a comprehensive collection of original work is to be found in the source books [Sm29, St69]; for more recent summaries see [DP94] and [KN98]). The coordinate system as a means for the graphical representation of functions became an inherent part of mathematical thought (for the history of this, see [Bo59, Fo77, DP94, KN98]). Before long, functional relations came to be investigated and characterized, and gained great importance as a result; but they also sparked a debate regarding the definitive concept of the function which continued into the 19th century [Du82, Sp00, Th00].

5 The infinitesimal calculus

But since a sum of points will not yield a line, nor a sum of lines a surface, the points are *immediately* assumed to be *linear*, just as the lines are assumed to be two-dimensional. But again, since linear elements *ought not* to be lines yet, which they

---

[3] Abraham Gotthelf Kästner's four-volume work [?] is a treasure-house of (today rather forgotten) connections and rare pre-17th century books of pure and applied mathematics.

[4] *The ancients took pains to avoid the name of the infinite and anything associated with it in any way, which tries our patience, yet Descartes somewhat tremulously applied the word indefinite,* indefinitum, *to it.* [?, Preface, p. 2]

[5] *Isaac Barrow was the first inventor of the Infinitesimal Calculus; Newton got the main idea of it from Barrow by personal communication; and Leibniz also was in some measure indebted to Barrow's work, obtaining confirmation of his own original ideas, and suggestions for their further development, from the copy of Barrow's book that he purchased in 1673* [Ba16, J.M. Child's preface, p. viii]. Isaac Barrow discovered most of the rules of differentiation. He proved the fundamental theorem of differential and integral calculus in 1667 (see [Ba16, We56]).

would be if they were taken as quantum, they are represented as *infinitely small*. [...]
It is the need to get hold of this moment of qualitative transition and for this reason
to have recourse to the *infinitely small* that must be regarded as the source of all
the mental pictures which, though meant to smooth out every difficulty, themselves
present the greatest difficulty. [He65, p. 377]

In the year in which Hegel's *Logic* was published (1812), almost 130 years after the first publication by Leibniz of the the infinitesimal calculus, discussions about a definition of the differential quotient (coefficient) were in full swing and nowhere near a conclusion. Georg Wilhelm Friedrich Hegel (1770–1831) put forward the thesis that analysis as a mathematical discipline must transcend itself. With the calculus of infinity, traditional mathematics had reached some sort of limit.

Figure 5: Isaac Barrow, Stahlstich um 1860

The determination of quantity and quality, of finiteness and infinity, can be discovered in the totality of the differential quotient, a self-contained entity, that cannot be subordinated to a higher totality. According to Hegel, two opposites, being and nothingness, meet in unity in the concept of becoming. Thus the concept of becoming is characterized by means of a mathematical concept, that of the differential quotient.

Abbildung 6: Gottfried Wilhelm Leibniz, copper engraving, around 1820

The differential calculus was created by Gottfried Wilhelm Leibniz (1646–1716) and Isaac Newton (1643–1727) [Le20, Ge48, Ne04].

By 1650 all these facts were on hand. But only a man of the next generation, Isaac Barrow, recognized in 1667 the basic relation which appeared here – the *fundamental theorem*. [...] In his Preface he acknowledges the help given him by his student Isaac Newton. Barrow had originally been a theologian. Later on problems of the calendar and of biblical chronology led him to take an interest in astronomy; and, since this could not be done without mathematics, he began to study Euclid and the other Greek mathematicians and eventually had become [a] teacher and researcher in mathematics [...].

But then a strange thing happened: after having published the *Lectiones geometricae*, which contained all the discoveries mentioned above, he gave up his teaching position, handing it over to young Newton, while he himself returned to his clerical career, at first in humble circumstances, but gradually rising to a leading position in the Anglican church. Only in his leisure hours did he still occupy himself with Euclid and the other ancients. In the meantime Newton continued to develop the infinitesimal calculus in various directions. He infused it with the theory of infinite series, in which he had made his first discoveries, and used it in connection with his discovery of the law of gravitation. But in his publications on this law he circumvented the infinitesimal calculus and published nothing on the calculus itself. [...] [Leibniz] was already in possession of the differential calculus, the first suggestions of which he had found in Pascal. [...] He too did not publish anything for quite a while. Only when year after year passed without Newton's publishing anything did Leibniz in 1684 begin publishing his results. Then much later, only after 1700, that unhappy priority dispute broke out which embittered the declining years of both men. [...] We are interested in the question of the substance of the dispute. The basic discoveries could all be found in Isaac Barrow's work published in 1669. But the mathematical public had learned the new calculus in the form published by Leibniz and worked with his differentials. In fact, a "mathematical public" came into being only through these publications. [...] And when all this began to sail under the flag of "Leibniz", English mathematicians recalled that Barrow and Newton had already been in possession of it. Thus the quarrel started. This in itself does not interest us. [...] We may speculate that it is somewhat absurd for the priority dispute to have raged between Newton and Leibniz rather than between Barrow and his successors. [To49, pp. 96, 128ff]

"I consider the undetermined quantities as in continuous movement, waxing and waning, that is to say as ebbing or flowing," said Newton. If in the case of a quantity y dependent on x, we call the increase in x, Δx, and the corresponding change in y, Δy, then the so-called derivative, i.e. "the ultimate ratio of evanescent increments" is the limiting value of $\frac{\Delta y}{\Delta x}$ in case Δx tends to zero. As a result Δx and Δy become infinitely small. Leibnitz called these infinitely small quantities dx and dy. The derivative was therefore $\frac{dy}{dx}$, a notation we still use today[6]. "The differential dx of the variable x has real existence as final, indivisible element of the axis of abscissas." So said Leibniz. He thus saw dx has a quantity smaller than any other quantity, yet not zero. He spoke of "actual infinitely small quantities".

---

[6] *In this way we obtain a definite value for $\frac{dy}{dx}$, dependent purely on the form of the function, which is thus called vanishing quotient.* [Ku31, p 196]

Abbildung 6: Isaac Newton, copper engraving, around um 1820

Leibniz and Newton struggled to understand what they had created. It was especially difficult for their successors to entertain such ideas. A metaphysical mood is evinced by the question of the philosopher George Berkeley (1685–1753) from the year 1734 about the nature of "evanescent increments":

> And what are these same evanescent increments? They are neither finite quantities, nor quantities infinitely small, nor yet nothing. May we not call them the ghosts of departed quantities ... ? [Sm29, p. 633]

Notwithstanding that with Leibniz and Newton the tangent problem and motion respectively took center stage[7], the difficulty for contemporaries and also for later mathematicians lay in coming to terms with what is essentially a numerical phenomenon. Both in numerator and denominator there is a variable quantity which approaches arbitrarily close to zero. Locher-Ernst called these "nascent zeros" [*werdende Nullen*] [Lo48, p. 163]. We thus see two nascent zeros whose quotient (as simultaneous limit) takes on a definite numerical value. The information that we have two nascent zeros *on its own* betrays nothing about the result to be expected. In general a ratio of two nascent zeros can take any numerical value, but it can also be infinite or even indeterminate. Only the *quality* of the becoming zero in numerator and denominator seen together determines the result.

This concludes our account of the origin of the differential calculus. At this point we make special mention of five books. The various editions of H.B. Lübsen's classic (see e.g. [?]) are particularly suitable sources since the metaphysics of the infinitely small and the so-called limit method are brought to bear side by side. Courant and Robbins [CR67] give a comprehensive insight into the origin of the infinitesimal calculus. Otto Toeplitz [To49] gives a lively treatment of the calculus using the genetic method. Egmont Colerus [Co57] recounts simply (so that everyone can understand it) how starting from the basics one can arrive at the integral. The two volumes of Karl Snell [Sn46] are very detailed, readable and worth reading.

What were the implications of the discovery of the infinitesimal calculus, and what prospects does handling this newly-won mathematics offer today?

---

[7] *Englishmen availed themselves of Newton's Calculus of Fluxions. [...] They wanted to accuse Leibniz of having had prior knowledge of Newton's method from correspondence; yet this accusation is quite unproven, Leibniz's famous character is contrary to it, and the fact that each in his calculus used quite different concepts as a basis, the one differences, the other velocities, seems to add weight to the idea that each came to his Calculus through his own thought.[...] The concept of Fluxions, and the word* fluere *itself are to be found in Napier's 1614 work* Mirifici canonis logarithmorum descriptio, *as MacLaurin's* Treatise on Fluxions *admits. [...] Furthermore the first applications of Fluxions and the Differential Calculus to the drawing of tangents were made.* [?, pp. 28, 29, 59]

6 Mathematics and physics

Figure 7: Pierre Simon de Laplace, copper engraving around 1830

The infinitesimal calculus branched out in the course of the centuries (see e.g. [Ba69, Bo51, Bo71, GO64, Kl72, Di85, HW96, Gr00, Gr98, Sa02]). The works of Leonard Euler (1707–1783) [Eu83], Joseph Louis de Lagrange (1736–1813)[La98], Pierre Simon de Laplace (1749–1827) [La97, La86] and Augustin Louis Cauchy (1789–1857) [Ca36] influenced the mathematical understanding of our time.

At the same time, in the broader history of ideas, the rational comprehension of nature which has emerged since the 17th century derives from the same mathematical ideas. Since that time, physical processes are described in the classical ideal as being predetermined and continuous in space and time.

Classical physics is based on this assumption of the possibility of arbitrarily small quantities, the assumption that in essence all changes in the world proceed "smoothly", that fundamentally there are no "jumps" [GG02, p. 20].

Laplace's abstract thesis of physical predetermination therefore is the continuation of an inner attitude that, taking its start in the age of the reformation, has spread its influence into our mechanized world.

Abbildung 8: Joseph Louis de Lagrange, copper engravin around 1830

The theologian Calvin (1509–1564) said: "We thus learn to relate the whole of the natural order to the special providence of God". The physicist Laplace said: "A spirit, knowing for its given moment all the forces active in nature, and the mutual positioning of the beings of which nature consists, if it were otherwise sufficiently comprehensive to subject this information to analysis, would grasp the motions of the heaviest world-body and the lightest atom in the same formula. Nothing would be incalculable for it, and future and past would be present to its gaze".

Predestination, *mathesis universalis* and Laplace's demon stood in an intellectual-historical relationship stretching from theology to physics and whose actual carrier was the spirit of mathematics. The Calvinist god of asceticism on a grand scale and Laplace's demon – an abstractionism on a grand scale – were both reflected in the history of mathematical ideas. [Be46, p. 118, 120, 123]

With Descartes, philosophy parted company with theology. Mathematics, as form and as calculational tool, has had an effect on philosophical and natural scientific thought ever since Leibniz. As a result, the archetypal phenomena of mathematical qualities receded behind abstraction, the key element of this new development. Thinking was called into question afresh for that very reason.

> In fact the severing of mathematics from its empirical starting point opened up quite new horizons to its development. If not earlier, then certainly with the discovery of the infinitesimal calculus by Gottfried Wilhelm Leibniz (1646–1716) and Isaac Newton (1643–1727) mathematics finally overcame the purely perceptual and soared aloft to the grasping of laws that eluded representation in perceptible form. [...] only now did one begin to discover and learn to think relationships that flatly contradicted naive perception. [Zi00, p. 121]

Since the appearance of Newton's mechanics, the seriousness and objectivity of science and knowledge has been measured by the extent that concepts are detached from our consciousness and subjective feeling. The differential equations of physics strengthen the view that, to paraphrase Einstein, the world-view of every scientist is permeated by a causality underlying everything that happens[8].

The existence of a "fundamental reality" whose common-sense meaning can no longer be grasped, is now forced upon us. And so the knowledge process must play itself out in "so-called fictitious realities" [Sc02]. As a result the possibility of an imaginative understanding is pushed into the background.

If we observe how our thinking comprehends limits of numerical sequences, we are bound to say that a special cognition awakens precisely though the fact that, at the threshold of the infinite, its qualitative content leaves the realm of the sense-perceptible. We are referred to a perceivable certainty beyond the reality revealed by the ordinary senses.

Seen in this way, the archetypal phenomena of the infinitesimal calculus, considered in their essential significance, are primarily spiritual experiences; they allow the human being to enter a reality, in which he can experience the activity of his spirit. It is the reality of a free, creative spirituality permeating our actions and our will. In this reality, the world as a whole comes into being, we apprehend and shape it, especially in our response to the variety of spiritual agents.

Are mathematical insights discovered? To put it another way, do we discern existing laws, as Platonists would have it, or are mathematical principles constructed and put together like an architecture of thoughts, which is the fundamental tenet of formalism (see for example [Sc02])?

Do we become capable, after many and diverse observations of the spiritual world, of making judgments about the meaning of what is perceived? Can spirit be experienced through mathematics? Can the horizon of natural science be expanded through "experimental" spiritual science?

---

[8] We are still committed to this basic feeling. The phenomena of quantum physics nevertheless make new demands on our deterministic understanding of reality stamped as it is by the "Laplacian world spirit". A physics of relationships comes to the fore and challenges the flexibility of our thinking afresh. See [Gö99].

Galileo's experiments lead to a reliable concept of the behavior of a stone under gravity. The infinitesimal reveals to us the ideal content of a clear and living phenomenology of the spirit – active Platonism. So mathematics does not serve exclusively for the description of nature, it is also a field for the practical evaluation of thought-qualities. Seen in this way, spiritual experiences enable us to acquire freedom of personal judgment.

> The next stage announces itself in an impression many have at a quite early stage, but which must be cultivated further. It can be suggested somewhat in the following way. If one has had insight into a mathematical truth, one exclaims perhaps: It's as clear as day! Yet afterwards the feeling often arises inwardly: How wonderful! Tending this further, one trains oneself to revere the spiritual laws shaping the world. And the inner demand on the human being speaks ever more insistently to him or her, pointing to the distant goal of harmonizing his conduct with the powers prevailing in the cosmos. [Lo73, p. 59]

7 Mathematics and living nature

Looking back to the Greeks once more: *They did not create the modern science for which they prepared. Because in all their desire for knowledge they thought of the world as the one familiar to themselves, and they thought it through to the end.*[Ga00, p. 106]

Today we are very remote from that. Nevertheless, we are not shut out from the possibility to feel wonder and awe at Nature's coming into being and to listen, to eavesdrop on its phenomena.

> The naturalist Eugène Marais breached a termite mound. Between the two parts of the mound he drove into the ground a steel plate considerably taller and wider than the termite mound itself so that what was now effectively two mounds were, naturally, completely isolated from each other. The termites of one mound knew nothing of those of the other mound. The termites rebuilt columns and arches in both. The astonishing thing was that when the plate was removed and the gap was closed, the two parts matched exactly. This result allowed only one conclusion, namely, that a complete building plan existed which the termites simply executed. [Sc02, p. 39]

Going further, can we grasp the ideal principles implied by this wonderful experiment? Is the location of a possible certainty in this case perhaps close to that of the differential quotient? This question is not to be understood in the abstract. It is more a matter of attentively observing thought-processes and finding, through our own activity, descriptions leading out of the isolation of perceptual or sense-based thinking.

> The moment we rise from the purely mineral to the plant or other kingdoms of nature, in that moment the mathematical method of treatment as we are accustomed

to it leaves us in the lurch. Someone who intends to rise to the imaginative level of cognition wants to produce something in his soul life that encompasses not merely geometrical constructs or numerical relationships, he wants to produce forms that will live in his soul in exactly the same way as do these mathematical forms, but which go beyond the mathematical in their content. [...] In fact the best preparation for developing imaginative cognition is to have been engaged as much as possible with the activity of mathematizing – not so much to reach particular mathematical insights as to experience clearly *what the human soul actually does when it moves in mathematical forms*. This fully conscious activity of the human soul must now be applied in another area: it must be applied in such a way that out of our inner forms – if I may use this expression in a wider sense – we construct, just as we do in mathematics, other forms so that we can penetrate into plant life or permeate plant life in the same way that we permeate mineral nature, chemical-physical nature and so on with mathematical forms. [St91, p. 48ff].

8 Outlook

The differential quotient is the concept for a numerical phenomenon of the form

$$\frac{0}{0}$$

in the sense of the ratio of two nascent zeros. A quality expressible as

$$\infty \cdot 0$$

constitutes the integral concept, where again zero is understood as something *becoming* zero, a nascent zero. The infinity ∞ is something *becoming* infinite, a potential infinite. When we grasp these concepts through the living convergence of finite, infinitely great and infinitely small, above all in practical ways in the classroom, the geometrical interpretation (tangent, area, volume, etc.) is no longer the starting point of our thought process but a practical and fascinating consequence.

> For sense-perception, the differential is a point, a zero. For spiritual comprehension, however, the point becomes alive, the zero becomes an active cause. Thus for our spiritual perception space itself is called to life. Conceived materially, its points, its infinitesimally small parts, are dead; but if we understand these points as differential quantities, an inner life awakens in the dead juxtaposition. [St84]

The supply of pure thought experiences has dwindled more and more in our time in favor of a flood of formalisms, images and vacuous clarity. Through the approach presented here, we take advantage of an opportunity to counteract this trend, and to create confidence in spiritual impulses once more. We go beyond the understanding of the world gained through discussions of the period since Newton and Leibniz: we understand aspects of the current situation by developing fields of activity in which pupils can even experience the intuitive thinking of a Greek or Egyptian.

The archetypal phenomena of the infinitesimal calculus as a path to a hermeneutics of mathematical principles, prove in active inner perception of our spirit to be a reality closely related to life.

The enhancement of faculties and potentials by actively transforming and enlivening mathematics is the current challenge. Not just the understanding of a graphical calculus, but the conscious, productive study of fundamental mathematical entities, based on clear, sense-free perceptions, forms our free way forward in thinking.

References

[Ba69] Margaret E. Baron. *The Origins of the Infinitesimal Calculus.* Pergamon Press Ltd., Oxford 1969.

[Ba16] Isaac Barrow. *The Geometrical Lectures.* The Open Court Publishing Company, Chicago-London 1916.

[Be66] Oskar Becker. *Das mathematische Denken der Antike.* 2. Aufl., Vandenhoeck & Ruprecht, Göttingen 1966.

[Be46] Max Bense. Konturen einer Geistesgeschichte der Mathematik. Claaßen & Goverts, Hamburg 1946.

[Bo51] Bernard Bolzano. *Paradoxien des Unendlichen.* C. H. Reclam, Leipzig 1851.

[Bo34] Ernst Borchert. *Die Lehre von der Bewegung bei Nicole Oresme.* Verlag der Aschendorffschen Verlagsbuchhandlung, Münster 1934.

[Bo71] Nicolas Bourbaki. *Elements of the history of mathematics.* Springer, Berlin - Heidelberg, 1994.

[Bo59] Carl B. Boyer. *The History of the Calculus and its Conceptual Development.* Dover Publications, New York 1959.

[Br90] Emma Brunner-Traut. *Frühformen des Erkennens am Beispiel Altägyptens.* Wissenschaftliche Buchgesellschaft, Darmstadt 1990.

[Ca65] Moritz Cantor. *Vorlesungen über Geschichte der Mathematik.* Nachdruck der 3. Auflage von 1907, Johnson Reprint Corporation, New York, B. G. Teubner Verlagsgesellschaft, Stuttgart 1965.

[Ca36] Augustin-Louis Cauchy. *Vorlesungen über die Differenzialrechnung.* Meyer Verlag, Braunschweig 1836.

[Cl59] Marshall Clagett. *The Science of Mechanics in the Middle Ages.* The University of Wisconsin Press, Madison 1959.

[Co57] Egmont Colerus. *Vom Einmaleins zum Integral.* Paul Zsolnay Verlag, Hamburg-Wien 1957.

[CR67] Richard Courant, Herbert Robbins. *What is mathematics?* Revised by Ian Stewart, Oxford University Press, 1996.

[DP94] Amy Dahan-Dalmedico, Jeanne Pfeiffer. *History of mathematics: highways and byways.* Mathematical Association of America, Washington DC, 2010.

[Di85] Jean Dieudonné. *Geschichte der Mathematik 1700-1900.* VEB Deutscher Verlag der Wissenschaften, Berlin 1985.

[Di56] E. J. Dijksterhuis. *Die Mechanisierung der Weltbildes.* Springer Verlag, Berlin-Göttingen-Heidelberg 1956.

[GO64] Bernard R. Gelbaum, John M.H. Olmsted. *Counterexamples in Analysis.* Holden-Day, San Francisco 1964.

[Du82] Paul du Bois-Reymond. *Die allgemeine Functionentheorie, Erster Theil, Metaphysik und Theorie der mathematischen Grundbegriffe: Grösse, Grenze, Argument und Function.* Verlag der H. Laupp'schen Buchhandlung, Tübingen 1882.

[Ei77] August Eisenlohr. *Ein mathematisches Handbuch der alten Ägypter (Papyrus Rhind des British Museum).* J. C. Hinrichs' Buchhandlung, Leipzig 1877 (Sändig Reprint Verlag, 1999).

[Eu83] Leonhard Euler. *Beiträge zu Leben und Werk, Gedenkband.* Birkhäuser, Basel 1983.

[Fo77] Eric G. Forbes. *Descartes and the birth of analytic geometry.* Historia Mathematica **4** (1977), 141–151.

[Fu98] Heinz Fuhrer. *Feldmessen und Kartographie.* Justus Perthes Verlag, Gotha 1998.

[Ga00] Hans-Georg Gadamer. *Hermeneutische Entwürfe.* Mohr Siebeck, Tübingen 2000.

[Ge48] C. J. Gerhardt. *Die Entdeckung der Differentialrechnung durch Leibniz.* H. W. Schmidt, Halle 1848.

[Ge84] Helmuth Gericke. *Mathematik in Antike und Orient.* Springer Verlag, Berlin-Heidelberg-New York-Tokyo 1984.

[Ge90] Helmuth Gericke. *Mathematik im Abendland*. Springer Verlag, Berlin-Heidelberg-New York-London-Paris-Tokyo-Hong Kong 1990.

[Gö99] Thomas Görnitz. *Quanten sind anders*. Spektrum Akademischer Verlag, Heidelberg-Berlin 1999.

[GG02] Thomas Görnitz, Brigitte Görnitz. *Der kreative Kosmos*. Spektrum Akademischer Verlag, Heidelberg-Berlin 2002.

[Gr00] Ivor Grattan-Guiness. *From Calculus to Set Theory 1630-1910*. Neuauflage, Princeton University Press, Princeton-Oxford 2000.

[Gr98] Ivor Grattan-Guiness. *The Rainbow of Mathematics*. W.W. Norton & Company, New York-London 1998.

[HW96] E. Hairer, G. Wanner. *Analysis by Its History*. Springer Verlag, Berlin-Heidelberg-New York 1996.

[He65] Georg Wilhelm Friedrich Hegel. *Wissenschaft der Logik*. Sämtliche Werke, vierter Band, Friedrich Frommann Verlag (Günther Holzboog), Stuttgart-Bad Cannstatt 1965.

[Ju64] A. P. Juschkewitsch. *Geschichte der Mathematik im Mittelalter*. B. G. Teubner Verlagsgesellschaft, Leipzig 1964.

[KN98] Hans Kaiser, Wilfried Nöbauer. *Geschichte der Mathematik*. 2. Aufl., Verlag Hölder-Pichler-Tempsky, Wien 1998.

[Kä61] Abraham Gotthelf Kästner. *Anfangsgründe der Analysis des Unendlichen*. Verlag der Wittwe Vandenhoeck, Göttingen 1770.

[Kä70] Abraham Gotthelf Kästner. *Geschichte der Mathematik*. Nachdruck der Ausgabe Göttingen 1796, Georg Olms Verlag, Hildesheim-New York 1970.

[Kl72] Morris Kline. *Mathematical Thought from Ancient to Modern Times*. Oxford University Press, New York 1972.

[Ku31] Jakob Philipp Kulik. *Lehrbuch der höheren Analysis*. Kronberger und Weber, Prag 1831.

[La98] Joseph Louis de Lagrange. *Theorie der analytischen Funktionen*. F. Lagarde, Berlin 1798/99.

[La97] Peter Simon La Place (Pierre Simon de Laplace). *Darstellung des Weltsystems*. Varrentrapp und Wenner, Frankfurt am Mayn 1797.

[La86] Pierre Simon de Laplace. *Philosophischer Versuch über die Wahrscheinlichkeit*. Verlag von Duncker & Humblot, Leipzig 1886.

[Le20] Gottfried Wilhelm Leibniz. *Über die Analysis des Unendlichen*. Ostwald's Klassiker der exakten Naturwissenschaften Nr. 162, Akademische Verlagsgesellschaft m.b.H., Leipzig 1920.

[Lo48] Louis Locher-Ernst. *Differential- und Integralrechnung*. Birkhäuser Verlag, Basel 1948.

[Lo73] Louis Locher-Ernst. *Mathematik als Vorschule zur Geisterkenntnis*. 2. Aufl., Philosophisch-Anthroposophischer Verlag, Dornach 1973.

[Lü16] H. B. Lübsen. *Einleitung in die Infinitesimal-Rechnung*. 9. Aufl., Friedrich Brandstetter, Leipzig 1916.

[Ne04] Isaac Newton. *Abhandlungen über die Quadratur der Kurven*. Ostwald's Klassiker der exakten Naturwissenschaften Nr. 164, Wilhelm Engelmann, Leipzig 1908.

[Or66] Nicole Oresme. *De proportionibus proportionum and Ad pauca respicientes*. The University of Wisconsin Press, Madison-Milwaukee-London 1966.

[Pe74] Olaf Pedersen. *Logistic and the theory of functions. An essay in the history of Greek mathematics*. Archives internationales d'histoire des sciences **24** (1974), 29-50.

[RW84] H. L. Resnikoff, R. O. Wells. *Mathematics in Civilization*. Dover Publications, New York 1984.

[Sa02] Karen Saxe. *Beginning Functional Analysis*. Springer Verlag, Berlin-Heidelberg-New York 2002.

[Sc02] Wolfram Schommers. *Formen des Kosmos*. Die Graue Edition, Zug/Schweiz-Kusterdingen 2002.

[Sc62] Matthias Schramm. *Die Bedeutung der Bewegungslehre des Aristoteles für seine beiden Lösungen der zenonischen Paradoxie*. Vittorio Klostermann, Frankfurt am Main 1962.

[Sm29] David Eugen Smith. *A Source Book in Mathematics*. McGraw-Hill Book Co. Inc., 1929. Reprint: Dover, New York 1959.

[Sn46] Karl Snell. *Einleitung in die Differential- und Integralrechnung*. F. A. Brockhaus, Leipzig 1846/1851.

[Sp00] Detlef D. Spalt. *... und doch gibt es sie nicht: Der Begriff der reellen Funktion*. Rüdiger Thiele (Hrg.), Mathesis, Verlag für Geschichte der Naturwissenschaften und der Technik, Berlin-Diepholz (2000), 182–215.

[St25] Rudolf Steiner. *Das Christentum als mystische Tatsache und die Mysterien des Altertums*. 5. Aufl., Philosophisch-Anthroposophischer Verlag, Dornach, 1925.

[St84] Rudolf Steiner. *Mathematik und Okkultismus*. In: Philosophie und Anthroposophie, 2. Aufl., GA 35, Rudolf Steiner Verlag, Dornach 1984.

[St91] Rudolf Steiner. *Naturwissenschaft, Experiment, Mathematik und die Erkenntnisstufen der Geistesforschung*. 3. Aufl., GA 324, Rudolf Steiner Verlag, Dornach 1991.

[St89] Rudolf Steiner. *Die Naturwissenschaft und die weltgeschichtliche Entwickelung der Menschheit seit dem Altertum*. 2. Aufl., GA 325, Rudolf Steiner Verlag, Dornach 1989.

[St69] J. Struik, editor. *A Source Book in Mathematics*. Harvard University Press, Cambridge-Massachusetts 1969.

[Th00] Rüdiger Thiele. *Frühe Variationsrechnung und Funktionsbegriff*. Rüdiger Thiele (Hrg.), Mathesis, Verlag für Geschichte der Naturwissenschaften und der Technik, Berlin-Diepholz (2000), 128–181.

[To49] Otto Toeplitz. *Die Entwicklung der Infinitesimalrechnung*. Springer Verlag, Berlin-Göttingen-Heidelberg 1949.

[Tr03] Johannes Tropfke. *Geschichte der Elementar-Mathematik*. Verlag von Veit & Comp., Leipzig 1903.

[We56] Hermann Weissenborn. *Die Principien der höheren Analysis in ihrer Entwickelung von Leibniz bis auf Lagrange*. Verlag von H. W. Schmidt, Halle 1856. Reprint: Leipzig 1972.

[Wi14] Heinrich Wieleitner. *Zur Geschichte der unendlichen Reihen im christlichen Mittelalter*. Bibliotheca Mathematica 3. Folge, 14, 1914.

[Wi29] Heinrich Wieleitner. *Mathematische Quellenbücher IV, Infinitesimalrechnung*. Verlag Otto Salle, Berlin 1929.

[Zi00] Renatus Ziegler. *Mathematik und Geisteswissenschaft*. 2. Aufl., Philosophisch-Anthroposophischer Verlag, Dornach 2000.

Thinking in processes and threshold experiences in 12th Grade mathematics

DETLEF HARDORP

1 Mathematics and sense-free thinking

Mathematics is often experienced as abstract, remote from life. Many people find it simply incomprehensible. When talking with adults about their school experiences one can be struck by how clearly they remember their often ambivalent relationship to mathematics. Whether mathematics is a favourite subject or not is of course connected with the student's personal predilections but also depends to a great extent on how maths is taught and what goals are consciously pursued through the teaching of the subject.

Which mathematical skills should be learned? Everyone knows that mastering elementary arithmetical operations is indispensable in our civilization. Far less understood is the fact that a special kind of thinking can be schooled using mathematics.

Mathematical content can only be acquired in inner perception. The mathematician does not observe a natural process, nor perform any experiments: he or she is completely dependent on mathematical content brought forth conceptually in inner perception. Albert Einstein speaks of a mystery "which in all ages has disconcerted inquiring minds":

> How can it be that mathematics, being after all a product of human thought which is independent of experience, is so admirably adapted to the objects of reality? Is human reason, without experience and through mere thinking, able to fathom the properties of real things?[1]

In his critical works Karl Popper rightly rejects the view stemming from western empiricism that what is perceived by the senses has greater reality than concepts consummated in thought[2]. Concepts – so concludes empiricism – are abstracted from the sense world, are more or less summaries or pale copies of sense perceptions. According to this view, it is outer (sensory) perceptions that are objective – in fact, really only the "primary" qualities of position, extension and movement which is thought to underlie all sense perception. And ideas formed in thought, even more so all "hallucinations" of inner observation and "super-sensory perception" have a purely subjective character.

John Locke consciously formulated the paradigm of empiricism. Since his time if not before, it has lodged itself, in spite of Popper's critical rejection, deep in the fundamental attitude of

---

[1] Albert Einstein: *Sidelights on relativity*, "Geometry and experience", 1921, Dover publications, p. 28
[2] Karl Popper: *A world of propensities*, Thoemmes Press, 1997, 60 pp.

modern civilization. To a great extent unnoticed, this philosophical view ultimately conditions our conception of the world. For this reason it is difficult to view – and more especially to experience – the world in a different way.

Following the empiricist line of thought with logical consistency, the reality and scientific character of mathematics would have to be denied. Because the structure of mathematics is conceived and perceived in thought alone, it must have a purely subjective character.

Mathematics, it is true, has to be created by a thinking subject. Yet it has an obviously universal character.

This realisation plays a significant role already early on in Rudolf Steiner's anthroposophy, out of which Waldorf education arose. In 1904 Steiner wrote in his essay *Mathematics and occultism*[3]:

> It is only with difficulty that the human being can emancipate itself from material perceptions, as a simple experiment on one's own self will prove. Even when someone who lives in the every-day world withdraws into himself and does not allow any material impressions of the senses to work upon him, the residues of sense perception still linger in his mind. And someone who is as yet undeveloped, when he rejects the impressions which he has received from the physical world of the senses, he simply faces nothingness – the complete void within consciousness. Hence certain philosophers claim that there exists no thought free from sense-perception. They say: "However much someone withdraws into the realm of pure thought, he is still only dealing with the shadowy reflections of his sense-perceptions." This statement holds good, however, only for an undeveloped person. As soon as a human being acquires the ability to develop in his or herself spiritual organs of perception (as nature formed organs of sense perception), then thinking ceases to remain void when it rids itself of the contents of sense-perception.

Steiner does not hold the view that he discovered this, but that it has been known since antiquity:

> It was precisely such a mind emancipated from sense-perception and yet spiritually filled which Plato demanded from those who wanted to understand his theory of ideas. In demanding this, however, he demanded no more than what was always required of disciples by those who aspired to make them true initiates of higher knowledge. Until we experience within ourselves the full scope of what Plato implies here, we cannot have any conception of what true wisdom is.

Using the mathematical concept of the circle Steiner then explains how a materialised mathematical shape leads beyond itself, that such a shape is only "an image of a comprehensive spiritual fact":

---

[3] *Mathematik und Okkultismus*, detailed notes of an address to a congress of the Theosophical Society, Amsterdam, June 1904, in *Philosophie und Anthroposophie*, collected essays 1904–23, GA 35, p. 7 ff.
Translation is a revision of that of M. H. Eyre, ed. H. Collison, http://wn.rsarchive.org/Lectures/19040621p01.html

Now Plato looked upon mathematical science as a means of training for life in the world of ideas free of sense-perception. Mathematical forms hover on the border-line between the material and the purely spiritual world. Think of a "circle". When we do this we do not think of a particular sense perceptible circle which perhaps has been drawn on paper, but of any circle which can ever be depicted or met in nature. So it is in the case of all mathematical objects. They relate to the sense-perceptible, but they are not exhausted by it. They hover over innumerable, diverse sense-perceptible forms. When I think mathematically, I am indeed thinking about something my senses can perceive, but equally I am not thinking *in* the sense-perceptible. It is not the sense perceptible circle which teaches me the laws of the circle, it is the ideal circle that exists only in my mind and of which the sense perceptible form is a mere image. I could learn the identical truths from any other sense image of a circle. The essence of mathematical perception is that a single sense-perceptible form leads me beyond itself; that it can only be an image, an allegory of a comprehensive mental-spiritual fact. And there is the possibility that, in return, I bring what is mental-spiritual into a sense perceptible form. From the mathematical form I can learn to know supersensible facts by way of the sense-world. This was the all-important point for Plato. We must see the idea purely spiritually if we want to cognise it in its spiritual reality. We can train ourselves to do this if we practice first steps of this activity in the mathematical realm, if we understand clearly what it is that we really gain from a mathematical figure. "Learn to emancipate yourself from the senses through mathematics, then you can hope to rise to the comprehension of ideas independent of the senses": this was what Plato strove to impress upon his disciples.

Sense-free understanding already starts with arithmetical ability. We cannot grasp the system of numbers without consciously dealing with inwardly generated spiritual content, since a number only becomes real when we think it. On the other hand a first experience of numbers is not an intellectual act: twoness already lives in the experience of the separation between yourself and the world. And in every rhythm live the most diverse number relationships, as they do in the musical intervals. This generally remains in the unconscious, nevertheless the whole realm of music is a living source of numerical relationships.

It is educationally appropriate to "make sense-perceptible that which is mental-spiritual in substance",[4]. The crucial question is, however, *in what way* this is done.

Does sense-perception serve to spark off something spiritual in the student (the "aha experience"), or do spiritual-mental abilities get encased in vestiges of sense-perception, impeding an increasingly free supersensible exploration? Do live musical processes (for example rhythmical clapping) bring number relationships to consciousness in the first class of the lower school? Or does one start exclusively from a dead world of things, with objects being grouped into sets whose

---

[4] ibid

cardinality is meant to introduce numbers? Cardinality is additive and less appropriate to the world of numbers, which is multiplicative in its core. The concept of cardinality leans toward intellectual abstraction and is thus less suitable for a child, calling forth dreariness. Because of that, set theory fundamentally failed as a basis for primary school arithmetic in the seventies of the last century.

A deeper understanding of the essence of mathematics is eminently important when teaching it. The misconceived approach to mathematics based on a purely formal understanding of the subject (e.g. in the sense of "learning by applying rules") denies its spiritual dimension and should be called into question, also because the way the subject is taught can leave its decisive mark on the relationship of the human being to the spiritual. When, three years after the opening of the first Waldorf school, Rudolf Steiner was invited to a congress at Oxford on the theme of spiritual values in education and social life, he opened his observations on the teaching of arithmetic with the following words[5]:

> Children are able to take in the elements of arithmetic at a very early age. But it is just in arithmetic that we can observe how only too easy it is for an intellectual element to get into the child too early. Mathematics in itself is not really alien to anyone at any age. It arises from human nature, and the alienation that occurs between human faculties and the letters of the alphabet in a subsequent intellectual development cannot occur between these faculties and the arithmetic operations. What is of immense importance, however, is that children be introduced to arithmetic in the right way. And this can really only be judged by those who can observe the whole of human life from a certain spiritual standpoint. — Teaching arithmetic and moral principles are two things that seem logically far removed from each other. We don't usually associate teaching arithmetic with moral principles, because the logical connection is not obvious. But to those who don't view the matter simply logically but in a living way, it *is* obvious that a child who is introduced to arithmetic in the right way will have a very different sense of moral responsibility in later life than a child who is not introduced to arithmetic in the right way.

Whoever learns to inwardly create rules with their own mental-spiritual strength, in accord with the universal spiritual realities in which those rules are grounded, can really understand mathematics. Something similar could be said about genuine moral action. Without inner reference, mathematics – like morality – is an outer straight-jacket which one either fits into – or does not. But what is done inwardly can only originate freely in an individual human being, it can neither be extorted nor programmed.

Are human mental-spiritual capacities (and mathematical capacities are entirely mental-spiritual) tied to thought templates free of any real content, tending to inhibit individual spiritual striving?

---

[5] *Die geistig-seelischen Grundkräfte der Erziehungskunst* [*Basic soul-spiritual forces in education*], GA 305, p. 109 ff., lecture of 21 August 1922.
Translation adapted from: http://steinerbooks.org/research/archive/spiritual_ground_of_ed/spiritual_ground_of_ed.pdf

If so, the individual burgeoning of the will – be it in thought or be it in moral action – would dwindle into a disruptive influence which would eventually stall. Mathematics and also morality would wither away to an observing of "drummed-in" rules prescribed outwardly without being inwardly understood. As a result the human being would fall into a bondage of rules and tend to turn into a (spiritual) cog in a (spiritual) machine[6].

2 Infinitesimal calculus

In high school students develop the desire to find an individual approach to the world. In class 12, they are most apt to have developed capacities for this. By the end of school, freely moving in thought-forms not based on outer perception will be a new kind of experience within their reach, if they are suitably stimulated. This can be accomplished in mathematics teaching in particular by work with differential calculus and projective geometry. Penetrating the infinitely small and the infinitely large stimulates going beyond intellectual thinking underpinned by outer perception and to plunge into thinking in terms of *processes*. This way of thinking was only developed in modern times and is not found even in the great Greek mathematicians with their thinking shaped as it was by the intellectual soul[7]. This thinking in processes requires that the mentally occurring thought process is concurrently experienced as a process of will.

He/she who plunges into the inner dynamic of the basic concepts of differential and integral calculus whilst simultaneously witnessing their own inner activity can notice something will-like that has the tendency to "liquefy" or "evaporate" that which was hitherto formed conceptionally, whereby the threshold from the formed to the formless is crossed. When the formed loses its

---

[6] Steiner continued the above-quoted observations in Oxford with a rather drastic, seemingly paradoxical statement that we – according to Steiner – should not shrink back from:

> What I am about to say may seem completely paradoxical to you. But I am speaking of realities and not of the illusions of our age, and I do not want to shy away from paradoxes just because the reality of our age often seems paradoxical. Had we as human beings known how to immerse the soul in arithmetic instruction in the right way during the last decades, we would not have Bolshevism in Eastern Europe today. This is the outcome, this is what we see inwardly: with what strength the faculty expressed in arithmetic is bound up with what apprehends morality in the human being.

A statement like this may surprise, startle or even anger. The connection Steiner makes is at the very least unusual. Yet reports based on personal experience of the seizure of power by the Bolsheviks (e.g. that of Vladimir Lindenberg in his book *Bobik im Feuerofen. Eine Jugend in der russischen Revolution* [*Bobik in the fiery furnace. A youth in the Russian revolution*] clearly show the effect – shattering to life and culture – that utterly abstract ideas can have: extermination algorithms are invented and implemented that presuppose a mechanized intelligence which excludes healthy human soul impulses. Later Stalin regarded whole peoples as sets which could be reassigned geographically completely arbitrarily.

Here – as also in mathematics – it is a question of the working of the human will. Is the will abstractly intellectually determined and thereby mechanized and deadened to spiritual realities, or is it grounded in the impulses of an *individual* opening up to the spiritual? Only the latter can be a basis for healthy instruction in arithmetic and mathematics. And only the latter can be a basis for a healthy social order. As a teacher of mathematics one could ponder on such relationships.

[7] In his book "Modes of Thought" (New York, 1938, p. 112) A.N. Whitehead compares Greek and modern thought: "In those days, mathematics was the science of a static universe. Any transition was conceived as a transition of static forms. Today we conceive of forms of transition. The modern concept of an infinite series is the concept of a form of transition, namely, the character of the series as a whole is such a form." The only exeption to this rule seems to have been Archimedes' squaring the parabola.

coalesced form in this way, what remains is not a nothingness but an extremely potent *weaving of forces* with form-creating power. Steiner points to this in his essay *Mathematics and Occultism*[8]:

> Euclidean mathematics expresses by mathematical formulae only what can be described and constructed within the field of the finite. What I can state in terms of Euclidean mathematics about a circle, a triangle or about the relationship of numbers is constructable within the finite realm and can be surmised with the aid of sense-perception. This is no longer possible with the differential with which Newton and Leibniz taught us to calculate. The differential still possesses all the properties that render it possible to calculate with it; but it in itself eludes sense-perception. In the differential, sense-perception is brought to a vanishing point; and then we get a new basis – free from sense-perception – for our calculation. What is sense-perceptible is calculated out of what is no longer sense-perceptible. Thus the differential is something infinitely small as opposed to the finitely sensible. The finite is referred back mathematically to something quite different from it, namely to what is intrinsically infinitely small. With the infinitesimal calculus we stand at an important boundary. We are led mathematically beyond what is sense-perceptible, and yet we remain so much within what is real that we calculate what is imperceptible. And when we have calculated, the perceptible shows itself to be the result of our calculations out of the realm of the imperceptible. Indeed, in applying infinitesimal calculus to natural processes in mechanics and physics, we accomplish nothing else than calculating the sensible out of the supersensible. We apprehend the former out of its supersensible beginning or origin. For sense-perception, the differential is but a point, or a zero. For the mental-spiritual apprehension, however, the point becomes alive, the zero becomes an active cause. Space itself thus becomes enlivened for mental-spiritual apprehension. Apprehended by the senses, all its points, its infinitesimally small parts, are dead; if, however, we apprehend these points as differential magnitudes, inner life radiates into the dead juxtaposition. Extension itself becomes the product of the extensionless. Thereby through infinitesimal calculus, life came into the comprehension of nature. The sense realm is led back to the point of the supersensible.

In this passage Steiner describes precisely the transition from Greek (Euclidean) mathematics to the mathematics of the modern age, which is grounded in a realm that eludes sense-perception. Modern mathematics is however remarkably well suited in describing that inner aspect of physics that eludes the sense-world – for example quantum mechanics. It thereby does not, in fact, depart from reality, but points to the fact that that which causes effects in the world is often not to be found in the realm of the phenomena. It is, however, imminent in the latter, if we turn our inner gaze upon itself. Philosophy of science made this step of understanding science at the latest with Popper when it turned away from empiricism and realised that, in fact, all empirical observations

---

[8] *Mathematik und Okkultismus*, GA 35, p. 12 f..

"are themselves theory-laden"[9].. This insight stands in stark contradiction to popular belief in empirical science, which is unfortunately often uncritically taught in school and cemented later by popular scientific journalism.

Since the quoted essay of Steiner's is part of a report on a theosophical congress in Amsterdam, it is not surprising that he also uses theosophical vocabulary a little further on in the essay. Today these words may seem antiquated; they were also not common at the time. But the vocabulary is not essential: Steiner's deliberations are also comprehensible without the theosophical vocabulary. Out of an understanding of modern mathematics the meaning of "Rupa" and "Arupa" (elsewhere called "lower and upper spiritual world" by Steiner) becomes clear in what follows. The word "occultist" shouldn't disturb us either: in Steiner's sense a physicist becomes an occultist when he/she uses science-appropriate higher mathematics.

> No one can become an occultist who is not able to accomplish within himself the transition from thought permeated with sense perception to thought emancipated from sense-perception. For this is the transition where we experience the birth of the "higher manas" from the "kama manas". It was this experience which Plato demanded from those who wanted to become his disciples. But the occultist who has experienced *this*, must also experience something still higher. He must also find the transition from thinking - emancipated from sense-perception - in forms to formless thinking. The thought of a triangle, of a circle, etc. still retains form, even though this form is not directly informed by sense perception. Only when we pass from what lives in finite form to what does not yet possess form but contains within itself the possibility of form-creation, are we able to understand what the realm of Arupa is, in contrast to the realm of Rupa. On the lowest and most elementary field we have an Arupa reality before us in the differential. When we calculate with the differential we always stand at the place where Arupa gives birth to Rupa. Therefore we can train ourselves through infinitesimal calculus to grasp the nature of Arupa and the relationship it has to the field of Rupa. One only needs to once integrate a differential equation with full consciousness in order to sense something of the force of the fountainhead that lives where the Arupa borders against the Rupa.[10]

Although we owe the genesis and development of some of the most important mathematical ideas to the ancient Greeks, the infinitesimal remained a mystery to them. They came close to it repeatedly, but were not able to see through it with conceptual clarity. Squaring the circle, Zeno's paradox, the irrationality of square roots: the rational thinking of antiquity[11] in the end remained

---

[9] cf. the Stanford Encyclopedia of Philosophy on Karl Popper (http://plato.stanford.edu/entries/popper/ under 4. The Growth of Human Knowledge, d.)

[10] GA 35, p. 14 f.

[11] Steiner always spoke of the thinking of the "intellectual soul", in contrast to modern thinking of the "consciousness soul"

too static to be able to penetrate the infinitesimal[12].

The key to differential calculus is *thinking in processes*, without which the existing ratio of two vanishing numerical quantities cannot be thought. This dynamic in thinking, kindled by the will, eludes normal reflection, but it can develop consciousness of the spiritual location where willing becomes thinking and thinking becomes willing. Rudolf Steiner writes an experiential narrative on reflection in chapter three and on the melding of thinking and will in chapter nine of his *Philosophy of freedom*, there in the domain of philosophy rather than mathematics. However it concern the same spiritual threshold. Everything mathematical is spiritual, and to that extent everyone who learns to think mathematics becomes a student of the spirit. This is where the student of the spirit crosses the threshold from a lower to an higher spiritual world, one which can no longer be grasped with the thought forms that are used to constitute the sensory realm into a meaningful world. In its essence formless, but thereby not devoid of content, the higher spiritual world is a world of form-creating germination. Someone who truly learns to think a differential begins to develop consciousness, within the domain of mathematics, of the spiritual region of incipient forms.

Through the mathematical process of integration, out of the germs of form (which can be imagined as a vector field) something formed once again arises. The purely mental-spiritual experience can again become sense-perceptible, it can be represented for example as flow-curves of a vector field, which are not hard for students to grasp geometrically. Thus mathematics remains within everyone's reach.

Steiner's expression "student of the spirit" may sound antiquated. Yet it describes precisely what should take place in a math lesson: a schooling of the spirit. Or still more precisely: performing purely mental-spiritual exercises through which students can unfold consciousness of self-illuminating self-evidence in locations of pure spirit. To what extent this is successful will certainly depend on the one hand on the individual student, on the other, however, also decisively on the extent to which the teacher is engaged in schooling the spirit within him/herself. In this volume, Klaus Labudde has written an article on the so-called "higher senses", one of which is the so-called "sense of thinking". While listening, the latter enables a momentary taking into oneself of the living thinking of another person just as if it were one's own thinking. This is not possible when reading a book, there the reader is obliged to think the thoughts entirely for him or herself.[13] In teaching higher mathematics, these mysterious "higher senses" of the human being also enable a student a submersion into thinking qualities which he or she would initially hardly

---

[12] See also William Mills Ivins: *Art and Geometry: A Study in Space Intuitions*, in particular the chapter: "The Greeks again and what they missed". Archimedes came closest to the infinitesimal calculus for example with his calculation of the area of a parabolic section. In his *Sand Reckoner* treatise on the finite nature of the number of grains of sand needed to fill the universe he used the idea of a mathematical upper bound, which later played a role in the infinitesimal calculus. Thus Archimedes touched on many crucial elements that later became important tools for infinitesimal calculus. He is rightly regarded as the (solitary) forerunner of differential calculus, which only came into existence in modern times through a newly born thinking in processes. See also the chapter "Infinity in Greek mathematics" in John Stillwell: *Mathematics and its History*.

[13] See also Detlef Hardorp: Thinking and sense of thinking, in Newsletter 39 of the Pedagogical Section, Michaelmas 2010.

be able to think alone.

This of course presumes that the teacher introduces these thoughts in a lively way and allows them to unfold in the student. On the one hand, the teacher should be capable of expressing the mathematical thoughts in a way that make an impact on the students and allows them to take teacher-aided walks in the spirit realm of mathematical thought. On the other hand, the teacher must give students the chance to practice walking unaided by leaving students free to their own devices so that they can begin to intuit mathematics autonomously. In this way mathematical understanding begins to breathe out of the swinging back and forth in class discussions between taking hold of the thinking that streams forth from the other and into the student through the sense of thinking – and the students own independent intuitive thinking. The other's thinking is always grasped as if in deep sleep, which remains unnoticed, however, by the listener only because he or she is filled with the content of the other's thinking[14]. On the other hand, every attempt of a student's intuitive thinking to "walk on its own" is wide awake and fully conscious. The latter can only be successful if the attempts to "walk on one's own" give rise to genuine questions individually posed by each student. Holding the balance in class discussions between listening and your own thinking is a difficult undertaking for students: on the one hand, it is impossible to really listen when engaging your own thinking; on the other hand, proper listening will repeatedly lull your own thinking. Conversation becomes "more refreshing than light" (cf. Goethe's Fairy Tale) insofar as listening and thinking relate to each other in a healthy kind of breathing, in and out. Learning right breathing is the source of life for invigorating educational practice[15].

One will hardly be able nor want to "explain" the spiritual background of mathematical thinking. An awareness thereof on the part of the teacher will, however, allow for a more skilful teaching. The less one is aware of the spiritual background of mathematics, the greater is the danger of analysis deteriorating into a learning of rules of differentiation and integration without the student beginning to engage in processual thinking. If differential calculus is already introduced in class 11, it is questionably whether the students thinking has sufficiently matured to begin to autonomously think in processes as described above. It is in any case also not to be expected that all students of class 12 will succeed to do this on their own. Seriously attempting it or at least having caught a glimpse with the help of the teacher or through the classroom discussion will, however, have an effect on the development of all pupils, an effect that should not be underestimated.

If differential calculus is introduced in class 10 (as has happened in Germany insofar as the Abitur was moved from the end of class 13 to the end class 12), the necessary soul maturity in thinking for an adequate in-depth understanding of the basis concepts of differential calculus is very unlikely to exist. The proper place for a sustainable instruction which goes beyond the acquisition of

---

[14] See also the first appendix (written in 1918) in Rudolf Steiner: *The Philosophy of Freedom*.
[15] This of course has many dimensions which can not not be deepened here. On the one hand, conversational dynamic can also develop between students; on the other hand, completely different soul levels quite independent of the educational classroom themes generally tend to play into student conversations and will be acted out. The teacher should sensitively observe all the various threads being woven between souls in the classroom. As conductor, the teacher sometimes needs to put down the baton and allow the ensemble to go on playing alone for a while.

superficially understood rules of differentiation is the 12th year of school. In the US, "calculus" is traditionally not taught until college (apart from "advanced placement" courses in class 12).

3 How can we introduce the derivative in school?

The derivative is a measure of the instantaneous rate of change of a function. In approaching this concept it makes sense to look for where we experience it in life. The classic example is a moving body where the distance covered is thought of as a function of time. The derivative of this function is measure of the instantaneous speed of the body.

If we take the example of a bicycle with a speedometer, we can ask how the speedometer measures the speed. Modern speedometers receive discrete impulses from a magnet attached to a spoke of the rotating wheel. When installing the speedometer you need to enter into the device the distance the wheel rolls during one full rotation of the wheel. How does the speedometer calculate the speed? The device simply divides the entered distance by the time, measured by a built-in clock, that it takes for the wheel to complete one rotation rotation, that is $\frac{\Delta s}{\Delta t}$. But this is not an instantaneous speed, it is an average speed. Just consider what happens when we brake heavily within one of these rotations of the wheel.

How could we measure the speed more accurately? Instead of one magnet on one spoke we could attach magnets to every spoke and feed the speedometer with the distance the wheel rolls from one magnet to the next magnet. Clearly this distance is smaller, as is the corresponding time interval. Nonetheless we are still measuring the average speed $\frac{\Delta s}{\Delta t}$, , although with smaller values in numerator and denominator.

What needs to be done in order to obtain the value of the instantaneous speed? If we halve the distances between the spokes (by having twice as many spokes) the average speed would approach the instantaneous speed still more closely. Thus it would be best if we were to let the distance between the magnets vanish completely by fitting a continuous magnetic ring to the wheel. In that case, the distance entered into the speedometer would shrink to zero.

That this is not workable is likely to quickly dawn on the students. However by continuously diminishing the distance between the spokes, the speed calculated by the speedometer approaches the instantaneous speed ever more closely. Mathematically speedometers with arbitrarily small distances between spokes can be imagined - the principle of how speed is measured remains the same all the while. Yet it remains an average speed throughout because the distance- and time-intervals remain discrete, however small they may have become.

In order to to approach the value of the instantaneous speed we have to get involved with the *unlimited* process of becoming smaller *as a whole*[16]. But as a *process*: if we were to go straight to the final state, we would be dividing zero by zero. That, however, does not yield a meaningful

---

[16]Once again, compare Whitehead's characterisation in footnote 7: "The modern concept of an infinite series is the concept of a form of transition, namely, the character of the series as a whole is such a form."

result. Thus we have to learn to think processually in such a way as to actually execute a limit. What thereby occurs in the human soul has already been characterised above. Steiner described it thus in 1904 (as previously quoted above): "The differential still possesses all the properties that render it possible to calculate with it; but it in itself eludes sense-perception. In the differential, sense-perception is brought to a vanishing point; and then we get a new basis – free from sense-perception – for our calculation." [17]

It is helpful to then work this out in mathematical detail using an example. If instead of a bicycle we take a stone falling in a vacuum,[18] then mathematically we are calculating the derivative of a quadratic function. This is best done first for specific points in time, before proceeding to calculate it at once for all points in time. When proceeding with the latter, care should be taken to avoid confusion between the actual variable and the point in time in general position.

These examples give mathematical conceptualisation a footing that can be linked to existing experience. This footing may also be viable for later concepts, such as the second derivative, since everyone will have experienced acceleration. But dwelling on the derivative *as measure of the instantaneous rate of change of a general mathematical function*, i.e. to comprehend the concept *purely mathematically*, should not be neglected. The variables will then be x and y rather than t and s[19].

This is described more fully elsewhere in this volume. Walter Hutter writes in his article "The differential quotient as numerical phenomenon":

> Numerical differences which tend to zero are put into relationship with corresponding small differences of functional values. How do fractions behave where numerator and denominator are small and interdependent differences?

He goes into this question with the help of various examples of functional relationships, using actual numerical examples of sequences that tend to zero, thereby calculating the derivative of functions like $y = f(x) = x^3$, x^4, x^5 up to x^n as the corresponding limit – there is no other way. If this is done for linear combinations of the above as well, students can discover the rules for differentiating polynomials themselves.

---

[17] See footnote 8 or 3. – It is sometimes called into question whether it is appropriate to introduce the purely mathematical concept of the derivative by starting from a so-called "application", in this case a physics problem (for example the concept of speed). It seems quite appropriate to me because a more sense-imbued problem makes it even clearer how the derivative "eludes" sense-imbued thinking. Steiner had inferred from the example of the circle (as previously quoted above): "The essence of mathematical perception is that a single sense-perceptible form leads me beyond itself; that it can only be an image, an allegory of a comprehensive mental-spiritual fact. And there is the possibility that, in return, I bring what is mental-spiritual into a sense perceptible form." When thinking a circle, mental-spiritual fact and sense perception relate more strongly to each other than in the case of a derivative. "Indeed, in applying infinitesimal calculus to natural processes in mechanics and physics, we accomplish nothing else than calculating the sensible out of the supersensible." This can also be experienced by students. They can then see how, "through infinitesimal calculus, life came into the comprehension of nature. The sense realm is led back to the point of the supersensible."

[18] Physically more vivid than a falling stone is a steel ball rolling on a gently sloping incline (for example a U-shaped aluminium bus bar). Then the movement is slower and thereby easier to follow.

[19] It is advantageous to work with $x - x_0$ instead of h in the denominator, so that the quotient of differences is more apparent.

Local minima and maxima of functional values can be considered right away. What is the derivative, that is to say the instantaneous rate of change, of a function when it passes through a maximum?[20] How does it vary as it passes through a minimum? This can be answered conceptually *without* referring to the graph of the function. When treated this way, we remain within the inherent dynamic of the given function. Ultimately a numerical function is nothing other than a dynamic relationship between numbers: a dependent numerical variable is assigned to an independent one. Therefore every functional relation of numbers can be thought of intrinsically purely as a relationship of number. If the function gets illustrated by a graph, however, the danger immediately arises that the inherent functional dynamic is forsaken by looking at the graph extrinsically as a form from the outside.

Traditionally school textbooks introduce the derivative by calculating the slope of tangents to the graph of a function. Teaching in high schools is generally structured accordingly. There are even teachers in Waldorf schools who teach according to such text books. This not only ignores Waldorf education but also the current state of modern didactical research. We should ask ourselves to what extent pupils actually understand differential calculus – and to what extent an attempt is made to teach it in accordance with its true character. In their 2006 book *Analysis verständlich unterrichten* [*Teaching analysis intelligibly*], the authors Rainer Danckwerts (Professor of mathematics education at the University of Siegen) und Dankwart Vogel (Head of mathematics at the Bielefeld teacher training college) analyse the pitfalls of the conventional school approach to the derivative using tangents. They write:

> The teaching of analysis should give an adequate answer to the question of what constitutes the concept of the derivative. This task is not unproblematic, particularly since on closer inspection the classical school approach by means of tangents is full of traps. A more suitable approach is approaching the derivative as a *local rate of change*. It accentuates the affinity to applications (basic experiences).

They then offer a five-page analysis [21] of the difficulties that arise when one defines the derivative as the steepness of a curve, using the tangent line, which, in turn, is defined as the limiting position of a family of secants. It's worthwhile to read their remarks in the original. They don't mince words when stating their conclusions:

> In face of this analysis the question needs to be asked, Why is the approach to the derivative concept via the tangent still a preferred approach? There are of course reasons for this: it has a long tradition in the history of mathematics and every teacher

---

[20] Obviously what is meant here is a function which is differentiable at least once. However, pupils will find it confusing if the teacher insists on formally watertight mathematical statements all the time, as this tends to complicate issues. If a clever student discovers that in the case of a non-differentiable function it is not a necessary condition that the derivative be zero at a local maximum, then this can be discussed. With such maxima the derivative vanishes not because it becomes zero, but because it is no longer well-defined.

[21] Rainer Danckwerts and Dankwart Vogel: *Analysis verständlich unterrichten*, München, 2006, pp. 45–50

is familiar with it, from his own school years. Nevertheless, the fact remains that this approach is characterised by a multitude of difficulties, which may be mitigated by methodological measures, but are, in principal, unresolvable.

In the differential calculus, it's not to be recommended, from a didactic point of view, to start by considering tangents, because such a geometrical, external representation is merely an outer reflection of the inner dynamics of numerical relationships inherent in the calculus; a dynamic in which the ratio of two vanishingly small numbers reaches a well-defined limiting value precisely when the numbers in that ratio transcend the realm of sense related mental pictures. To be able to think of this appropriately – as a process – requires considerable maturity in thinking, which in turn can ripen further through a deepened immersion in the calculus. This thinking succeeds in proportion to our success in setting out from living movement rather than from a fixed form.

In 1924 Rudolf Steiner proposed the following to the teachers of the first Waldorf school:

> I do not consider that it is advantageous for general mathematical education for differential and integral calculus to be linked to geometry, but to be linked to quotients. I would start from the calculus of *differences*, that is from $\frac{\Delta y}{\Delta x}$, regarding this as a quotient and, merely through the dividend and divisor becoming smaller and smaller, purely out of number, I would move on to developing the differential quotient. I would not start from this continuity relationship, from that you get no concept of the differential quotient, I would not start from the differential but from the differential quotient. If you start from series, then only go over to geometry with the tangent problem, i.e. go over from the secant to the tangent, at the very end. And when the differential quotient is properly grasped purely numerically, purely as computation, only then pass on to the geometrical, so that the pupil comes to understand that the geometrical is only an illustration of the numerical. You then get integrals as the reverse process. Then you develop the possibility of starting, not from calculation as something fixed by geometry, but from geometry as an illustration of calculation. This should be taken heed of more generally. For example one should not regard the positive and negative integers as things in themselves, but take the sequence of integers as $5-1$, $5-2$, $5-3$, $5-4$, $5-5$, $5-6$: now I don't have enough because 1 is lacking, which I write as -1. Make the deficit real without using the number line. Then you remain in the numerical. The negative number is the amount that is not there, the lack of minuend. There is much more inner activity in that! This way it's possible to stir up the pupils' faculties which are much more real than when you do everything just from geometry.[22]

---

[22][*Conferences with teachers*], GA 300a–c, Dornach 1975, p. 154.
Translator note: Differential coefficient may be used in technical math works, but differential quotient seems clearly better for the present context.

Thinking which clings to the world of fixed forms versus thinking which reaches out to sense the form-creating forces active in the living world: these give rise to different kinds of thinking and teaching. This is just as true for introducing differential calculus as is is for introducing negative numbers. The goal of teaching mathematics can and should be to stimulate real faculties in the pupil, though "much more inner activity" is, of course, needed for this.[23]

The more it becomes inwardly transparent, the more does mathematical activity become a joy. The apparently greater demands of penetrating the material in the deepest possible way pays off in the persistence of the acquired understanding alone: the less you see into the heart of something, the sooner it is forgotten again. Genuine understanding builds far less on learning a particular set of rules; it is a matter first and foremost of acquiring competence, of increasing one's capacity to think through an intellectual content, self-reliantly and with certainty.

This can be practiced with extreme values problems. At a maximum the function remains momentarily unchanged (thus the derivative equals zero). But how does the derivative itself change in the neighbourhood of a maximum? It is possible to revisit the bicycle example and ask what happens when you slow down. The class soon arrives at the idea that, when going from a higher to a slower speed, the instantaneous rate of change of the instantaneous rate of change must be negative.

Recurring links to practical experience as well as down-to-earth examples ensure that what is dealt with in the lesson does not evaporate into difficult to grasp intellectual exercise. Care needs to be taken, however, that the concept of the derivative is not "glued" to instantaneous speed or some other real-life experience. To the contrary: In the end, mathematical concepts must also be thought purely as (inner) functional relationships – which are, in essence, relationships of number.

Even though plotting graphs is not essential, it can become an aid *if* the student does it *for himself*, not simply imitating the teacher. Here we have two completely different gestures: In the first, the unaided pupil gives expression to his will. In that case, drawing the graph effectively helps him to *think his will*. In the second, a *product of the teacher's will* is given. In order to grasp *this*, the student needs to first grasp it by inwardly bringing it to life. Here, a very different gesture is necessary in order for understanding to alight.

Mathematical understanding is encouraged when the teacher is, to begin with, frugal with graphical representations. Often, the opposite is the case! In particular in German-speaking areas, engaging in differential calculus is often named "Kurvendiskussion", i.e. a "discussion of curves" (which incidentally has no counterpart in English usage). This shows how far we have, as a rule, distanced ourselves from the inner functional relationship. Instead of inwardly trying to experience the instantaneous rate of change of a given function, one speaks of the "slope" of an externally represented curve. From a functional point of view, it is legitimate to speak of the rate of increase of the values, but not of the "slope" as such, since the latter derives solely from a graph, as do the terms "peak" and "valley".

---

[23] See also the article closely related to these observations entitled *The mathematical as bridge to the spiritual* by Uwe Hansen.

Even though all derivatives can be externalised graphically, dynamic thinking kindled out of the will by calculus eludes ordinary reflection, as the above discussion was meant to made clear. The key to the differential calculus is *thinking in processes*. It is easily usurped by the standardised methods of discussing externally represented curves, an approach that has been taken to an extreme by the German *Abitur* system[24] for many decades. Only recently has this approach begun to be partially called into question through an increasing emphasis on the *acquisition of competences* (as opposed to the acquisition of mere skills).

4 Not to forget the imagination...

The full dimension of thinking, moulding ever-changing forms as flowing water carves a riverbed, only comes to expression beyond the hardened paths of narrow logical deduction. What then emerges are will-permeated points of germination of a (directed or exact) imagination[25]. Goethe spoke of an "incurable gap" if one forgets imagination as the primary force behind the human capacity to form mental pictures[26], as Kant did (and innumerable Kantianists in his wake):

> Here [in Kant's philosophy] the *sensory nature, judgement and reason* are represented as essential forces of our ***ideation***, but *imagination* is forgotten, as a result of which an incurable gap arises. Imagination is the fourth essential force of our spiritual nature, she makes the sensory nature complete in the form of memory, she submits our view of the world to our judgement, in the guise of experience she shapes or finds forms for the ideas of reason and thus reinvigorates Man's wholeness, which without her must founder in dull incompetence. But if imagination serves her three sibling powers in this way, then she is brought by the agency of these beloved kin into the realm of truth and reality. Sensory nature gives her clearly circumscribed, positive forms; judgement regulates her productive power; and reason makes her sufficiently confident that she is not playing with phantoms, but is grounded in ideas.[27]

The teaching approach runs the risk – in case it gives too much weight to sense-perception, judgement and reason – of failing to see the fundamental enlivening effect of an imagination which "is not playing with phantoms, but is grounded in ideas". Sensing the germinating force which has its source at the border of the formless with the formed can invigorate. Fostering this kind of

---

[24] In Germany, graduation from high school is accompanied by a comprehensive set of exams which have in recent years become more and more centralised and standardised.

[25] The original German term "Phantasie" is not directly translatable here; it denotes a more precise power of inner picturing far removed from the ordinary connotations of "fantasy" as something unreal or imprecise.

[26] Here the German word is "Vorstellung", which includes in this context not only the self-produced activity of "Phantasie" (previous footnote) but also those mental pictures arising in the soul as a result of sense perceptions.

[27] Goethe 1816/17, in a letter to the Grand Princess Maria Paulowna, quotation from the 1994 edition, p. 229 (German version).

mathematical thinking can help to actually tap deep sources of innovation and creativity (instead of merely paying the usual lip-service to these concepts).[28]

Nevertheless, threshold experiences remain largely unconscious, since as a rule the mathematical thinker is too preoccupied with the content of mathematics to observe his or her mental-spiritual state as well. This seldom seems to interest mathematical thinkers, just as someone enjoying an appetizing meal is barely conscious of the physiological processes of his digestion. They nevertheless take place, indeed are the basis of his digestion. But even when crossing the threshold to the higher spiritual world largely unconsciously, you move into mental-spiritual regions that can have a real effect – also when the reality of the threshold is not noticed.

5 Projective geometry

In the infinitesimal calculus the infinitely small becomes not nothingness but rather a living source of powerful mathematical insight. Similarly, in projective geometry the study of the infinitely large can break through the limits of our conventional mental pictures and grant us a dynamic overview of global geometric relationships. The mathematician Arthur Cayley called projective geometry "the mother of all geometries", since ordinary Euclidean geometry as well as all classical non-Euclidean geometries can crystallise out of projective geometry.[29] In its maternal role, it is not yet committed to any single crystallised form and is a geometry of the "measureless" (non-metrical) interweaving of planes, lines, and points, a weaving that extends even into the "infinite".

When set the goal of inventing the most economical geometry, the geometry which gets by with the most basic means possible, invariably this incidence geometry of free forms would be discovered. With this approach, students can be led to invent this geometry in class discussions, with the teacher, using the Socratic method, asking questions and recording what is said. This exercise brings into plain view, however, that the most elementary simplicity brings with it many obstacles of understanding, since our imagination is so tightly strait-jacketed by the metric of Euclidean geometry. It turns out to be quite difficult to think logically in geometries which are, in fact, conceptually much simpler. But once this succeeds, thinking itself becomes mobile and fluid and learns to grasp dynamically metamorphosing configurations with mathematical precision.

Arnold Bernhard has shown this in his book *Projektive Geometrie,* which is highly recommended in preparing to teach projective geometry. The book begins with simple Euclidean exercises on the cube and then gradually frees projective geometrical thinking from the fetters of Euclidean geometry. It is a less radical approach than the one sketched above but more secure and more suitable for less experienced teachers.

---

[28] See also the description of creativity in Ernst Schuberth, *Erziehung im Computerzeitalter* [*Bringing up children in the age of the computer*]
[29] See for example http://www.physicsforums.com/archive/index.php/t-136763.html

But one can also risk jumping straight-away into the apparent void of "measureless" notions of space, in which only the most elementary relation of incidence (or mutual belonging) remains, from which, however, all of geometry can be developed "from scratch"[30]. It can be liberating, particularly for pupils of this age, to experience a world which comes into being in continuous metamorphosis, behind the seeming rigidity of geometrical forms, a world which can only be understood with a way of thinking made fluid and freed from measurement.

Projective geometry plays an important role in the history of mathematical thought. Johannes Kepler was the first to succeed in understanding the ellipse, parabola and hyperbola as different manifestations of the same form by thinking them in a metamorphic sequence. They are distinguished simply by having a different relation to the infinite.[31] Later in the same century Blaise Pascal proved a fundamental theorem about these forms, so fundamental that many seemingly disparate theorems of the Greek mathematician Appolonius of Perga turned out to be special cases of Pascal's theorem. Nearly two hundred years later, Charles Julien Brianchon discovered a theorem with an identical logical structure but a polar opposite geometric meaning, in which the roles of point and line are consistently exchanged. Not much later Jean-Victor Poncelet discovered, during his Russian imprisonment, the *principle of duality*, a deep and well-hidden symmetry permeating all of projective geometry.

The principle of duality asserts that any statement in projective geometry has a dual partner which is true exactly when the original statement is true. Practising duality in projective geometry with students confronts them with one-sided aspects in everyday thinking. Far-reaching perspectives arise by dualising Euclidean geometry. One obtains a qualitatively new geometry called dual-Euclidean geometry (also known as *negative space*), in which, among much else, the role of periphery and centre are reversed[32].

Holistic thinking - in the true sense of the word - can be exercised particularly well through

---

[30] You can develop this geometry "from scratch" even including the introduction of coordinate systems via Moebius nets (see e.g. Louis Locher-Ernst: *Urphänomene der Geometrie* [*Archetypal phenomena of geometry*], Vol. 1). In these nets you can then draw parabolas and really see how the line at infinity is a tangent to the (closed!) parabola.

[31] In a short work of Kepler's appearing in 1604, "points at infinity" are spoken of for the first time, pictured with the help of families of conic sections, whereby line and parabola are transitional stages, with families of ellipses and hyperbolas lying in between. Kepler was the first mathematician to describe hyperbola, parabola, ellipse and circle as curves that transform continuously into one another. Using his beloved "principle of analogy," he wrote the first treatise in which the projective plane, including its points at infinity, becomes an object of thought. A deeply poetical, mathematically brilliant treatise which has remained largely unknown, it only appeared in German translation in 1990, published by its translator. Johannes Kepler *De coni sectionibus/Über die Kegelschnitte* [*On the conic section*], Neujahrsgabe 1990, Latin/German, Verlag Thomas Dittert. An English translation was only published ten years later and can be found in Johannes Kepler *Optics. Paralipomena to Witelo & Optical Part of Astronomy*, Green Lion Press, 2000, p. 106-110.

[32] Once again, see William Ivins' excellent study *Art and geometry: a study in space intuitions*. Also relevant to this theme are the books *The Plant between Sun and Earth*, by George Adams and Olive Whicher, *Man and Matter* by Ernst Lehrs, and *The Sun: The Ancient Mysteries and a New Physics*, by George Blattmann. Each of these books explores, in a different direction, possible applications of negative space to a modern understanding of the riddles of man and the universe. Most of this research can be traced back to the three natural science lecture cycles given by Rudolf Steiner for the teachers of the first Waldorf School (GA 320, 321, and 323). Teachers who are able to develop a connection to this research on negative space may then develop a sense that projective geometry, in contrast to analytic geometry, is still a "young" geometry, containing important seeds for civilisation. Such an insight can inspire the teacher and provide inner validation of the significance of teaching projective geometry.

synthetic projective geometry. It is recommendable to to lay some foundations for thinking in polarities already in class 10, in order to then bring it to fruition in class 11[33]. As a Waldorf teacher, I've also had good experiences of taking up and deepening projective geometry in a further main lesson block in class 12[34]. Note that this was in Bavaria, where in the end-of-school examination (the *Abitur*) questions on analysis, linear algebra and probability have been centrally set for decades. I believe that my pupils, thanks to their competence in thinking developed through extensive work with projective geometry, ultimately did better in the *Abitur* than they would have, had I – following a false sense of relevance – slanted my instruction in class 12 explicitly towards the three problem-areas of the centrally-set *Abitur*.

6 Regarding teaching methods

Mathematics instruction is inevitably enriched when one brings in the biographies of the mathematicians who shaped new mathematical concepts. Examples need not be restricted to the classical ones. Descartes – as father of the universally taught analytical geometry – can be compared with Kepler, Desargues and Pascal as fathers of projective geometry – that even then quickly fell into oblivion. It is also largely forgotten that the derivative was already introduced in 1629 by Fermat, as was the integral calculus in 1655 by Wallis. Not until 1669 and 1671 did Newton submit his seminal work on the calculus for publication by the Royal Society – which however turned it down (!). Leibniz's fundamentally important work on the calculus only appeared in 1684. [35]

Mathematical concepts find their historical reflections in the thoughts of the great mathematicians. But entering into another's thought challenges the thinker to independent insight. Considering a concept "in relation to the phenomena from which it is won" (see below) is the essence of the *genetic* teaching method[36]. This method is the living source of a pedagogy which encourages independent understanding and does not make students grow pale from an overconsumption of abstract concepts.

Following Goethe, the young Steiner once made the following remark:

> A concept is esoteric when it is considered in relation to the phenomena from which it is won. It is exoteric when it is considered for itself in isolation, as an abstraction.[37]

---

[33] See also *Topics in mathematics for the 11th Grade* in the same series as this book.

[34] Also see the article "The Free Geometry of Plane Curves" in Volume II of the 12th grade book (to appear), which presents a possible direction for such a main lesson.

[35] A highly recommended book about the history of calculus – and the history of mathematics as a whole – is John Stillwell, *Mathematics and its history*. See also the article *The meaning of the infinitesimal calculus* by Walter Hutter in this volume (p. 71) for more on the history of calculus as well as the excellent treatise by Otto Toeplitz *Die Entwicklung der Infinitesimalrechnung*, Springer 1949.

[36] On this theme see also Rolf Rosbigalle's article in this volume entitled *Teaching mathematics: some basic ideas – Facts, suggestions and hints from practical experience*. See also Manfred Kronfellner *The indirect genetic approach to calculus*, in John Fauvel, Jan van Maanen (Ed.) *History in Mathematics Education: An ICMI Study*, p. 71ff. Furthermore Ildar S. Safuanov *Psychological aspects of genetic approach to teaching mathematics*, http://www.kurims.kyoto-u.ac.jp/EMIS/proceedings/PME28/RR/RR100_Safuanov.pdf. Also see Peter Gallin, Urs Ruf *Dialogic Learning From an educational concept to daily classroom teaching* , www.ecswe.org/wren/documents/Article3GallinDialogicLearning.pdf

[37] Thus wrote Steiner, the editor, in a footnote to *Sprüche in Prosa [Prose maxims]* in Vol. 117 of Kürschner's complete

One of the worst things a teacher can do is to confront pupils at the start with abstract concepts, without developing these concepts from the phenomena underlying them and from which they were "abstracted". Martin Wagenschein criticized this tendency emphatically ("Understanding what can be understood is a human right" [38]) and, in the same spirit, specifically recommended the Waldorf approach to education. Wagenschein makes the case for a method which develops scientific concepts gently but with exactness, from those natural phenomena which led to coining the concepts in the first place. One could, following Steiner, call this an "esoteric" approach.[39]

In the mathematical sphere, there is a corresponding tension: solely mathematical objects, created and experienced in thought, can "congeal" into rules, formulas, and graphs. What is the right way to deal with these by-products of mathematical activity? Are they experienced as path-markers in the mental landscape of thinking out of which they were formed, or are they delivered as finished products before students have themselves had sufficient opportunity to wander through this landscape?

If life is not "taught by what is alive"[40], misunderstandings soon arise and, not surprisingly, a hatred toward the mathematical can develop in students – because the concepts do not appear transparent to the students. To avoid this, everything possible should be done in order to allow mathematical insight to alight as reason *in the students themselves*.

---

edition of Goethe (1883 – 1897), referring to Goethe's statement that "It does not do to dally too long in the realm of the abstract – what is esoteric is only damaging when it strives to be exoteric. Life is best taught by what is alive." (Goethe, *Maxims and reflexions* 728). This highlights the significance Steiner attributed to the word "esoteric".

[38] The Wagenschein website www.martin-wagenschein.de is sub-titled with the slogan: "The understanding of what can be understood is a human right". See also Heinrich Schirmer *Im Einzelnen aufs Ganze gehen – Martin Wagenschein zum hundertsten Geburtstag* [*Going all out into the particular – Martin Wagenschein's centenary*], in *Erziehungskunst*, a monthly publication on Rudolf Steiner's pedagogy, issue 12, December 1996, pp. 1310 – 1320.

[39] See also the detailed explanation of the sequence *conclusions from experience–judgement–concept* [*Schluss–Urteil–Begriff*] in Stephan Sigler's article: "Can the principle of Experience–Judgement–Concept be applied to mathematics instruction?" Whether we call it "genetic", "esoteric" or something else, the concept that is elaborated does not stand at the beginning of the sequence but at the end *after* conclusions drawn from experience. First conclusions are drawn – as far as possible from "direct and immediate" experiences in which the "whole human being is involved" – conclusions which in turn stimulate the mental activity of judgement, out of which the concepts finally crystallise. These may, as one perhaps notices in hindsight, have been mentally latent and therefore active from the beginning. But you can only genuinely work with them if you have actually walked the road yourself. Here lurks a great danger for teachers: since they have already gone through the process, the concepts are evident to them from the start. If the teacher does not succeed in calling this "self-evidence" into question once more, there is a danger of imposing concepts on students, who will not properly understand them for that reason.

[40] See footnote 32

Developing the concept of number from the 1st to the 12th grade

KLAUS LABUDDE

The world of numbers is gradually made accessible to the children and young people in the course of their school years as the essential basis of arithmetic and mathematics. They make their first acquaintance with the simplest, the natural numbers as it were playfully and without a specific aim. Then in real life calculations, for example in Building in the Third school year, they learn to make practical use of numbers. When they reach a new level in numbers, as happens in the Fourth year with fractions and the Seventh with negative numbers, practical applications follow immediately. In fact an application can even be the starting point for formulating a problem leading to new numbers, as in the case of money when negative numbers are introduced.

Then in the High School when it time to deal with trigonometry, it is essential to have the continuum of real numbers at one's disposal. This is an important reason for scheduling the theme of "irrational numbers" in the curriculum for the Ninth school year. The continuously varying number, the "variable" must be available certainly in trigonometry but also in analytic (or co-ordinate) geometry and still more clearly in the infinitesimal calculus. Then we can make practical use of numbers. As we all know this happens in abundance in real life, and in the final year our pupils get to know plenty of these applications.

The usefulness of numbers to the human being is meant here in a completely *outwardly* practical sense.

But there is another, less conspicuous current which accompanies the school children through the world of numbers. This current, if we want to perceive it, has more to do with the qualitative side of of the various kinds of numbers. The intention is not to set up a main lesson block in the High School specifically for this. I want rather to point to a supplementary, more inwardly directed guideline or policy for the math lesson – above all in the High School. Again and again experience shows that situations arise in the classroom where this can be contemplated. To make this possible is the ultimate aim of what follows.

When a Waldorf schoolboy or -girl gets to the 9th Grade, the rational numbers in the setting of the maths lessons hitherto have become familiar to him or her as *the* numbers pure and simple. In the First school year it was just the natural numbers. He got to know them from various aspects: number in the sense of a number used to grasp a set, without regard to the quality of the elements of the set; then number as a means of establishing a particular ordering of a set's elements (naturally neither aspect in the garment of the abstract conceptuality used here); finally also – at least in examples of individual numbers – what we can summarize under the heading of the "essence of a number". The specifics of what this could mean I am deliberately leaving open. To name just one example, Threeness: as we meet it outside in nature, in the human being and in the Christian religion.

Naturally this brief suggestion does not refer to the ways and means of *how* the Class Teacher shapes this introduction of the qualitative. Opportunely from monthly festivals, but above all from conversations with Class Teachers we can learn that the rhythmical element plays an important role here, also combined with intensive exercise of the limbs.

Feeling and will especially are appealed to, while the unfolding faculty of thought is little required as yet. The children learn how the measuring numbers become useful to the human being for instance in the Building block and in connection with a widening of their "horizon" in the Local History and Geography lessons. The first, far-reaching expansion of the number concept takes place from the Fourth year with the introduction of fractions and the arithmetic of fractions. An oft-repeated experience, also from conversations with older pupils, suggests that a considerable number of them do not consider fractions really to be numbers. For them fractions and natural numbers are fundamentally very much of two different kinds; for them the word "number" is inextricably linked to the concept of natural number. Quite often one even discovers that with such children awareness of the distinction between a number as such and how it is represented is too little developed. Here the Class Teacher will be able to take preventative measures by familiarizing his or her class in a pictorial way in the History lesson, or even earlier in the lower school, with Roman numbers or even earlier number symbols. Even the study of different place-value systems, in year Nine at the latest, can contribute something to this.

The next significant advance into the world of the real numbers consists in the introduction to negative numbers in year Seven, for the Class Teacher probably the greatest challenge in teaching arithmetic. The sequence of these advances is adapted to the pupil's development. It takes into account the totally different qualities between the transition to fractions and later the transition to negative numbers. The step from the whole to the part is of course already prepared in the lowest classes in that the four operations of arithmetic are introduced analytically. A fractional part of a whole always has the character of a thing in itself as well of course.

The transition from the positive to the negative numbers has a quite different quality. As is well known, it is important *not* to take this step in a formal way, say by extending the number line beyond zero, nor even as a numerical means of understanding temperatures below the freezing point of water.

The most convincing way of expressing the essence of the negative number is probably in relation to money. The best example of the quality of the negative number may be debt as an expression of deficit or lack, as contrasted with money in hand.

Then, in the Ninth grade, one of the tasks of the Class Teacher is to introduce the irrational numbers and thus expand the hitherto known realm of the rationals. Here, as can be inferred for example from the relevant essays in the 9th Grade main lesson book or from conversations with specialist teachers amongst one's colleagues, two key aspects play a role: the occurrence of the irrationals in regular polygons, and the possible ways of calculating approximate values for the irrationals. As a rule, just irrational roots of natural numbers (surds) will serve for this, but if need be also the number π. The use of π for the practical calculation of the circle, sphere and related figures is admittedly more to the fore than its irrationality.

For work on the theme of "irrational numbers" in the 9th Grade it is not a question of extensive discussion of the concept, but rather of approaching, i.e. approximating, them numerically. Think for example of the algorithm for calculating square roots; or nested interval methods, which the pupil her- or himself could discover. What is common to both examples of course is that one *could* continue them ad infinitum, but sooner or later must simply stop.

As a result we end up with rational numbers again as practicable approximate values of the irrationals. It was exactly the same earlier with the use of logarithm tables, and is today with a calculator. I am convinced of the importance of pupils calculating as much as possible by hand at this stage so that their staying power is challenged and their will used intensively. We can see in this a first, age-appropriate step in preparation for the limit concept, which the pupil will anyway encounter consciously later, but then at a more intellectual level. For the 9th Grade pupil what matters is that a sure feeling develops into certainty that in this process one comes ever nearer to something quite new. How naturally this new thing is seen as a number is of course related to the choice of examples. If the irrational number is the length of a particular segment, e.g. the diagonal of a square, or the height of an isosceles triangle, then there must be a measurement for it and thus a measuring number. The so-called square root snail or spiral is a beautiful example of the fact that the square root of any natural number can be seen as the number measuring the length of a segment.

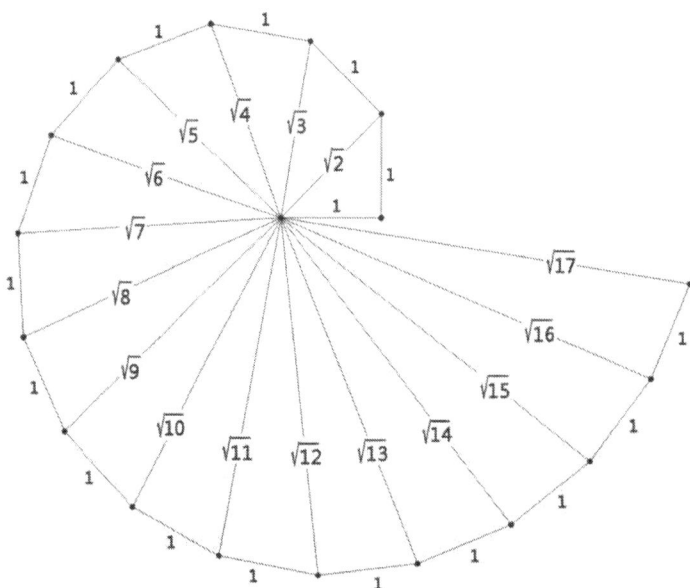

Similarly with π. It is quite natural to the students that this Greek letter denotes a particular number because of the geometrical problem that leads to it. After all, there must be a number to multiply the diameter of a circle by to give the length of its circumference. Even the 8th Grader often gets to know the number π in this sense, though only as an approximate value for practical purposes. The question of this number's irrationality is raised in the Ninth school year at the earliest, if it is thought at all important. For the students the number π is, in my view, first and foremost for practical use.

Time and attention is given to the distinction between algebraic irrationals and transcendental irrationals only towards the end of the school time, if at all.

What I consider essential is that, with the transition to the irrationals, the expansion to the continuum of all real numbers takes place. In the consciousness of pupils of the 9th and 10th Grade, as a rule this plays a secondary role. Although in principle irrational numbers occur in the calculations they have carried out in their exercises, in effect they nevertheless calculate with rational approximations. Pupils of this age are predominantly oriented to the practical.

It is certainly different in the Eleventh school year with analytic (co-ordinate) geometry. Working in this geometry makes little sense if we don't take the continuum of the reals and their one-to-one relationship with the points of the real line as basis. A complete correspondence between the lines and curves on the one hand and the equations representing them on the other, is only possible if we have the continuum at our disposal for the variables in those equations. Although this is an indispensable assumption, it does not constitute the essence of analytic geometry. The students rightly see the essence in the fact that it is possible to pursue geometry by algebraic means. In other words, to see an equation with two variables as equivalent to a definite line or curve, and to see certain calculations as equivalent to particular steps of a geometric construction. The real continuum so to speak runs alongside, without intruding into the pupil's consciousness.

It is quite otherwise when the infinitesimal calculus is introduced towards the end of the Eleventh or in the Twelfth year. The concept of function fundamental to this calculus rests, at least in the context of school mathematics, on the continuum of real numbers in that it – or a portion of it – is the domain of definition. This fact alone may still not necessarily draw the pupil's attention to the real numbers as such. This is more likely to be done by following Rudolf Steiner's advice and developing the derivative concept purely numerically rather than starting from the tangent problem. Here it is a question of investigating a particular quotient – we describe this by the expression

$$\frac{f(x+\Delta x)-f(x)}{\Delta x}$$

as is often done. Does this tend to a limit as Δx tends to zero, and if so what limit? In practice a first answer is often found by letting Δx go through definite null sequences[1], to be precise those with purely rational terms. If we go through this process a few times then a sure feeling awakens in the student that there is actually *one quite definite limit*. A rigorous proof is needed to show that this limit results when Δx is *any* null sequence.

In actual practice, I've allowed Δx to tend to zero continuously. Mathematically this may be open to question, but it is justifiable I think from important educational points of view.

---

[1] Sequences which tend to zero.

My concern was to prompt the students to think of a number as continuously varying in order to experience the numerical structure given by a function as something freely moving in itself. This assumes that the real numbers form a continuum. Thus there is a problem with a clear central theme here which the math teacher must get to grips with at the latest with the introduction of the infinitesimal calculus. In my experience there is no need to devote a great part of the main lesson block to this theme.

I consider it important that by looking back over their time at school the students get an overview of the kingdom of the real numbers and how it was built up over that time, beginning with the natural numbers in the First year. What has proved of value is having the students report from memory what was brought forward during that time. This quite often provokes satisfied smiles and helps many students by giving them the feeling of throwing a bridge to a theme that with a prosaic scientific approach can prove very dry and unattractive.

At this stage of math education one should clearly emphasize that with the construction of the set of real numbers a certain conclusion is reached. Conclusion in the sense that now, without exception, the numbers can be related one-to-one with the points of a number line.

Now we know of course that this conclusion is not definitive. As teachers we are faced with the question of whether expanding the concept of number as far as the complex numbers should be dealt with in the classroom, whether from educational conviction or because exam considerations suggest it in any case. A well-known curriculum item of Steiner's states that one should deal with the complex numbers as far as de Moivre's theorem. I do not know of any statement by Steiner containing a more detailed explanation of this. So can a motive be found which induces us to deal with this theme in class? I see such a motive in the belief that concept-forming should be planned educationally in such a way that further development of the concept is possible.

In progressing from the real to the complex numbers two different new things arise. On the one hand the expansion from the number line to a number plane (the Argand diagram) enables the pupils to remain with something intuitive, except that now each one of the new numbers can be related in a one-to-one correspondence to a point of a plane. In this sense the totality of these new numbers can be represented by the points of a plane. The real numbers they've known up to now prove to be embedded even pictorially in the totality of the complex numbers. Things are quite different and for many students certainly very strange when we come to the fact that we can no longer say of two different complex numbers, which is the greater. Here we have something that seems to contradict the hitherto valid concept of number, even though this concept is usually only unconsciously present. What actually are the basic properties of numbers? – is a question that can arise at this point. This can be historically illuminating even, in that we can point to the discovery of the irrationals in antiquity for example, or to that of mathematical *structures* underlying not only numbers but also quite different mathematical objects.

Among the latter I'm thinking particularly of the projective and affine transformations which many colleagues like to deal with in the 12th or 13th Grade, both constructively and analytically. Here of course the relationship to the real numbers lies deeper than is the case with the relation between the real and complex numbers. In the geometry of projective transformations one studies to begin with individual concrete transformations by applying them to various geometrical forms. What has changed, and what properties of the form are preserved by the transformation? Here we have an object (the form) and a precisely determined action which is performed on the latter (i.e. we are seeing the transformation as a process). Comparison with the numbers and the arithmetic operations is immediately obvious. But it is quite different when we consider projective transformations from an (algebraic) structural point of view. The transformation as such – i.e. what the student experiences as a process – is the object. And the operation, usually called composition, is what "occurs" between two such objects. But in fact this is no real occurrence. The occurrence consists in the fact of the *successive execution* of the transformations, where only the "succession" is the "occurrence". The "execution" – there are actually two of them – has the character of object here.

So one could say that with this way of looking at things, in comparison with the numbers and the arithmetic operations, object (element) and action (operation) are exchanged.

Experience has shown that it is possible with the pupils of the top classes to work on exercises in which the composition of projective transformations, or more generally, the group of these transformations plays a role. Here it is admittedly mainly a question of their formal subjection to certain rules. To me it was more important in our context to track down something of the inner quality of the group of projective transformations in comparison with the numbers and their computations.

Certainly only a proportion of the students of a class will be able to follow the ways of thinking pursued here.

If we try to review the path through the realm of numbers in the course of the entire school time, we can picture the development from the natural to the real numbers like a progressive densification. Beginning with the positive direction of the natural number line, then with the negative numbers eventually comprehending the whole line, finally with the real numbers covering every point without exception of the entire number line. The further one can go *beyond* the real numbers the more clearly does a quite different tendency appear. For example the relationship structure between the complex numbers has become looser as a result of order properties ceasing to apply; with projective transformations we have a system of simple composition with successive execution as single basic operation. Here too there's a kind of loosening. The step beyond the realm of the reals appears to be inevitably connected with relinquishing one or the other property that until now one has seen as indispensably associated with all numbers. The question of whether further steps are possible can be left open at the end of the school time.

We return in conclusion to the key phrase "progressive densification up to the continuum of the real numbers", together with the question of whether and how far is it possible to picture what this means and thus to make it in principle accessible to inner intuition.

This is simple enough with the whole numbers which we can picture as a chain of equidistant points on the number line. Not completely of course, for we certainly cannot grasp the totality of *all* these points. It becomes essentially harder with the rational numbers. All the same we can imagine for example how, by continually bisecting intervals, we can insert further points between two distinct points. But even here, sooner or later we reach the limit of our ability. An inner infinity exists as well as an expansive infinity. An additional difficulty. The rational numbers make the number line so to speak "black" with points, because between two of them, however close together they are, there are in fact always more points. The next and last step of this kind comes with the discovery that the number line is far from being completely filled by the "rational points". This is only done when the irrational numbers or rather their points are added. Grasping the totality of the rational points in our imagination was already impossible, but grasping the totality of absolutely *all* the points – this is the epitome of impossibility. Whereas the rational and irrational points (or numbers) can be distinguished from each other in thought, please note that here we are concerned with the *totality* of points of both types. First as two sets of quite different elements, then as the union of these two sets. The fact that we are in a position to construct any amount of rational and irrational points in our imagination, and thus in a certain sense allow them to become concrete, does not contradict the above since in reality the set of these constructed points can only be finite. Such sets have no bearing at all on the above argument.

Considerations such as these bring the imagination comparatively strongly to the fore. Here we can speak of the "spatialization" of numbers. This is a result of the fact that in analytic geometry Cartesian co-ordinates are at least introduced if not used all the time. This produces, certainly in this domain, an association between what is actually in question, namely geometrical forms and their properties and relationships, and the method used to investigate these forms. So a question predominately spatial by its very nature. This even expresses itself in the fact that the co-ordinates axes are nothing other than number lines.

By contrast, what is process-like and hence time-like in numbers enters our consciousness less when we are active in the domain of analytic geometry. This temporal element is intensified again when in the differential calculus we introduce the concept of derivative paying heed that we develop it without borrowing anything from geometry. In my understanding, Rudolf Steiner's indications about this even show that one should not start from the tangent problem when introducing the derivative concept.

Finally we can sum up with this assertion: We can certainly grasp the totality of real numbers in thought. But we cannot picture this totality, i.e. every single one of them, as points. As pure ideal content the reals are a reality. But they do not belong to the realm of what can be grasped with the senses. So one can even see the path through the realm of the numbers during the school years as a path which opens up the possibility of sense-free thinking. Or, in the words of the title Louis Locher-Ernst gave to a collection of articles: *Mathematics as preparatory school for spiritual knowledge* [*Mathematik als Vorschule zur Geist-Erkenntnis*][2]. These articles can, even today, be enriching and encouraging for every mathematics teacher.

---

[2] published by Philosophisch-Anthroposophischen Verlag Dornach (Switzerland), second edition, 1973

Introducing the Derivative

UWE HANSEN

At the start of a main-lesson block it is a good idea to present a problem which is not too simple and in relation to which key aspects of that block can be developed. To introduce the differential quotient[1] for example, one can begin with the following problem. **Example 1:** A box (without a lid) of greatest possible volume is to be made from a square metal sheet, edge length $a = 30$ cm, by cutting off squares at the corners and folding up the side faces (Figure 1). What height h must be chosen?

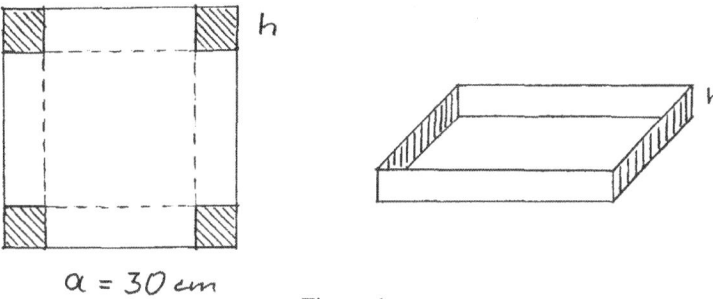

Figure 1

Many students will make the obvious guess that the height h must be 10 cm since this gives a cube. A height $h = 10$ cm gives a volume $V = 1000 \, cm^3$. But they will also suspect that a wider box would give a greater volume. Since this means a height smaller than 10 cm, the case of say $h = 8$ cm is checked. Then we get a volume of

$$V = 8 \cdot 14 \cdot 14 \, cm^3$$
$$= 1568 \, cm^3$$

---

[1] or differential coefficient, as it is usually called

This leads to the drawing-up of a table showing dependence of volume on height h.

Height h in cm	Width	Volume	in cm³
1	28	$1 \cdot 28 \cdot 28$	$= 784$
2	26	$2 \cdot 26 \cdot 26$	$= 1352$
3	24	$3 \cdot 24 \cdot 24$	$= 1728$
4	22	$4 \cdot 22 \cdot 22$	$= 1936$
5	20	$5 \cdot 20 \cdot 20$	$= 2000$
6	18	$6 \cdot 18 \cdot 18$	$= 1944$
7	16	$7 \cdot 16 \cdot 16$	$= 1792$
8	14	$8 \cdot 14 \cdot 14$	$= 1568$
9	12	$9 \cdot 12 \cdot 12$	$= 1296$
10	10	$10 \cdot 10 \cdot 10$	$= 1000$

At first the student is convinced that a height of $h = 5$ cm gives the greatest volume. But the height we're looking for doesn't have to be in a simple ratio to the edge length $a = 30$ cm, so the greatest volume *could* occur for values close to $h = 5$ cm. We have:

$$
\begin{aligned}
h &= 4.8 \text{ cm} & V &= 1997.568 \text{ cm}^3 \\
&= 4.9 \text{ cm} & &= 1999.396 \text{ cm}^3 \\
&= 5.1 \text{ cm} & &= 1999.404 \text{ cm}^3 \\
&= 5.2 \text{ cm} & &= 1997.632 \text{ cm}^3
\end{aligned}
$$

Almost every student will be satisfied with this result. However we can't exclude the possibility that the height we're looking for is closer to 5cm than we've so far checked. That is to say, it's not generally possible to prove by calculating individual volumes that $h = 5$ cm is the required height. Interestingly, only a conceptual proof is possible. We have to show that any change — however small — in the height $h = 5$ cm leads to a smaller volume. This is done by calculating the volume for $h = 5$ cm $+ \varepsilon$ where ε is a small positive or negative length. If the height is $h = 5$ cm $+ \varepsilon$ then the width of the box will be $b = 30 - 2(5 + \varepsilon) = 20 - 2\varepsilon$ (units are omitted from now on). The volume comes to

$$
\begin{aligned}
V(5 + \varepsilon) &= (20 - 2\varepsilon)^2 \cdot (5 + \varepsilon) \\
&= 2000 - 60\varepsilon^2 + 4\varepsilon^3 \\
&= 2000 - \varepsilon^2 \cdot (60 - 4\varepsilon)
\end{aligned}
$$

If $\varepsilon < 15$ then the factor $60 - 4\varepsilon$ is positive. Thus for $\varepsilon \neq 0$ something will always be subtracted from 2000. Therefore we have proved that the volume is maximal when $h = 5$ cm. Arguing in this way is unfamiliar but nevertheless comprehensible for students. What is important is that by means of this algebraic manipulation, that is to say by a purely conceptual argument, the infinite number of possible deviations from the value $h = 5$ cm can be taken into consideration.

The students will feel a need to understand the solution discovered still better. Figure 2 shows one possibility. The area of the upper (imagined) face of this square cuboid is 400 cm². This face has the same area as the four side faces together. This equality of areas accounts for the maximal volume, as we shall see.

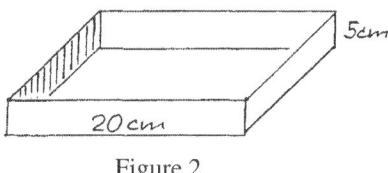

Figure 2

For comparison we consider the case $h = 4 + \varepsilon$ and calculate the corresponding volume

$$V(4+\varepsilon) = (22-2\varepsilon)^2 \cdot (4+\varepsilon)$$
$$= 1936 + 132\varepsilon - 72\varepsilon^2 + 4\varepsilon^3$$

or

$$V(4+\varepsilon) - 1936 = \left(132 - 72\varepsilon + 4\varepsilon^2\right) \cdot \varepsilon$$

Since $1936 = V(4)$ (see Table above), we can also write this equation in the form

$$\Delta V = \left(132 - 72\varepsilon + 4\varepsilon^2\right) \cdot \varepsilon \qquad (2)$$

where ΔV is an abbreviation for the volume difference $V(4+\varepsilon) - V(4)$. From this equation (2) we can develop the basic idea of the differential calculus by first considering the factor

$$132 - 72\varepsilon + 4\varepsilon^2$$

in more detail. For this it is necessary to go back to work done in the 11th Grade, especially what was learnt about reckoning with sequences that tend to zero, so-called null sequences. It might even be necessary to revise a few of these lines of thought at this point. If ε takes on the values of a null sequence then the factor $132 - 72\varepsilon + 4\varepsilon^2$ approaches a limiting value of 132. The special difficulties of the differential calculus consist in the fact that this process of the vanishing of ε, that is, the vanishing of the height difference, is taken into consciousness as something distinct and compared with the simultaneous vanishing of the volume difference ΔV.

Since we could use Δh to denote the height difference ε, we replace ε with dh to express the vanishing. This so-called differential dh thus denotes a quantity tending to zero, a "vanishing quantity" as it's sometimes called. Since the quantity ΔV also tends to zero (whenever ε tends to zero) and so is denoted dV, as a result of Equation (2) and by using the limiting value 132 we have the relation

$$dV = 132 \cdot dh \qquad (3)$$

So clearly, this introduction of differentials only makes sense for a *ratio* of differentials. Differentials can only be understood in context.

The transition from Equation (2) to Equation (3) often elicits from the students the justifiable question, Why does the "eventually" in the factor of Equation (2) no longer play a role – we replace the factor by the limiting value of 132 after all – even though we consider the differential dh, which is of course an abbreviation for ε, as a vanishing but non-zero quantity?

This question shows that it's not just a matter of limiting values but of how we form them, in particular it's a matter of comparing two limiting processes. Equation (2) states that the smaller the change in the height h, the more precisely is the change in volume 132 times as great as the change in height. To put it another way: If the height h (at the point $h=4$) changes by an amount that tends to zero, then the change in volume is 132 times as great. To grasp this thought demands special mental activity – ultimately we're comparing two "impulses of change". We're examining two activities, two movements in the moment of their coming into being.

At this point one can go back to what was discussed in the 11th Grade. For example, the two sequences (a_n) and (b_n) where

$$a_n = \frac{2n+1}{n^2} \qquad b_n = \frac{n-1}{n^2}$$

are null sequences, and

$$\lim_{n \to \infty} \frac{a_n}{b_n} = 2$$

is true. In other words, if n becomes infinitely large, then the change in a_n is eventually twice as great as that of b_n.

Equation (3) leads to another question. In this equation dV has the dimension of a volume and dh the dimension of a length. This means 132 must have the dimension of an area. Which area is it? This area can be explained using Figure 3. For a height of 4 cm the width of the box is 22 cm, giving a side-face area of 88 cm^2, so that the four side faces together have an area of 4 times 88 cm^2 = 352 cm^2. The non-existent upper face of the cuboid has an area of 22^2 cm^2 = 484 cm^2. But 484 cm^2 − 352cm^2 = 132cm^2. Now if the height $h=4$ cm increases by the zero-tending amount dh, the result is a volume increase of 484 cm$^2 \cdot$ dh at the top. This is only true for a constant base area, that is to say in the limit. Yet on the other hand, since as a result of the height increase the four edges of the base square move inwards by dh, the cuboid undergoes a volume decrease on four sides of 4 times 88 cm$^2 \cdot$ dh = 352cm$^2 \cdot$ dh. Therefore the overall volume increase is $(484 - 352)$ cm$^2 \cdot$ dh = 132 cm$^2 \cdot$ dh. Thus for $h=4$ cm the greatest volume has not been reached, since an increase in h leads to an increase in V.

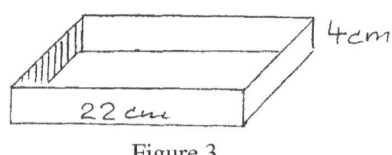

Figure 3

Let's take up the case $h = 5$ cm once more. Since in this case, as already mentioned, the two areas are equal, even a minimal increase in h does not lead to an increase in V. The increase at the top and the decrease at the sides balance each other out. Exactly the same is true for a decrease in h. Therefore, as already proved, the maximal volume must occur at $h = 5$ cm.

If we investigate a height of $h = 6 + \varepsilon$ we come by means of a similar calculation to the relation

$$dV = -108dh$$

Here a minimal increase in h leads to a decrease in the volume.

On further examination we are led to the following summary:

h in cm	V in cm^3	$V(h+\varepsilon)$	dV
3	1728	$1728 + \varepsilon(288 - 84\varepsilon + 4\varepsilon^2)$	$288dh$
4	1936	$1936 + \varepsilon(132 - 72\varepsilon + 4\varepsilon^2)$	$132dh$
5	2000	$2000 + \varepsilon(-60\varepsilon + 4\varepsilon^2)$	$0dh$
6	1944	$1944 + \varepsilon(-108 - 48\varepsilon + 4\varepsilon^2)$	$-108dh$
7	1792	$1792 + \varepsilon(-192 - 36\varepsilon + 4\varepsilon^2)$	$-192dh$

The special case $h = 5$ is instantly recognizable.

In a math class the question arose of whether dV could be calculated for general h. For the volume we have

$$V = (30 - 2h)^2 \cdot h$$
$$= 900h - 120h^2 + 4h^3$$

One student had the following idea: When h increases by dh, the factor before dh must be equal to the difference between the area of the imagined upper face and the area of the four side faces:

$$dV = \left((30 - 2h)^2 - 4h(30 - 2h)\right) \cdot dh$$
$$= (30 - 2h)(30 - 6h) \cdot dh$$
$$= (900 - 240h + 12h^2) \cdot dh$$

This factor is zero if $h = 15$ or $h = 5$. When $h = 15$ the cuboid contracts to the segment of a line; the volume is minimal. When $h = 5$ we have the maximal volume. So we come once more to the same result.

If we ask the students to compare the two expressions

$$V = 900h - 120h^2 + 4h^3$$
$$dV = (900 - 240h + 12h^2) \cdot dh$$

119

there will always be students who will guess the well-known power rule of differentiation in this one example.

The train of thought outlined here will only be understood if accompanied by specific activities. Yet it corresponds completely to what a 12th Grade requires. The differential quotient, which is a ratio of "vanishing" quantities, eludes the realm of the imagination; it cannot be understood by inner perception, "face to face". It can only be grasped by means of inwardly experienceable will processes, will impulses. Will impulses which are co-ordinated with each other. This co-ordination happens inwardly — a definition of the differential quotient as the gradient of a tangent doesn't grasp the essence. This first example must be complemented with others. It makes sense first to consider a very similar case.

Example 2: The square metal sheet is replaced by a rectangular one (see Figure 4). The problem is the same as in Example 1: the maximal volume is to be determined.

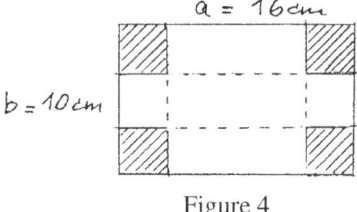

Figure 4

As before a table is drawn up:

Height in cm	Base area in cm^2	Volume in cm^3
1	14·8	112
2	12·6	144
3	10·4	120
4	8·2	64

This table leads to the conjecture that the volume is maximal when $h = 2$ cm. The following calculation confirms this. Let $h = 2 + \varepsilon$. Then

$$V(2+\varepsilon) = (2+\varepsilon) \cdot (12-2\varepsilon) \cdot (6-2\varepsilon)$$
$$= 144 - 28\varepsilon^2 + 4\varepsilon^3$$
$$= 144 - \varepsilon^2 \cdot (28 - 4\varepsilon)$$

For $\varepsilon < 7$ something will always be subtracted from 144 provided $\varepsilon \neq 0$. Thus for $\varepsilon = 0$, $h = 2$ the volume is maximal. Like in Example 1 we calculate the volume at $h = 1 + \varepsilon$:

$$V(1+\varepsilon) = (1+\varepsilon) \cdot (14-2\varepsilon) \cdot (8-2\varepsilon)$$
$$= 112 + \left(68 - 40\varepsilon + 4\varepsilon^2\right)\varepsilon$$
$$\Delta V = \left(68 - 40\varepsilon + 4\varepsilon^2\right)\varepsilon, \quad \text{since } 112 = V(1)$$

Introducing the Derivative   Uwe Hansen

If now ε tends to zero, we replace ε by dh and obtain

$$dV = 68 dh$$

A minimal rise in h leads to an increase in V, thus the volume must achieve its maximum at a greater height than $h = 1\,\text{cm}$. Similarly for $h = 3 + \varepsilon$ we get the equation

$$dV = -44 dh$$

With this value for h we've already gone past the maximum. A minimal rise in h leads to a decrease in the volume. For this second example too it is a good idea to compare V with dV:

$$V(h) = h(16 - 2h) \cdot (10 - 2h)$$
$$= 160h - 52h^2 + 4h^3$$

From the difference of the upper face area and the sum of the side-face areas we get

$$dV = ((16 - 2h)(10 - 2h) - 2h(16 - 2h) - 2h(10 - 2h)) \cdot dh$$
$$= \left(160 - 104h + 12h^2\right) \cdot dh$$

Here again talented students will succeed in seeing the connection between V and dV.

This example can also be generalized. If the rectangle has edges a and b, then the volume is maximal when the height is

$$h_{max} = \frac{1}{6}\left(a + b \pm \sqrt{a^2 + b^2 - ab}\right)$$

If one wants to give individual students separate exercises one can choose for example:

$a =$	21	8	16	15	30	21	15	11
$b =$	16	3	6	7	14	5	8	35
$h_{max} =$	3	$\frac{2}{3}$	$\frac{4}{3}$	$\frac{3}{2}$	3	$\frac{7}{6}$	$\frac{5}{3}$	$\frac{5}{2}$

In the two examples described, the required height was ascertained by means of a simple table. If one chooses for the edge-lengths $a = 15\,\text{cm}$ and $b = 7\,\text{cm}$, the required height is $h = 1.5\,\text{cm}$. If one takes $a = 18\,\text{cm}$ and $b = 6\,\text{cm}$, the sought-after height is irrational; it is $4 - \sqrt{7} \approx 1.35$.

In these cases determining the sought-after height is more complicated. The value of h is to be determined for which the factor before dh in the equation $dV = (\ldots) \cdot dh$ equals zero. In this case – a fact we've used many times already – the area of the upper face equals the sum of the areas of the side faces. This condition leads to a quadratic equation whose solution yields the required height.

The steps are briefly indicated:

In **Example 3:** $a = 15\,\text{cm}$ and $b = 7\,\text{cm}$. Then

$$V = h(15 - 2h) \cdot (7 - 2h)$$
$$= 105h - 44h^2 + 4h^3$$
$$dV = \left(105 - 88h + 12h^2\right) \cdot dh$$
$$= (3 - 2h)(35 - 6h) \cdot dh$$

Thus $h_1 = \frac{3}{2}$ and $h_2 = \frac{35}{6}$.

In **Example 4:** $a = 18\,\text{cm}$ and $b = 6\,\text{cm}$. Then

$$V = h(18 - 2h) \cdot (6 - 2h)$$
$$= 108h - 48h^2 + 4h^3$$
$$dV = \left(108 - 96h + 12h^2\right) \cdot dh$$

Hence $h_{1,2} = 4 \pm \sqrt{7}$.

We broaden our investigation and replace the rectangle with an equal-sided triangle. Here too the remit is to produce a "box", without lid, of maximal volume. We obtain the same result as in Example 1 with a square base, namely, that the volume is maximal for $x = \frac{a}{6}$ (see Figure 5).

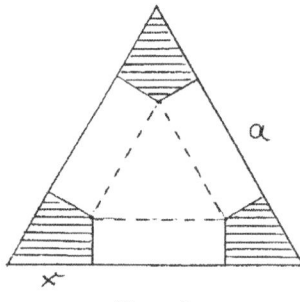

Figur 5

Example 5 is very simple. Which rectangle with perimeter 20 cm has the greatest area? It should be obvious to students that it's a square. So that the students can internalize the newly introduced method, it would be a good idea to apply the train of thought we've described to this problem too. Simple calculation results in the table

Height in cm	Width in cm	Area in cm^2
1	9	9
2	8	16
3	7	21
4	6	24
5	5	25
6	4	24

We start by calculating the area for $h = 5 + \varepsilon$:

$$A(5+\varepsilon) = (5+\varepsilon) \cdot (5-\varepsilon)$$
$$= 25 - \varepsilon^2$$

Thus the area is maximal for $\varepsilon = 0$. The result is a square as expected. For comparison we now choose $h = 4 + \varepsilon$. Then

$$A(4+\varepsilon) = (4+\varepsilon) \cdot (6-\varepsilon)$$
$$= 24 + 2\varepsilon - \varepsilon^2$$

or

$$A(4+\varepsilon) - A(4) = (2-\varepsilon) \cdot \varepsilon$$
$$\Delta A = (2-\varepsilon) \cdot \varepsilon$$

If ε tends to zero, this equation becomes

$$dA = 2dh$$

This result is immediately plausible. If the height $h = 4$ cm increases by a minimal amount dh, the upper edge is moved upwards, the right edge inwards – the lower left corner of the rectangle remaining fixed (see Figure 6).

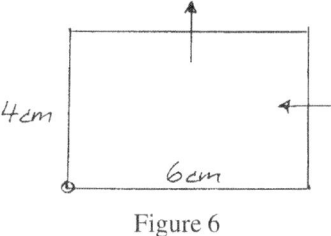

Figure 6

Therefore the gain in area is

$$dA = 6dh - 4dh = 2dh$$

From this it follows that if the sides of a rectangle of constant perimeter have different lengths, an enlargement of the smaller side leads to an increase in area. So a square must have the greatest area.

Here the general calculation is very simple:

$$A(h) = h(10-h) = 10h - h^2$$
$$A(h+\varepsilon) = (h+\varepsilon)(10-h-\varepsilon)$$
$$= 10h - h^2 + (10 - 2h - \varepsilon) \cdot \varepsilon$$
$$A(h+\varepsilon) - A(h) = (10 - 2h - \varepsilon) \cdot \varepsilon$$

If ε tends to zero, we have
$$dA = (10 - 2h) \cdot dh$$
That the area is maximal when $h = 5$ is also shown by the factor $10 - 2h$.

This result also follows immediately from the theorem about the altitude of a right triangle (Figure 7). Since height h and width b together amount to 10cm, this figure with the Thales circle is the result. The rectangle with sides h and b has the same area as the square on the segment H. But this square has greatest area when H is greatest, that is to say when h and b are equal.

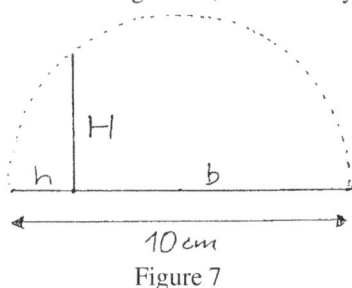

Figure 7

In this last example it's again clear that with the "differential ratio" or "differential quotient" the important thing is the observation of one's own will activity. One must inwardly increase the height "a little" – it's a question of will impulse – and realize that the gain in area (at $h = 4$ cm) is twice as great as – or more precisely 2 cm times as great as – the gain in height.

Whether more examples are added for consolidation purposes is discretionary – it depends on the teaching situation. A comparison of the next two examples can be quite helpful.

Example 6: Put inside the isosceles triangle of Figure 8 a rectangle of maximal area. Again a table is made which causes us to guess that the solution is $h = 2$ cm.

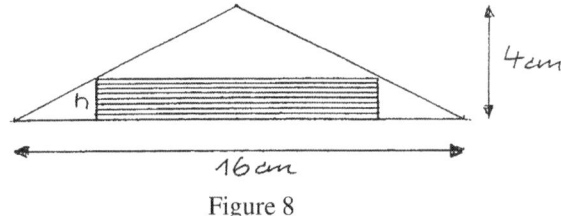

Figure 8

This is established by the following calculation:
$$A(2+\varepsilon) = (2+\varepsilon) \cdot (16 - 8 - 4\varepsilon)$$
$$= 16 - 4\varepsilon^2$$

What is important here is that increasing the height by dh causes both side-edges to shift by $2dh$ inwards. This means that in the maximal situation the upper edge must be twice as long as the sum of the lengths of the two side-edges. For $h = 2$ cm the gain in area above balances the loss in area at the sides. This equality is the critical one.

For arbitrary h we have
$$A = h(16 - 4h)$$
$$= 16h - 4h^2$$
$$A(h+\varepsilon) = (h+\varepsilon)(16 - 4h - 4\varepsilon)$$
$$= 16h - 4h^2 + (16 - 8h - 4\varepsilon)\varepsilon$$
$$A(2+\varepsilon) - A(h) = (16 - 8h - 4\varepsilon)\varepsilon$$
$$dA = (16 - 8h) \cdot dh$$

Here too we see that the area is maximal when $h = 2\,\text{cm}$.

This exercise can be made spatial, the problem becoming that of putting a cylinder of maximal volume inside a cone of radius $R = 8\,\text{cm}$ and height $H = 4\,\text{cm}$. (In Figure 8 rotate the triangle about the vertical axis of symmetry.) Here the maximizing height is smaller, namely $h = \frac{4}{3}\,\text{cm}$.

This result is comprehensible as a greater radius takes effect forwards *and* sideways.

For a height of $h = \frac{4}{3}\,\text{cm}$ the following holds: With a "minimal" increase the top surface moves half as fast upwards as the vertical surface does inwards. Since in this case the top surface has double the area of the vertical surface, volume gain and volume loss balance each out out.

We can put the results together to get an overall view:

Example 1	V	$= 900h - 120h^2 + 4h^3$
	dV	$= (900 - 240h + 12h^2) \cdot dh$
Example 2	V	$= 160h - 52h^2 + 4h^3$
	dV	$= (160 - 104h + 12h^2) \cdot dh$
Example 3	V	$= 105h - 44h^2 + 4h^3$
	dV	$= (105 - 88h + 12h^2) \cdot dh$
Example 4	V	$= 108h - 48h^2 + 4h^3$
	dV	$= (108 - 96h + 12h^2) \cdot dh$
Example 5	A	$= 10h - h^2$
	dA	$= (10 - 2h) \cdot dh$
Example 6	A	$= 16h - 4h^2$
	dA	$= (16 - 8h) \cdot dh$

The students see immediately that if
$$V = a \cdot h^3 + b \cdot h^2 + c \cdot h \quad \text{then}$$
$$dV = (3 \cdot a \cdot h^2 + 2 \cdot b \cdot h + c) \cdot dh$$

and if

$$A = a \cdot h^2 + b \cdot h \quad \text{then}$$
$$dA = (2 \cdot a \cdot h + b) \cdot dh$$

To represent functional dependences we generally use the letters x and y. Then we have:

$$y = a \cdot x^3 + b \cdot x^2 + c \cdot x$$
$$\text{implies} \quad dy = (3 \cdot a \cdot x^2 + 2 \cdot b \cdot x + c) \cdot dx$$

This process – namely determining dy as a function of dx for a given functional dependence of y on x – is called *differentiation* (one starts by forming differences after all).

Students will appreciate it if these results are elucidated once more with some simple examples:

1. If $y = 3x$, then

$$y(x+\varepsilon) - y(x) = 3(x+\varepsilon) - 3x$$
$$\Delta y = 3\varepsilon$$
$$\text{thus} \quad dy = 3dx$$

It is immediately evident that the increase in x is tripled as well. Geometrically we can represent y as the area of a rectangle with sides 3 and x. If x increases then the rectangle increases on the right side. The increase in area is always three times the increase in the side x. Similarly if $y = cx$, then $dy = cdy$.

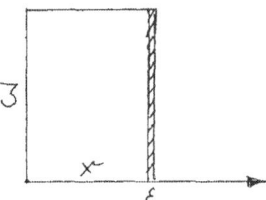

2. Let $y = x^2$; the rule developed above then gives

$$dy = 2x \cdot dx$$

This also follows from the following algebraic argument:

$$y(x+\varepsilon) - y(x) = (x+\varepsilon)^2 - x^2$$
$$\Delta y = (2x+\varepsilon)\varepsilon$$
$$\text{If } \varepsilon \text{ tends to zero we have} \quad dy = 2x \cdot dx$$

This result can also be explained with a square of edge length x; y is then the area of the square. The square's lower left corner is kept fixed as x increases. The square thus grows at its right and top sides. The result is two "thin" rectangles each of area $x \cdot dx$, in total therefore $2x \cdot dx$. Thus the increase in area is $2x$ times as great as the increase in the square's side.

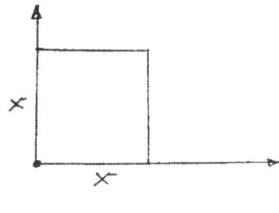

3. Let $y = x^3$, then $dy = 3x^2 \cdot dx$.

   Consider a cube with edge of length x, thus of volume x^3. Then an increase in x causes the cube to grow at three faces of area x^2, namely rightwards, upwards and forwards (the rear lower left corner remaining being fixed). Therefore the gain in volume is $3x^2$ times as great as the gain in the cube's edge. Thus three square cuboids of volume $x^2 dx$ are continuously arising.

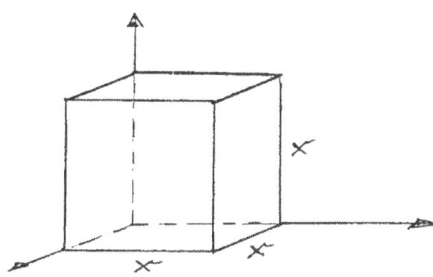

In the lesson a practice exercise component could now follow in which simple polynomials in the variable h or x are differentiated.

In the second part of the block one could deal with the graphical representation of a function and the geometrical interpretation of the differential quotient. Exercises of the following kind are suitable as an introduction.

Let $y = 9x - x^2$. At which point is the change in y exactly as great as that in x? At which point is the change in y twice (three times) as great as that in x? For which value of x is y greatest?

Calculate the y-values for $x = 0, 1, 2, \ldots, 9$ and draw the graph of the function.

We have $dy = (9 - 2x) dy$. The factor before dx is abbreviated as y'. One could then draw up the following table:

x	$y = 9x - x^2$	$y' = 9 - 2x$
0	0	9
1	8	7
2	14	5
3	18	3
4	20	1
5	20	-1
6	18	-3
7	14	-5
8	8	-7
9	0	-9

This table shows that at the point $x = 4$ the change in y is exactly as great as that in x; at the point $x = 5$, the loss in y is as great as the gain in x. At the point $x = 4.5$, $9 - 2x = 0$. So that is where y achieves its maximum (20.25). At $x = 3.5$, $y' = 2$, so here y's variation is twice as great as x's. At $x = 5.5$, the loss in y is twice as great as the gain in x since $y' = -2$ here. At $x = 3$, y's variation is three times as great as x's since $y' = 3$ here. At $x = 6$, $y' = -3$.

After these considerations, we can look at the graphical representation. As preparation we could simply draw the y-axis with the corresponding x-values. We experience the rise and fall of the y-values particularly well with this representation (left in the Figure). It is a very satisfying experience for the teacher when the students can see from the equality $dy = dx$ at the point $x = 4$ that there the graph has gradient $m = 1$, and so the tangent is parallel to the bisector of the angle between the positive axes. That is, with this gradient the change in y at every point is exactly as great as the change in x. The other results can be interpreted geometrically in a similar way.

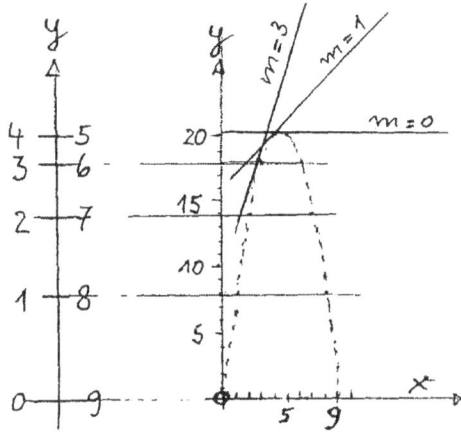

For the train of thought followed in this contribution the connection between y' and the tangential

Introducing the Derivative

gradient is not a definition but is a relationship that can be deduced. This enables a better understanding of the concept "tangential gradient". This happens because we start not from a picture – the tangent – but from two related will impulses. This way of proceeding also complies with Rudolf Steiner's call to develop the differential quotient from the numerical, and to transfer from there to the geometrical aspect; the student should gain the idea that "the geometrical aspect is in the end only an illustration of the numerical" (Teachers' conference, 30.4.1924).

As a first example of graphical representation one could also start from the function

$$y = -0.5x^2 + 4x - 3.5$$

whose tangents are easier to draw. We have the following table:

x	y	y'
0	−3.5	4
1	0	3
2	2.5	2
3	4	1
4	4.5	0
5	4	−1
6	2.5	−2
7	0	−3
8	−3.5	−4

The following sketch can be produced using the table. In this connection one could also take up the examples in the first part and draw the graphs of the volume and area functions.

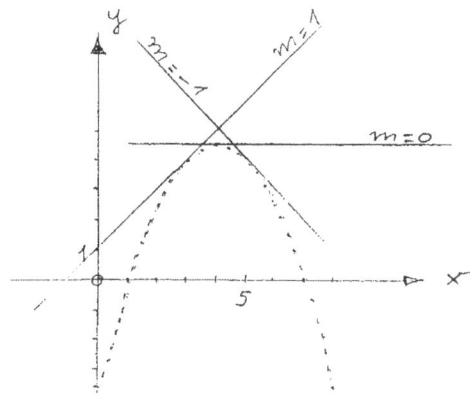

Appendix

Understanding the differential quotient can be deepened by the following.

For the area of a circle we have

$$A = r^2 \pi$$

which implies $\quad dA = 2r\pi \cdot dr$

This equation states that the circumference indicates how many times greater the area of the circle grows than does the radius, if the radius increases "a little".

Similarly a sphere has a volume of

$$V = \frac{4}{3} r^3 \pi$$

which implies $\quad dV = 4r^2 \pi \cdot dr \quad$ with $\quad A_{\text{sphere}} = 4r^2 \pi$

So the sphere's surface area indicates how many times greater the volume of the sphere grows than does the radius, if the radius increases "a little".

The volume of a cylinder is

$$V = r^2 \pi h$$

Thus we have $\quad dV = r^2 \pi \cdot dh$

and also $\quad dV = 2r\pi h \cdot dr$

If the cylinder's height grows, then the base area is the factor by which we multiply the height increase to get the volume increase. If the cylinder's radius grows, then the curved surface area is factor by which we multiply the radial increase to get the volume increase.

The differential quotient as numerical phenomenon

WALTER HUTTER

In this article we shall develop the concept of the differential quotient (also known as the derivative). The discussion focuses on phenomena which appeared in mathematics beginning with the 17th century. We abstain from introducing graphical representations too soon, preferring to let it become clear that the derivative concept is, essentially, a numerical phenomenon, one amenable to thinking.

When we consider the underlying significance of the differential quotient, we find that it has to do with the acceptance and precise formulation, in thought, of the infinitely small. The infinitely small in turn presupposes something continuous that can be infinitely divided.

> It is remarkable that at the very start of his brilliant career Lagrange was led to the discussion of the validity of the principles of the infinitesimal calculus, something that preoccupied him right until his last years [...]. He gave an outline of his new method in a paper of 1772 [...]. In the intervening period (in 1784), through the agency of the Berlin Academy whose chairman he was, he invited academics throughout the world to solve the all-important problem; [...] We want to report in some detail on the prize problem mentioned. "A lucid and rigorous theory of what in mathematics is called *the infinite*" was requested. "Higher geometry", read the invitation, "frequently uses infinitely great and infinitely small quantities, yet academics of old carefully avoided the infinite and some famous analysts of our time declare that the words *infinite quantity* are contradictory [...]." The prize was awarded to *Exposition élémentaire des principés des calculs supérieurs* [*Elementary exposition of the principles of the higher calculus*] (Berlin 1786). The author of this treatise was Simon Antoine Jean Lhuilier who was born in Geneva in 1750 and died there in 1840 [...]. (Moritz Cantor *Vorlesungen über Geschichte der Mathematik* [*Lectures on the history of mathematics*], Vol. IV, 2nd ed., B. G. Teubner Verlagsgesellschaft, Stuttgart 1965, p. 644ff)

Starting from very practical problems we want to try to develop this realm of the continuum of numbers, without recourse to formalism or to geometrical over-simplification. The path described here gives an impression of what pupils can and want to understand in discussions of this sort.

1 Maximum and minimum

> According to Diogenes Laertius, "another of Pythagoras' doctrines was, that of all solid figures the sphere was the most beautiful; and of all plane figures, the circle". Although this quote is not to be construed as claiming that the Pythagoreans were

concerned with the isoperimetric problem, it's still true that such studies were, in their own way, quite advanced. For example, at the beginning of the 2nd century BC a substantial work of Zenodorus outlines a great number of important propositions of this theory. [...] According to Zenodorus, for given perimeter, a regular polygon has greater area than an irregular one with the same number of sides [...]. A circle has the greatest area. [...] Later (Greek) mathematicians did not advance beyond Zenodorus' findings, hardly any of his propositions being mentioned in later writings (according to von Bradwardinus, †1349 in Avignon). Only in modern times was the ancient theme taken in hand again. We have to thank Lhuillier 1782 and Steiner 1841 for taking it up again. (Johannes Tropfke *Geschichte der Elementar-Mathematik* [*History of elementary mathematics*], Vol. II, Verlag von Veit & Comp., Leipzig 1903, p. 461)

How must a field be cultivated so as to maximize the harvest? How can we choose a shortest route through the hundreds or thousands of streets of a town? Problems about maxima and minima have been the focus of discussion since antiquity. But the mundane character of these problems can hide their deeper nature. The following examples will go into such problems in detail and provide a first acquaintance with the infinitely small.

The city wall

A rectangular enclosure with an area of 450 m² is to be marked out against a town wall and fenced. How can this be done so that the cost of the fence is as small as possible?

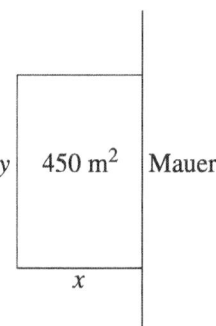

Solution:
The fenced-in area is equal to $A = x \cdot y = 450$ m². This gives a relation between the sides x and y of the enclosure:
$$y = \frac{450}{x}.$$

The length of the fence then equals $l = 2x + y = 2x + \frac{450}{x}$, the last expression for the length depending on x alone. We emphasize this by writing:
$$l(x) = 2x + \frac{450}{x}.$$

The differential quotient as a numerical phenomenon

For what value of the argument x is $l(x)$ minimal? Intuitively, x must become neither too small nor so large that y becomes too small. In both cases we would enclose an uneconomically narrow area with a great deal of fence. To find the right x-value we use trial and error.

$$x = 12 \Rightarrow l(12) = 61.5$$

$$x = 13 \Rightarrow l(13) \approx 60.615$$

$$x = 14 \Rightarrow l(14) \approx 60.143$$

$$x = 15 \Rightarrow l(15) = 60$$

$$x = 16 \Rightarrow l(16) \approx 60.125$$

$$x = 17 \Rightarrow l(17) \approx 60.471$$

$$x = 18 \Rightarrow l(18) = 61$$

The shortest fence-length occurs when x is close to 15 m. We investigate the behavior of the fence-length in the neighborhood of $x = 15$:

$$x = 15.1 \Rightarrow l(15.1) \approx 60.0013245$$

$$x = 15.01 \Rightarrow l(15.01) \approx 60.00001332$$

$$x = 15.001 \Rightarrow l(15.001) \approx 60.00000013$$

$$x = 15.0001 \Rightarrow l(15.0001) \approx 60$$

$$\ldots$$

$$x = 14.9999 \Rightarrow l(14.9999) \approx 60$$

$$x = 14.999 \Rightarrow l(14.999) \approx 60.00000013$$

$$x = 14.99 \Rightarrow l(14.99) \approx 60.00001334$$

$$x = 14.9 \Rightarrow l(14.9) \approx 60.00134228$$

Pupils now feel sure that the length is minimal for $x = 15$ and $y = \frac{450}{x} = 30$, the minimal length being $l(15) = 60$ m. To substantiate this, we consider $2x + \frac{450}{x}$ where x has a general value of $x = 15 + h$:[1]

$$2(15+h) + \frac{450}{15+h} = 60 + \frac{2h^2}{15+h} > 60 \text{ for small } |h|.$$

The expression tends towards the minimal value of 60 as h approaches the value zero. This evidence follows only after careful examination of the length function $l(15+h)$, suitably refor-

---

[1] $2(15+h) + \frac{450}{15+h} = \frac{(30+2h)(15+h)+450}{15+h} = \frac{900+60h+2h^2}{15+h} = \frac{60(15+h)+2h^2}{15+h} = 60 + \frac{2h^2}{15+h}$

mulated, as $h \to 0$.

The maximal area consists of two squares. The fence-length is therefore minimal when a semicircle can be inscribed in the area.

Inscribed cylinder

A cylinder of maximal volume is to be inscribed in a sphere of radius $r = 4\sqrt{3}$. How high must the cylinder be?

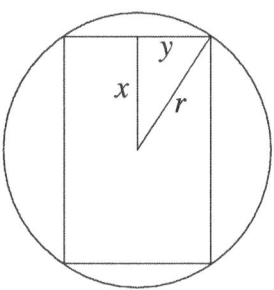

Solution:

The volume of the cylinder is equal to $\pi y^2 \cdot 2x = \pi(r^2 - x^2) \cdot 2x = 2\pi(r^2 x - x^3)$ where $r = 4\sqrt{3}$. Hence

$$V(x) = 2\pi(48x - x^3).$$

As we approach the argument $x = 4$ we find the maximal volume:

$$x = 4.1 \quad \Rightarrow \quad V(4.1) \approx 803.4874539$$

$$x = 4.01 \quad \Rightarrow \quad V(4.01) \approx 804.2401732$$

$$x = 4.001 \quad \Rightarrow \quad V(4.001) \approx 804.2476439$$

$$x = 4.0001 \quad \Rightarrow \quad V(4.0001) \approx 804.2477186$$

$$x = 4.00001 \quad \Rightarrow \quad V(4.00001) \approx 804.2477193$$

$$x = 4.000001 \quad \Rightarrow \quad V(4.000001) \approx 804.2477193$$

$$\ldots$$

$$x = 3.999999 \quad \Rightarrow \quad V(3.999999) \approx 804.2477193$$

$$x = 3.99999 \quad \Rightarrow \quad V(3.99999) \approx 804.2477193$$

$$x = 3.9999 \quad \Rightarrow \quad V(3.9999) \approx 804.2477186$$

$$x = 3.999 \quad \Rightarrow \quad V(3.999) \approx 804.2476439$$

$$x = 3.99 \quad \Rightarrow \quad V(3.99) \approx 804.2401858$$

$$x = 3.9 \quad \Rightarrow \quad V(3.9) \approx 803.5000203$$

The cylinder has a maximal capacity of

$$V(4) \approx 804.2477193.$$

Just as in the first example, here the impression should *not* arise that the numerical trial and error carried out with the arguments closing in on $x = 4$ qualifies as the proof of an extreme value. What matters more is to cultivate a basic sense for extreme values and how they come about. Then the feeling will arise in the classroom, that the found value is a plausible maximum, along with a dim awareness that something must nevertheless be said to justify it. At that moment, the pupil can find his way to the analysis of the problem. The investigation of $2\pi(48x - x^3)$ for general $x = 4 + h$ follows:

$$2\pi \left[48(4+h) - (4+h)^3\right] = 2\pi \left(128 - 12h^2 - h^3\right) = 256\pi - 2\pi h^2(12+h) < 256\pi$$

for small $|h|$. This expression tends to the maximal value of $256\pi \approx 804.2477193$ as h approaches the value zero.

The volume is thus maximized when $x = 4$ and $y = \sqrt{r^2 - x^2} = \sqrt{48 - 16} = 4\sqrt{2}$. The height of the cylinder is $2x = 8$. Generally, $\frac{y_{max}}{x_{max}} = \sqrt{2}$.

Silo with domed roof

A silo is in the shape of a cylinder with a hemispherical top. What must the radius r and the overall height a be so that for a given total volume of $V = 45\pi$ m³, the material needed to construct it is minimal?

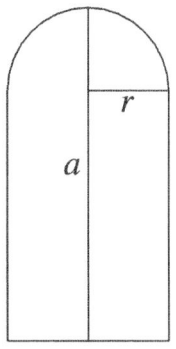

Solution:

First we consider the silo's capacity.

$$\begin{aligned} \text{total volume } V &= \text{cylinder volume + hemisphere volume} \\ &= \pi r^2(a-r) + \frac{2}{3}\pi r^3 \\ &= \pi r^2 a - \pi r^3 + \frac{2}{3}\pi r^3 \\ &= \pi r^2 a - \frac{\pi r^3}{3} \end{aligned}$$

We make a the subject.

$$\pi r^2 a - \frac{\pi r^3}{3} = V$$

$$\pi r^2 a = V + \frac{\pi r^3}{3}$$

$$a = \frac{V}{\pi r^2} + \frac{r}{3}$$

$$a = \frac{45}{r^2} + \frac{r}{3}$$

Now we can investigate the surface area of the construction.

$$\begin{aligned} S &= \text{cylindrical surface + hemisphere + base surface} \\ &= 2\pi r(a-r) + 2\pi r^2 + \pi r^2 \\ &= 2\pi r a - 2\pi r^2 + 2\pi r^2 + \pi r^2 \\ &= 2\pi r a + \pi r^2 \end{aligned}$$

By substituting $\frac{45}{r^2} + \frac{r}{3}$ for a in the latter formula, we obtain the surface area S as a function of r only.

$$\begin{aligned} S(r) &= 2\pi r \left(\frac{45}{r^2} + \frac{r}{3} \right) + \pi r^2 \\ &= \frac{90\pi}{r} + \frac{5\pi r^2}{3} \end{aligned}$$

We conjecture that the smallest value of $S(r)$ is given by $r = 3$.

$$r = 3.1 \quad \Rightarrow \quad S(3.1) \approx 141.525371$$

$$r = 3.01 \quad \Rightarrow \quad S(3.01) \approx 141.3732367$$

$$r = 3.001 \quad \Rightarrow \quad S(3.001) \approx 141.3716851$$

$r = 3.0001 \Rightarrow S(3.0001) \approx 141.3716696$

$r = 3.00001 \Rightarrow S(3.00001) \approx 141.3716694$

$r = 3.000001 \Rightarrow S(3.000001) \approx 141.3716694$

...

$r = 2.999999 \Rightarrow S(2.999999) \approx 141.3716694$

$r = 2.99999 \Rightarrow S(2.99999) \approx 141.3716694$

$r = 2.9999 \Rightarrow S(2.9999) \approx 141.3716696$

$r = 2.999 \Rightarrow S(2.999) \approx 141.3716851$

$r = 2.99 \Rightarrow S(2.99) \approx 141.3732437$

$r = 2.9 \Rightarrow S(2.9) \approx 141.5323601$

The area then equals
$$S(3) \approx 141.3716694 \, \text{m}^2.$$

Finally the proof that this value is minimal is as follows. For small $|h|$ the expression[2]

$$\frac{90\pi}{3+h} + \frac{5\pi(3+h)^2}{3} = 45\pi + \frac{5\pi h^2(9+h)}{3(3+h)} > 45\pi$$

and it therefore tends to the minimal value $45\pi \approx 141.3716694$ as h approaches zero. In general $a_{\max} = 2r_{\max}$. So the hemispherical top of the silo, extended to a complete sphere, would touch the floor of the silo.

The ideal box

A cylindrical metal box with volume (V) equal to 0.45 liter is to be made with minimal use of material. What size must the radius r and the height x of the box be?

Solution:
The surface area equals $S(r,x) = 2\pi r^2 + 2\pi rx$. Substituting $x = \frac{V}{\pi r^2} = \frac{450}{\pi r^2}$, we have

$$S(r) = 2\pi r^2 + \frac{900}{r}.$$

We search for the radius which causes the surface area to be minimal:

$r = 2 \Rightarrow S(2) \approx 475.13$

$r = 3 \Rightarrow S(3) \approx 356.55$

---

2 $\quad \frac{90\pi}{3+h} + \frac{5\pi(3+h)^2}{3} = \frac{270\pi + 5\pi(3+h)^3}{3(3+h)} = \pi \cdot \frac{405 + 135h + 45h^2 + 5h^3}{3(3+h)} = \pi \cdot \frac{135(3+h) + 5h^2(9+h)}{3(3+h)}$

$$r = 4 \quad \Rightarrow \quad S(4) \approx 325.53$$

$$r = 5 \quad \Rightarrow \quad S(5) \approx 337.08$$

$$r = 6 \quad \Rightarrow \quad S(6) \approx 367.19$$

By further trial and error, one finds in fact that $r = 4.15283$ is a more precise minimum point. At the same time, one has the impression that the shrinking down towards the sought-after radius value will never end. The problem, in stark comparison to preceding examples, is that the required value for r arises only approximately from the numerical experiment. Escape from this impasse is provided by the following proposition:

The surface area $S(r)$ is minimal for

$$r_m = \sqrt[3]{\frac{225}{\pi}} \approx 4.152830592...$$

Proof: We substitute $r = r_m + h$ in the formula for the area:

$$\begin{aligned} S(r_m + h) &= \frac{2\pi(r_m+h)^3 + 900}{r_m+h} = \frac{2\pi r_m^3 + 6\pi r_m^2 h + 6\pi r_m h^2 + 2\pi h^3 + 900}{r_m+h} \\ &= \frac{6\pi r_m^3 + 6\pi r_m^2 h + 6\pi r_m h^2 + 2\pi h^3}{r_m+h} \\ &= 6\pi r_m^2 + 2\pi h^2 \frac{3r_m + h}{r_m+h} \end{aligned}$$

The fractional term is positive for small $|h|$ and tends to zero as $h \to 0$. Hence, as $h \to 0$, $S(r_m+h)$ tends to the minimal value $6\pi r_m^2 \approx 325.0794777...$. The optimal height turns out to be

$$x_m = \frac{450}{\pi r_m^2} = \frac{450}{\pi \left(\sqrt[3]{\frac{225}{\pi}}\right)^2} \approx 8.305661184...$$

In general $r_m = \sqrt[3]{\frac{V}{2\pi}}$ and $x_m = \sqrt[3]{\frac{4V}{\pi}}$, hence $x_m = 2r_m$.

However convincing this proof is, we have still not fathomed why the value of r_m is supposed to be precisely

$$\sqrt[3]{\frac{V}{2\pi}} = \sqrt[3]{\frac{225}{\pi}}.$$

A practical aspect for further work arises from this:

Motive 1. How are minimum or maximum points found analytically? Can we anticipate an extreme value directly from the network of operations from which an expression is formed?

The newly ßwon familiarity with decimal numbers which occurred at the end of the 16th century is the historical basis for the foregoing considerations.

> We look [...] toward the origin of the concept of number as an infinite decimal fraction. It is around 1600 that we find that concept in the form and usage to which we are accustomed. Sine tables were then systematically transformed into decimal notation—by Viète in 1579 and by Stevin in 1585—with the invention of the decimal point. The inventors of logarithms soon cast these into the form of decimal fractions. The discoverers of the infinitesimal calculus tacitly or subconsciously adhered to this number concept throughout the seventeenth century. (Otto Toeplitz *The calculus: a genetic approach*, University of Chicago Press, Chicago 60637, 2007, p. 15)

Hence, we can confirm that our method up to now for finding extreme values has provided verifiable answers. It was based on the picture that the numbers form a continuum and that we can think of an arbitrarily close (that is, infinitely fine) approximation to a particular number. This is the basis for all the limits accompanying the mathematical analysis in this article.

Motive 2. The quantity h appeared in the examples as a small numerical deviation which tends to zero. The corresponding calculated deviations from the sought-for maximum or minimum values also tended to zero. How are these mutually-determined vanishing deviations related?

In sections 3–5 we answer these questions. First we need to define a term.

2 The function

> *Functio quantitatis variabilis est expressio analytica quomodocunque composita ex illa quantitate variabili et numeris seu quantitatibus constantibus.*
> A function of a variable quantity is any analytic expression whatsoever made up from that variable quantity and from numbers or constant quantities. (Leonhard Euler: Introductio in Analysin Infinitorum (1748). Opera Omnia, ser. I/8, Section 4, Teubner Verlag, Leipzig 1922, p. 18)

The examples of the last section lead us to what is, since the time of Leonard Euler, the most important concept of mathematics. It is the concept of function – the idea that a relation between two variables can be described.

A function is an unambiguously defined relation between two variable quantities.

> To express the fact that a quantity depends on one or more others, be this through arbitrary operations or even by relationships which, though not specifiable algebraically, nevertheless have definitely specified conditions for their existence, one says that the first is a function of the others. The use of this word will elucidate its meaning fully. (S. F. Lacroix *Handbuch der Differential- und Integralrechnung* [*Handbook of differential and integral calculus*], Realschulbuchhandlung, Berlin 1817, p. 3)

For example the equation $V(x) = 2\pi(48x - x^3)$ describes a well-defined relationship between x and V. For each x-value there is exactly one V-value $V(x)$, which depends on x. The relationship V is a function.

For functions f (other letters may be used as well) one uses a standard notation appropriate to graphical representation in a coordinate system:

$$y = f(x), \text{ where } f(x) = 2\pi(48x - x^3).$$

The independent variable x is called the *abscissa*. There is no restriction on the values of x. The dependent variable y is called the *ordinate*. The values of $y = f(x)$, the function values, arise according to the choice of x in conformity with a rule.

> The concept of functional value – fundamental to that of function, and therefore for analysis – existed already in the 19th century. But it was Augustin Louis Cauchy (1789–1857) who recognized and clarified its central significance for analysis. (Detlef D. Spalt: *Der Begriff der reellen Funktion* [*The concept of the real function*], in Mathesis, Verlag für Geschichte der Naturwissenschaften und der Technik, Berlin-Diepholz 2000, p. 212)

With the process of closing in on the desired number we came as close as we wished to a number x and observed the behavior of the corresponding functional value.

> Imagine x to be a variable quantity which, little by little, can take on all possible real values, and that a single value of the undetermined quantity y is associated with each of its values, then y is known as a function of x; and if while x goes steadily through all values between two fixed values, y varies steadily as well, then this function is called *continuous* within this interval. (Bernhard Riemann *Grundlagen für eine allgemeine Theorie der Functionen einer veränderlichen complexen Größe* [*Basic principles of a general theory of functions of a complex variable*], inaugural dissertation, Göttingen 1851, p. 1)

Arbitrarily small variations of the functional value could be achieved with sufficiently small variations in the associated x-value. Such a relationship is called a *continuous function*.

> When one sees infinitely small quantities subjected to strict criticism and control in this way, while the concept of continuous variation is left unchallenged, one cannot help thinking of the saying: one hangs the little thieves and lets the big ones get away. (Karl Snell *Einleitung in die Differential- und Integralrechnung* [*Introduction to differential- and integral calculus*], Part I, F.A. Brockhaus Verlag, Leipzig 1846, p. 120)

A parabola, for example, is continuous. Even the hyperbola $y = \frac{1}{x}$, which consists of two diverging branches, is continuous in every point except $x = 0$.[3]

---

[3] We leave on one side the fact that when we include the line at infinity the hyperbola can be seen as a closed curve.

Without the assumption of continuous growth of the quantities by virtue of which, for any arbitrarily small change, infinitely many intermediate levels are passed through, the concept of mutually dependent variables would soon be exhausted and show itself as fruitless. The distinction between continuous and discrete quantities rests solely on the different ways they increase. If a continuous quantity [...] is increased by an arbitrarily small amount, then after the transition from one state to another, infinitely many intermediate levels [...] have actually been passed through.[...] The increase of [discrete] numbers is always a successive adding on of units of whatever sort which in this respect appear as finished parts, as atoms as it were, and the act of counting cannot exhaust and actually pass through the infinity of possible states of the quantities in an act of thought, but merely postulate or suppose them. The increase of continuous quantities is an object of intuition, the increase of discrete ones, an object of thought . (Snell, p. 30)

In the following examples the continuity of the curves can be confirmed or refuted by exact inspection.

The function q is given by

$$q(x) = \begin{cases} \sin\left(\frac{1}{x}\right) & \text{for } x \neq 0 \\ 0 & \text{for } x = 0 \end{cases}.$$

The form of the graph becomes compressed in the neighborhood of $x = 0$ at the same time oscillating between the y-values -1 and 1.

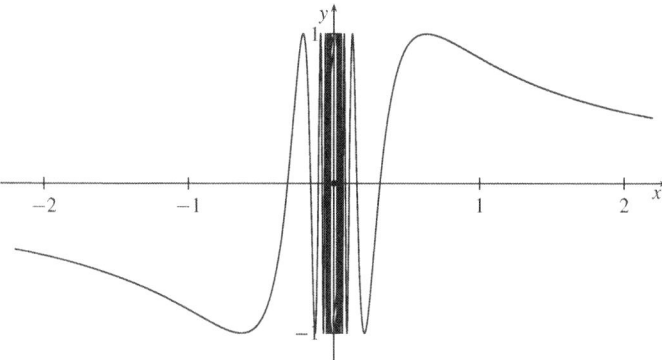

This function is not continuous at the point $x = 0$ (Cauchy, 1821). Yet if we damp the oscillations of the function values for $x \to 0$ by defining

$$g(x) = \begin{cases} x \cdot \sin\left(\frac{1}{x}\right) & \text{for } x \neq 0 \\ 0 & \text{for } x = 0 \end{cases},$$

then the function contracts steadily to a point at $x = 0$, the oscillations of the function values about the x-axis dying away completely as x approaches 0 and then growing again. The function g is continuous (Weierstraß, 1874).

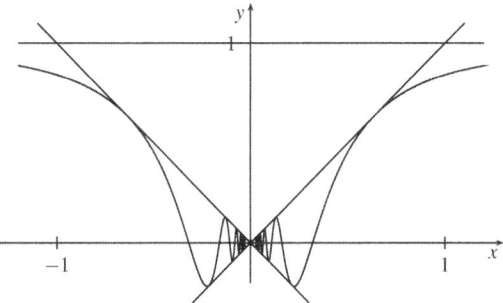

A still heavier damping of the oscillations occurs if we multiply the expression for g by x. The continuous function h given by

$$h(x) = \begin{cases} x^2 \cdot \sin\left(\frac{1}{x}\right) & \text{for } x \neq 0 \\ 0 & \text{for } x = 0 \end{cases},$$

assumes the following shape.

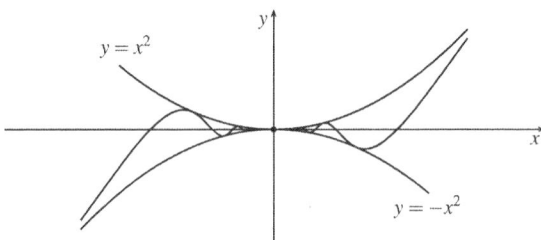

Likewise continuous is the function p which is again enveloped by two parabolas and has the following equation:

$$p(x) = \begin{cases} x + x^2 \cdot \sin\left(\frac{1}{x}\right) & \text{for } x \neq 0 \\ 0 & \text{for } x = 0 \end{cases}$$

The differential quotient as a numerical phenomenon   Walter Hutter

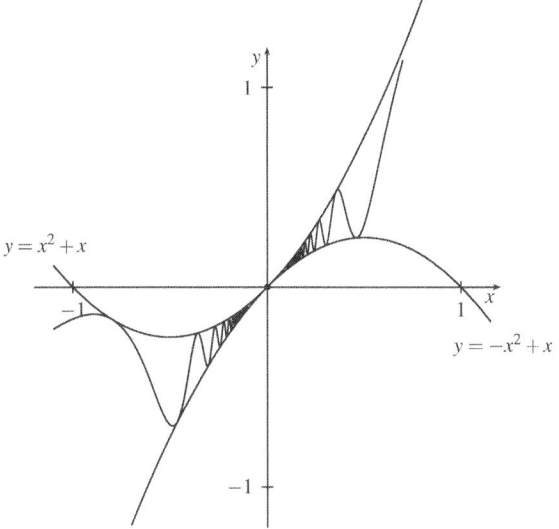

The mathematical concept of continuity goes beyond the picture ordinarily associated with the word "continuous". Not every continuous function can be thought of as one that can be drawn in one "go", without lifting the pencil from the paper, as it were. The next function d, known as the *Devil's staircase*, illustrates this.

$$d(x) = \begin{cases} \frac{1}{2} & \text{for } x \in \left[\frac{1}{3}, \frac{2}{3}\right] \\ \frac{1}{4} & \text{for } x \in \left[\frac{1}{9}, \frac{2}{9}\right] \\ \frac{3}{4} & \text{for } x \in \left[\frac{7}{9}, \frac{8}{9}\right] \\ \frac{1}{8} & \text{for } x \in \left[\frac{1}{27}, \frac{2}{27}\right] \\ \frac{3}{8} & \text{for } x \in \left[\frac{7}{27}, \frac{8}{27}\right] \\ \frac{5}{8} & \text{for } x \in \left[\frac{19}{27}, \frac{20}{27}\right] \\ \frac{7}{8} & \text{for } x \in \left[\frac{25}{27}, \frac{26}{27}\right] \\ \ldots & \ldots \end{cases}$$

It is defined piecewise as follows: The interval $[0, 1]$ of numbers between 0 and 1 (including 0 and 1) is divided into three. Over the middle third $[\frac{1}{3}, \frac{2}{3}]$ the function has the constant value $\frac{1}{2}$. The two outer thirds are again trisected, *their* middle thirds being assigned the function values $\frac{1}{4}$ and $\frac{3}{4}$ respectively. This process is continued. The next graph shows the beginning of the process.

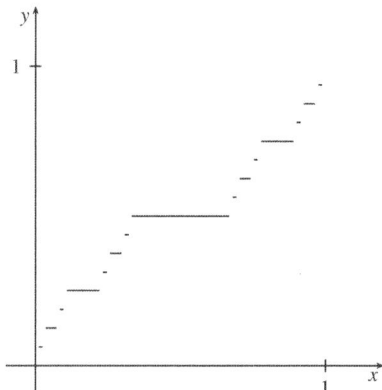

Surprisingly, the function d produces a non-decreasing, continuous curve, even though initially the piecewise, disjointed definition of the function gives a different impression. The infinitely many subintervals together produce the interval $[0,1]$:

$$\frac{1}{3} + \frac{2}{9} + \frac{4}{27} + \frac{8}{81} + \cdots = 1.$$

3 Instantaneous speed

If we now follow the history of the maximum and minimum problems further, we have first of all to remember the writings of the French writer Oresme (1323-1382), who plotted curves and studied them; among other things he at one point remarks [...] that at the highest point of a semicircle the speed of increase and decrease is at its slowest. If we consider what analytic importance the change of direction of a curve took on, some four hundred years later, in the differential quotient, we see here the first, admittedly very obscure foreshadowing of the fact that the differential quotient must vanish at a maximum point. (Tropfke, p. 462)

We return to the problem of section 1. Numerical differences, tending to zero, are put into relationship with the corresponding small differences of functional values. How do fractions behave, whose numerator and denominator are small and interdependent differences? We formulate a concrete problem around this question.

An object is thrown vertically from the ground into the air and falls back to the ground after a short while. The relation between time elapsed and distance covered is described by the function f with equation

$$f(x) = -5x^2 + 50x, \quad 0 \leq x \leq 10,$$

in the sense that the independent variable x represents the time elapsed in seconds (s), the dependent variable $y = f(x)$ represents the height of the object in meters (m) at time x. It turns out that when $x = 5$ s the height $f(5) = 125$ m is maximal.

1. How many meters has the object covered after 3.5 s?

2. After how many seconds has it traveled a distance 105 m from the start point?

3. What is its average speed between the end of the first and the end of the third second?

4. What is its average speed between the end of the first and the end of the second second?

5. What is its instantaneous speed at time $x = 1$ s?

Solution:

1. $f(3.5) = 113.75$ m

2. The quadratic equation $105 = -5x^2 + 50x$ has the two solutions $x_1 = 3$ and $x_2 = 7$. Thus the object passes the 105 m mark twice, once going up and once coming down.

3.
$$v_{1,3} = \frac{\text{displacement}}{\text{time elapsed}} = \frac{f(3)-f(1)}{3-1} = 30\,\frac{m}{s}$$

4.
$$v_{1,2} = \frac{f(2)-f(1)}{2-1} = 35\,\frac{m}{s}$$

5. The idea is to calculate the average speeds
$$v_{1,1+h} = \frac{f(1+h)-f(1)}{h} = \frac{f(1+h)-45}{h}$$
from time 1 to time $1+h$ for ever diminishing time-intervals h.

Time	h	0.1	0.01	0.001	0.0001	$\to 0$
	$1+h$	1.1	1.01	1.001	1.0001	
	$f(1+h)$	48.95	45.3995	45.039995	45.00399995	
Displacement	$f(1+h)-45$	3.95	0.3995	0.039995	0.00399995	$\to 0$
$v_{1,1+h}$	$\frac{f(1+h)-45}{h}$	39.5	39.95	39.995	39.9995	$\to 40$

The average speeds $v_{1,1+h}$ tend towards 40. In fact the quotient

$$\frac{f(1+h)-45}{h} = \frac{-5(1+h)^2 + 50(1+h) - 45}{h} = \frac{40h - 5h^2}{h} = 40 - 5h$$

tends to the value 40 as h tends to zero. This value is the sought-for instantaneous velocity v_1. The instantaneous velocity v_1 at time $x = 1$ is thus the limit of $\frac{f(1+h)-f(1)}{h}$ as $h \to 0$; in short

$$v_1 = \lim_{h \to 0} \frac{f(1+h)-f(1)}{h} = 40\,\frac{m}{s}.$$

We can determine the following instantaneous velocities as we did in part (e):

$$v_2 = 30\,\frac{m}{s} \qquad v_3 = 20\,\frac{m}{s} \qquad v_4 = 10\,\frac{m}{s} \qquad v_5 = 0\,\frac{m}{s}$$

$$v_6 = -10\,\frac{m}{s} \qquad v_7 = -20\,\frac{m}{s} \qquad v_8 = -30\,\frac{m}{s} \qquad v_9 = -40\,\frac{m}{s}.$$

Each velocity is the limit of a quotient whose numerator and denominator tends to zero. Speaking metaphorically, the denominator sounds the note, the numerator attunes itself to it and together they form a definite ratio. This can only happen since they have much in common.

> One will have noticed that this result is obtained from two quite heterogeneous concepts, the concept of an intuitively evident continuum on the one hand, and that of a function on the other, i.e. a formal combination of arithmetic operations in which of course the quantities can only be thought of as numbers. The increase of the continua considered for itself produces a content with an indeterminate value, and the increase of the values of the function considered for itself produces likewise an indeterminate value, and only the relation between the two – and the verification that they form a «good match» – gives an expression that is fully determined with respect to form and content, and with respect to quantity and meaning, namely the instantaneous, relative strength of the limiting value of the differential quotient, giving the growth of the function. (Snell, p. 90)

The rate of change of a quantity $f(x)$ which varies with time x was of great interest to Newton. He regarded time and instantaneous position as variable elements, as so-called *flowing* quantities. From them he let instantaneous speed arise as a mathematical concept. Of course, this speed can directly experienced whenever we move. On the other hand, as soon as we want to *measure* speed (as with radar) we resort to average speed. Instantaneous speed cannot be measured. In practice, since the difference between (1) average speed over a very small time interval and (2) instantaneous speed, is imperceptible, these two speeds are equated. However, assuming the average speed over an arbitrarily small time interval is known, instantaneous speed actually arises as a limiting process, as shown above. Mathematically, in the sense of our problem, we thus obtain instantaneous speed as an exact value.

> Thus with Newton the concept of speed already exists as basic principle before he starts any calculations. [... With Leibniz on the other hand the idea of speed, that a movement appears to be measured by it, is the result of calculation. (Prof. Dr. Paul Freyer *Studien zur Metaphysik der Differentialrechnung* [*Studies in the metaphysics of the differential calculus*], commissioned by W. Weber, Berlin 1883, p. 12)

4 The derivative

Following Leibniz one had advanced, roughly speaking, to the following. If $f(x)$ expressed a function, one formed $f(x+dx) - f(x)$ and rewrote it until one could factor out dx, giving $f(x+dx) - f(x) = g(x,dx)dx$. The result $g(x,0)$ was then the differential quotient; it was Lagrange who first spoke of derivatives. (Bernhard Riemann, Vita Mathematica 10, Birkhäuser, 1996, p. 63)

We have in mind the functions fx, called original functions in relation to the functions $f'x$, $f''x$ etc. which are derived from them, and the latter may be called derived functions in relation to the former. (Joseph Louis de Lagrange *Theorie der analytischen Funktionen* [*Theory of analytic functions*], Lagarde Verlag, Berlin, 1798)

In this concept of the infinite the quantum has truly achieved a qualitative existence. (Georg Wilhelm Friedrich Hegel *Wissenschaft der Logik I* [*Science of logic I*], complete works, Vol. 4, Friedrich Frommann Verlag (Günther Holzboog), Stuttgart-Bad Canstatt 1965, p. 310)

We divided differences of function values $\Delta f(x) = f(x+h) - f(x)$ by differences of x-values $\Delta x = (x+h) - x = h$. For a general function f we call the

limiting value of the difference quotient $\dfrac{\Delta f(x)}{\Delta x} = \dfrac{f(x+h) - f(x)}{h}$ as $h \to 0$

the *derivative* or the *differential quotient* of f at the point x. The derivative of a function is thus a process by which a relation is established between the changes in the abscissa and the associated changes in the ordinate, as both become infinitely small. According to Hegel (Logik I, p. 310) these infinitely small differences are

> no longer quanta, but only have meaning in their relationship, with purely momentary existence. They are no longer something, the something taken to be quantum, no longer finite differences; and yet not nothing, not indeterminate zeros. Apart from their ratios they are purely zeros, but they should be understood as only a *moment* of their ratios [...].

f can be differentiated at each point x. In the last example we chose as values of x: $1, 2, \cdots, 9$. The derivatives at these points were the instantaneous speeds. For each x-value there is thus a value of the derivative, which we denote $f'(x)$.

$$f'(x) = \lim_{h \to 0} \frac{f(x+h) - f(x)}{h}$$

Limes [lat.]: Limit

The derivative f' is thus itself a function. We notice the following about this function. In the last problem we had $v_5 = f'(5) = 0$, corresponding to the function value $f(5) = 125$. If the object achieves its maximum height, then the instantaneous speed is equal to zero. All function values at points around $x = 5$ are smaller than 125. Thus the function's maximal value is given when the derivative equals zero.

The points at which a maximal (or minimal) function value arises are zeroes of the derivative of the function.

The notation $\frac{df}{dx}$ for f' originates with Gottfried Wilhelm Leibniz. It is commonly used to this day and reminds us that f' arises from a quotient. In contrast to the symbol Δ usual for finite differences, he chose d to emphasize that a limiting process has occurred. Leibniz gave a separate meaning to the "differentials" df and dx as "actual infinitely small quantities", which however is not consistent with the way we have built up our concepts.

5 Nascent zeroes

> The ultimate Ratios with which synchronal Increments of Quantities vanish, are not the Ratios of finite Increments, but Limits which the Ratios of those Increments attain, by having their Magnitudes infinitely diminish'd.
> (John Walton *A Vindication of Sir Isaac Newton's Principles of Fluxions against the Objections Contained in the Analyst.* Dublin, 1735, p. 3,
> http://www.maths.tcd.ie/pub/HistMath/People/Walton/Vindication/Vindic.pdf)

Our examples led to limit processes within the continuum of numbers. With instantaneous speed, it was a question of quotients whose values in numerator and denominator tended to zero in a particular way. Such variable quantities tending continuously to zero we call *nascent zeroes*[4]. In this section we will study further qualitative differences in how such quantities approach zero.

Suppose we start with a variable h which tends to zero. Then h^2 tends to zero essentially faster. The expressions

$$\lim_{h \to 0} h = 0 \qquad \lim_{h \to 0} h^2 = 0$$

give no indication of this qualitative difference, however. Only when we consider quotients does the dramatic contrast appear:

$$\lim_{h \to 0} \frac{h^2}{h} = \lim_{h \to 0} h = 0$$

$$\lim_{h \to 0} \frac{h}{h^2} = \lim_{h \to 0} \frac{1}{h} = \infty$$

---

[4] Louis Locher-Ernst formed the concept of "nascent zero" [*werdende Null*] in his book *Differential- und Integralrechnung* [*Differential and integral calculus*], Birkhäuser Verlag, Basel 1948.

In what follows we shall form ratios from such nascent zeroes and observe the coordinated behavior of their values. Much finer distinctions than between 0 and ∞ arise as a result. The quotient of two nascent zeroes can be a real number. In the language of nascent zeroes the expression "$\frac{0}{0}$" has many meanings. The examples below are chosen so that the limiting quotients are, in fact, derivatives.

1. We investigate the genesis of $f'(2) = \lim_{h \to 0} \frac{f(2+h)-f(2)}{h}$ for $f(x) = x^2$.

$$\frac{2.1^2 - 2^2}{0.1} = \frac{0.41}{0.1} = 4.1$$

$$\frac{2.01^2 - 2^2}{0.01} = \frac{0.0401}{0.01} = 4.01$$

$$\frac{2.001^2 - 2^2}{0.001} = \frac{0.004001}{0.001} = 4.001$$

$$\ldots$$

$$\lim_{h \to 0} \frac{(2+h)^2 - 2^2}{h} = 4 = 2 \cdot 2$$

2. We investigate the genesis of $f'(3) = \lim_{h \to 0} \frac{f(3+h)-f(3)}{h}$ for $f(x) = x^2$.

$$\frac{3.1^2 - 3^2}{0.1} = \frac{0.61}{0.1} = 6.1$$

$$\frac{3.01^2 - 3^2}{0.01} = \frac{0.0601}{0.01} = 6.01$$

$$\frac{3.001^2 - 3^2}{0.001} = \frac{0.006001}{0.001} = 6.001$$

$$\ldots$$

$$\lim_{h \to 0} \frac{(3+h)^2 - 3^2}{h} = 6 = 2 \cdot 3$$

$$\ldots$$

$$\boxed{\lim_{h \to 0} \frac{(x+h)^2 - x^2}{h} = \lim_{h \to 0} \frac{2hx + h^2}{h} = \lim_{h \to 0} \frac{h(2x+h)}{h} = 2x}$$

3. We investigate the genesis of $\lim_{h \to 0} \frac{f(x+h)-f(x)}{h}$ for $f(x) = x^3$.

$x = 2$ $\quad \lim_{h \to 0} \frac{(2+h)^3 - 2^3}{h} = \lim_{h \to 0} \frac{12h + 6h^2 + h^3}{h} = 12 = 3 \cdot 2^2$

$x = 3$ $\quad \lim_{h \to 0} \frac{(3+h)^3 - 3^3}{h} = \lim_{h \to 0} \frac{27h + 9h^2 + h^3}{h} = 27 = 3 \cdot 3^2$

...

$$\lim_{h\to 0}\frac{(x+h)^3-x^3}{h}=\lim_{h\to 0}\frac{3x^2h+3xh^2+h^3}{h}=3x^2$$

4. We investigate the genesis of $f'(x)=\lim_{h\to 0}\frac{f(x+h)-f(x)}{h}$ for $f(x)=x^4$.

$x=2\qquad \lim_{h\to 0}\frac{(2+h)^4-2^4}{h}=\lim_{h\to 0}\frac{32h+24h^2+8h^3+h^4}{h}=32=4\cdot 2^3$

$x=3\qquad \lim_{h\to 0}\frac{(3+h)^4-3^4}{h}=\lim_{h\to 0}\frac{108h+54h^2+12h^3+h^4}{h}=108=4\cdot 3^3$

...

$$\lim_{h\to 0}\frac{(x+h)^4-x^4}{h}=\lim_{h\to 0}\frac{4x^3h+6x^2h^2+4xh^3+h^4}{h}=4x^3$$

5. In this example we go into what is called *continuous compounding* of interest in more detail. 1 dollar is to be invested at an annual interest rate of 100%. If we add the interest each month to the capital, then after the first month the sum of $\frac{1}{12}$ dollar is added to the initial capital. After the second month the capital would increase to

$$1+\frac{1}{12}+\frac{1}{12}\cdot\left(1+\frac{1}{12}\right)=\left(1+\frac{1}{12}\right)^2.$$

After one year, i.e. 12 months, there would be

$$\left(1+\frac{1}{12}\right)^{12}$$

dollars. If we divide the year into n compounding periods, then after a year has elapsed the capital amounts to

$$\left(1+\frac{1}{n}\right)^n$$

dollars.

$n=100\qquad \left(1+\frac{1}{n}\right)^n=2.704813829...$

$n=1000\qquad \left(1+\frac{1}{n}\right)^n=2.716923932...$

$n=10000\qquad \left(1+\frac{1}{n}\right)^n=2.718145927...$

$$n = 100000 \quad \left(1+\frac{1}{n}\right)^n = 2.718268237...$$

$$n = 1000000 \quad \left(1+\frac{1}{n}\right)^n = 2.718280469...$$

$$n = 10000000 \quad \left(1+\frac{1}{n}\right)^n = 2.718281693...$$

$$n = 100000000 \quad \left(1+\frac{1}{n}\right)^n = 2.718281815...$$

$$n = 1000000000 \quad \left(1+\frac{1}{n}\right)^n = 2.718281827...$$

$$n = 10000000000 \quad \left(1+\frac{1}{n}\right)^n = 2.71828128...$$

$$n = 100000000000 \quad \left(1+\frac{1}{n}\right)^n = 2.718281828...$$

The limit of $\left(1+\frac{1}{n}\right)^n$ as $n \to \infty$ we denote e (sometimes called Euler's number}).

$$e \approx 2.718281828$$

The number e is irrational. We now examine the limiting value $f'(0) = \lim_{h \to 0} \frac{f(0+h)-f(0)}{h}$ for $f(x) = e^x$.

$$\frac{e^{0.1} - 1}{0.1} = 1.051709181...$$

$$\frac{e^{0.01} - 1}{0.01} = 1.005016708...$$

$$\frac{e^{0.001} - 1}{0.001} = 1.00050017...$$

$$\frac{e^{0.0001} - 1}{0.0001} = 1.00005...$$

$$\frac{e^{0.00001} - 1}{0.00001} = 1.000005...$$

...

$$\boxed{\lim_{h \to 0} \frac{e^h - 1}{h} = 1}$$

6. The instantaneous rate of change of the capital value at the beginning of the investment period is thus equal to 1 (corresponding to the initial capital). With continuous compounding

of interest, in the course of the year, this rate is proportional to the current total capital[5]. This is shown in the next example.

6. We investigate how $f'(x) = \lim_{h \to 0} \frac{f(x+h)-f(x)}{h}$ is calculated for $f(x) = e^x$.

$$x = 2 \qquad \lim_{h \to 0} \frac{e^{2+h}-e^2}{h} = \lim_{h \to 0} \frac{e^2(e^h-1)}{h} = e^2 \lim_{h \to 0} \frac{e^h-1}{h} = e^2$$

$$x = 3 \qquad \lim_{h \to 0} \frac{e^{3+h}-e^3}{h} = \lim_{h \to 0} \frac{e^3(e^h-1)}{h} = e^3 \lim_{h \to 0} \frac{e^h-1}{h} = e^3$$

...

$$\boxed{\lim_{h \to 0} \frac{e^{x+h}-e^x}{h} = \lim_{h \to 0} \frac{e^x(e^h-1)}{h} = e^x \lim_{h \to 0} \frac{e^h-1}{h} = e^x}$$

7. The derivative of the function $f(x) = e^x$ is thus the function itself! Conversely, this property leads once more to the explicit evaluation of the number e. We have just shown that

$$f'(x) = e^x \cdot \lim_{h \to 0} \frac{e^h-1}{h}.$$

Assuming $f'(x) = e^x$ to be true, the number e must have the property that

$$\lim_{h \to 0} \frac{e^h-1}{h} = 1.$$

This means that for very small $|h|$, the expression $\frac{e^h-1}{h}$ is approximately equal to 1:

$$\frac{e^h-1}{h} \approx 1$$

$$e^h - 1 \approx h$$

$$e^h \approx 1 + h$$

$$e \approx (1+h)^{\frac{1}{h}}$$

and hence

$$e = \lim_{h \to 0}(1+h)^{\frac{1}{h}}.$$

---

[5] In reality an initial sum of k_0 is invested at an annual interest rate of $p\%$ (for example $p = 2.4$). By arguments similar to those used above it can be shown that if interest is compounded continuously the capital k after one year amounts to

$$k = k_0 \cdot e^{\frac{p}{100}}.$$

Furthermore after x years the ensuing capital is

$$k(x) = k_0 \cdot e^{\frac{p}{100}x}.$$

The well-known formula for e is thus established:

$$e = \lim_{n \to \infty} \left(1 + \frac{1}{n}\right)^n$$

8. The figure shows two examples of two orthogonal families of logarithmic spirals:

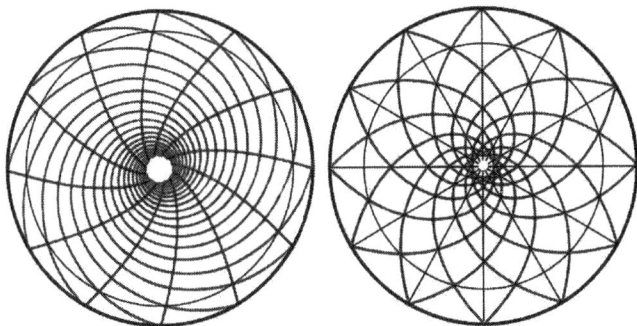

In the circle on the right both spirals have the same shape. From this double family we choose a right-handed spiral; we also choose one of this spiral's points to follow as it spirals out. Through this starting point a radius leads to the outer circle. This radius is now rotated clockwise about the circle's center so that its intersection with the circle's edge moves exactly one radius length. At the same time the outward-moving spiral point has moved further away from the center than it was at the start. For the spirals chosen here (left and right spirals are the same shape), the distance from the center increases by a factor of $e = 2.71828182845...$. Euler's number e (after Leonhard Euler, 1727) is arguably the most famous number in mathematics. It is the number of natural growth, i.e. continuous enlargement that preserves similarity. We speak, in fact, of *exponential* growth. Its characteristic is that the growth dynamic depends on the existing state: the more the formation has grown already, the faster it grows further (i.e. $f'(x)$ is proportional to $f(x)$). In the Nautilus shell, resembling the symmetric spirals above, this behavior is arranged circularly and realizes a logarithmic spiral. The number e is universal. The applications of what are called dynamical systems are closely involved with the number e. For these reasons we can speak of the symmetrical spirals as an archetype in mathematics[6].

9. We conclude this section with a look at trigonometry. In a right-angled triangle with hypotenuse of unit length, the sine of an acute angle is equal to the length of the opposite side. The radian measure of a very small angle in such a triangle is almost the same as the length of the opposite side, and hence as the sine of the angle. The smaller the angle, the better

---

[6]See Hermann von Baravalle *Goethes Prinzipien von Urbild und Metamorphose in der Mathematik [Goethe's principles of archetype and metamorphosis in mathematics]*, in Goethe in unserer Zeit, Hybernia Verlag, Dornach-Basel 1949, p. 163-174.

the agreement. This is reflected in the following example[7]. We investigate the formation of $\lim_{h \to 0} \frac{\sin h}{h}$.

$$\frac{\sin 0.1}{0.1} = 0.9983341665...$$

$$\frac{\sin 0.01}{0.01} = 0.9999833334...$$

$$\frac{\sin 0.001}{0.001} = 0.9999998333...$$

$$\frac{\sin 0.0001}{0.0001} = 0.9999999983...$$

...

$$\boxed{\lim_{h \to 0} \frac{\sin h}{h} = 1}$$

10. Using the formula $\sin \alpha - \sin \beta = 2 \cos \frac{\alpha+\beta}{2} \sin \frac{\alpha-\beta}{2}$ with $\alpha = x+h$ and $\beta = x$ we have

$$\frac{\sin(x+h) - \sin x}{h} = \frac{2 \cos \frac{2x+h}{2} \sin \frac{h}{2}}{h} = \cos \frac{2x+h}{2} \cdot \frac{\sin \frac{h}{2}}{\frac{h}{2}}$$

$$\boxed{\lim_{h \to 0} \frac{\sin(x+h) - \sin x}{h} = \cos x}$$

The differential calculus consists in the mutual relationship and inner union of two starkly contrasting quantities, the discrete and the continuous, the thought and the intuited. [...] In brief – from a methodological point of view – one can call the differential calculus the theory of the arithmetic or analytic treatment of the continuum. The world of quantity as objects of intuition is taken up into the world of mental pictures; being is brought into thinking. (Snell, p. 188)

Now that we have become familiar with differential quotients as quotients of nascent zeroes, we give a brief summary of what we have discovered.

---

[7]"If the ratio of two infinitely small quantities converges to a given limit, while each of them tends to zero, then the limit referred to is the so-called ultimate ratio of these infinitely small quantities. So for example the ultimate ratio of $\sin \alpha$ and α is unity." (Augustin Louis Cauchy *Vorlesungen über die Differenzialrechnung* [*Lectures on the differential calculus*], Meyer Verlag, Braunschweig 1836, p. 5)

6 Standard derivatives

> We shall now discuss with some detail the logical foundation of the differential calculus [...]. The principle idea is that the infinitesimal calculus is *only an application of the general notion of limit*. The differential quotient is defined as the limit of the quotient of corresponding finite increments of variable and function [...]. The scientific mathematics of today is built upon the series of developments which we have been outlining. But an essentially different conception of infinitesimal calculus has been running parallel with this through the centuries. What precedes harks back to old metaphysical speculations concerning the structure of the continuum according to which this was made up of ultimate indivisible infinitely small parts. [...] Leibniz, who shares with Newton the distinction of having invented the infinitesimal calculus, also made use of such ideas. [...] But there is a third direction for the mathematical ideas of Leibniz, one which is especially characteristic of him. It is his formal point of view. [...] His thought here is as follows. It makes no difference what meaning we attach to the differentials, or whether we attach any meaning whatever to them. If we define appropriate rules of operation for them, and if we employ these rules properly, it is certain that something reasonable and correct will result. (Felix Klein *Elementary mathematics from an advanced standpoint: arithmetic, algebra, analysis*, translated from the 3rd German ed., Dover, 2004, p. 211 ff.)

We have seen these examples of going over from a given function to its derivative:

$$f(x) = x \quad \leadsto \quad f'(x) = 1$$
$$f(x) = x^2 \quad \leadsto \quad f'(x) = 2x$$
$$f(x) = x^3 \quad \leadsto \quad f'(x) = 3x^2$$
$$\ldots$$
$$f(x) = x^n \quad \leadsto \quad f'(x) = n \cdot x^{n-1}$$

$$f(x) = e^x \quad \leadsto \quad f'(x) = e^x$$

$$f(x) = \sin x \quad \leadsto \quad f'(x) = \cos x$$

In a more abbreviated form this can be summarized as:

$$(x^n)' = n \cdot x^{n-1} \qquad (e^x)' = e^x \qquad (\sin x)' = \cos x$$

These basic continuous functions, the power function, the exponential function and the sine function, are so-called differentiable functions[8], functions whose derived function is defined (i.e. the differential quotient exists) for all x-values[9].

7 The tangent problem

> Through investigations of curved lines, geometers arrived at the differential calculus, which since then has been presented from quite diverse points of view. [...] By the law of continuity we have to understand what is observed when we describe curves through movement, and by which the points of one and the same curve succeed each other without any gaps. The approach to quantities in the calculus appears not to admit this law since one always assumes an interval between two successive values of the same quantity; yet the smaller this gap is the closer one approaches the law of continuity, with which the limit agrees fully. It is also by virtue of this law that increments, even if vanishing, still keep the character of ratio to which they have gradually – before vanishing – converged. [...] Geometrical considerations show in a very clear way that the ratio-character of the increases of a function and its variable can be described by limits. (Lacroix, p. 74-76)

The differential calculus has its origin in two main problems, (1) that of the instantaneous velocity of a moving body, (2) the so-called tangent line problem. We shall show that these are equivalent problems.

In section 3 we determined, for a distance-time function f, the instantaneous velocity

$$f'(x) = \lim_{h \to 0} \frac{f(x+h) - f(x)}{h}$$

at time x. For any function f the function f' (where it is defined) can be interpreted as a velocity function if f is regarded as a distance-time function.

Geometrically, seen in relation to the graph of a function f, the ratios

$$\frac{f(x+h) - f(x)}{h}$$

---

[8] Every differentiable function is automatically continuous. Differentiability is thus a stronger property than that of continuity.

[9] "Until recent times it was a common assumption that a single-valued continuous function of a real variable always possesses a first derivative whose value is defined and finite everywhere except possibly at isolated points. Even in the writings of Gauss, Cauchy, Dirichlet there is to my knowledge no certain evidence that these mathematicians, who in their scholarship were wont to exercise the most stringent criticism about everything, had held a different view." (Karl Weierstraß, see *Scherz und Ernst in der Mathematik* [Math in jest and in earnest], Teubner Verlag, Leipzig 1904, p. 49). In 1872 Weierstraß was the first since Bolzano to construct an example of a function on $\mathbb{R}$ which is continuous but nowhere differentiable.

are slopes of secants, which approach a particular value as $h \to 0$. This limit must be the slope of the tangent at the point x.

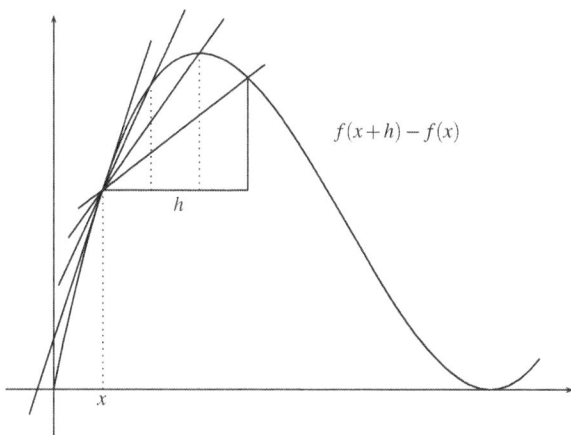

Slopes of curves can be described by the slopes of their tangents. Zeroes of the derivative, i.e. solutions of the equation $f'(x) = 0$, give the points where curves have horizontal tangents. This intuitive, geometrical interpretation of the transition from difference quotients (slopes of secants) to the differential quotient (slope of the tangent) confirms that *the points at which a maximal or minimal function value arises are zeroes of the derivative of the function.*

> The investigation is thus related to a process of becoming. If I consider the curve merely as the locus of the point $x\ y$, merely as a manifold of points, then I cannot apply the differential calculus. By its very nature, questions which concern only discrete quantities are far removed from its domain. (Freyer, p. 3)

Thus differentiability means we can construct tangents to curves. If the graph has a sharp corner then the function is not differentiable there. The function f given by $f(x) = |x|$ (the absolute value or modulus function)[10] is not differentiable at $x = 0$.

---

[10] Other examples were shown in section 2. The function q there is neither continuous nor differentiable at $x = 0$. The function g is continuous but not differentiable at $x = 0$. The function h is continuous and differentiable, though the derived function

$$h'(x) = \begin{cases} 2x \cdot \sin\left(\frac{1}{x}\right) - \cos\left(\frac{1}{x}\right) & \text{for } x \neq 0 \\ 0 & \text{for } x = 0 \end{cases}$$

is not continuous at $x = 0$. The function p is also both continuous and differentiable. From the graph one might ask whether in fact $p'(0) = 1$. Since $p(x) = x + r(x) \cdot x$ with $|r(x)| \leq |x|$, this is the case. Since for $x \neq 0$ the derivative is given by the formula

$$p'(x) = 1 + 2x \cdot \sin\left(\frac{1}{x^2}\right) - \frac{2}{x} \cdot \cos\left(\frac{1}{x^2}\right),$$

it follows that here too the derivative is discontinuous at the point $x = 0$. As regards the function d, the "Devil's staircase", there are infinitely many points at which the derivative does not exist, even though the function is continuous. Within each of the intervals of the step-wise definition the derivative is equal to zero.

8 Old problems solved anew

> In high school, this knowledge may be gathered together and treated as a whole, the result being that pupils come into complete possession of the beginnings of infinitesimal calculus. It is essential here to make it clear to the pupil that he is dealing not with something mystical, but with simple things that anyone can understand.
> (Klein, p. 223)

The whole secret of the differential calculus is finding the magnitude of the relative increase and decrease of two quantities whose interdependence is determined by a function. One imagines oneself as it were right in the flux of a continuous transformation. And the discrete, fleeting moment of transition from increase to decrease (or the other way round) corresponds to a vanishing slope.

The exercises at the beginning of this article can now be computed quickly using the differential calculus. The derivative is set to zero to find the required maxima or minima.

The city wall

A rectangular enclosure with an area of 450 m² is to be marked out against a town wall and fenced. How can this be done so that the cost of the fence is minimized?

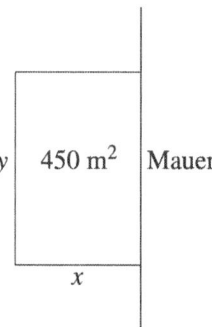

Solution:
The length function is given by the equation

$$l(x) = 2x + \frac{450}{x}.$$

Setting the first derivative

$$l'(x) = 2 - \frac{450}{x^2}$$

to zero gives $x = \pm 15$ and hence the physically meaningful solution $x = 15$ m. We obtain the required minimum of the length function when $x = 15$.

Inscribed cylinder

A cylinder of maximal volume is to be inscribed in a sphere of radius $r = 4\sqrt{3}$. How high must the cylinder be?

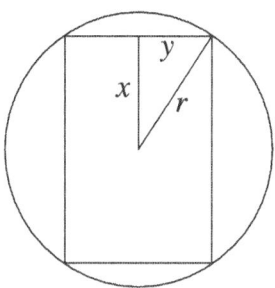

Solution:
The volume function V is given by

$$V(x) = 2\pi(r^2 x - x^3)$$

Setting the first derivative

$$V'(x) = 2\pi(r^2 - 3x^2)$$

to zero gives

$$3x^2 = r^2$$

$$x^2 = \frac{r^2}{3}$$

and from

$$y^2 = r^2 - x^2 = r^2 - \frac{r^2}{3} = \frac{2}{3}r^2$$

we have

$$\frac{y^2}{x^2} = \frac{\frac{2}{3}r^2}{\frac{r^2}{3}} = 2.$$

Thus the volume function is found to have a maximum when

$$x = \sqrt{\frac{r^2}{3}} = \sqrt{\frac{(4\sqrt{3})^2}{3}} = 4 \text{ and } y = 4\sqrt{2}$$

Silo with domed roof

A silo is in the shape of a cylinder with a hemispherical top. What must the radius r and the overall height a be so that, for a given total volume of $V = 45\pi$ m³, the cost of material is minimized?

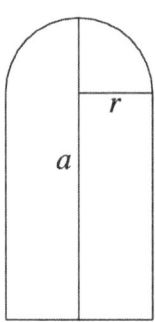

Solution:
The surface area function has equation

$$O(r) = \frac{2V}{r} + \frac{5\pi r^2}{3}.$$

Setting to zero the first derivative

$$O'(r) = -\frac{2V}{r^2} + \frac{10\pi r}{3}$$

gives

$$-6V + 10\pi r^3 = 0$$

$$r^3 = \frac{3V}{5\pi}$$

$$r = \sqrt[3]{\frac{3V}{5\pi}} = \sqrt[3]{\frac{3 \cdot 45\pi}{5\pi}} = 3.$$

Therefore the use of material is minimized when $r = 3$ m. We show furthermore that with *any* fixed volume, the silo constructed has minimal surface area when the height a is double the radius r. Using the expression for a found in section 1 we have:

$$\begin{aligned}
a &= \frac{V}{\pi r^2} + \frac{r}{3} \\
&= \frac{V}{\pi} \cdot \sqrt[3]{\frac{25\pi^2}{9V^2}} + \frac{1}{3} \cdot \sqrt[3]{\frac{3V}{5\pi}} \\
&= \sqrt[3]{\frac{125 \cdot 3V^3 \pi^2}{27 \cdot 5\pi^3 V^2}} + \frac{1}{3} \cdot \sqrt[3]{\frac{3V}{5\pi}} \\
&= \frac{5}{3} \cdot \sqrt[3]{\frac{3V}{5\pi}} + \frac{1}{3} \cdot \sqrt[3]{\frac{3V}{5\pi}} \\
&= 2\sqrt[3]{\frac{3V}{5\pi}} = 2r
\end{aligned}$$

In all the examples, we defined a function and investigated it in a particular way. The function was differentiated, the derivative was set to zero and a solution gave us the *x*-value of the function's extremum. In the nature of the problem we knew in advance whether the *x*-values give a maximum or a minimum value of the function.

The ideal box

The surface area formula to be investigated is

$$O(r) = 2\pi r^2 + \frac{900}{r}.$$

Setting to zero the first derivative

$$O'(r) = 4\pi r - \frac{900}{r^2}$$

leads to the equation $4\pi r^3 - 900 = 0$, i.e. the (minimal) radius $r = \sqrt[3]{\frac{225}{\pi}}$.

9 Summary and prospect

Given a function, can we deduce which extreme points are maxima and which are minima? The derivative of the derivative or *second derivative*, which describes the behavior of the curvature of the graph of the original function, is related to this question.

> [...] a curve is concave or convex towards the horizontal axis according as the ordinate and its second order differential quotient have the opposite or the same sign. (Lacroix, p. 81)

We can use this second derivative to investigate the graphs of many different functions, i. e. their intercepts with the coordinate axes, extreme points and points of inflection, which are points in which the sense of the curvature changes from anticlockwise to clockwise (or the other way round).

Questions of this kind can present themselves in classroom discussions surprisingly early. When this happens the intuitive value of geometrical images should be made available to the students. If for example a distance-time curve is seen or called for in a problem about instantaneous speed it can be included in the discussion: the pupils set the tone. At the same time, the form-giving character of the equation of a function can be reviewed by drawing its graph in various coordinate systems. So for example functions of the type $y = x^n$ can easily be represented in polar coordinates even. The resulting graphs are spirals. Cartesian curves are seen to be just one of many possible ways of representing functions.

Asymptotes introduced with rational functions are a novel concept. New too are the extended opportunities for forming derivatives using the Product-, Quotient- and Chain Rules.

If $u(x)$, $v(x)$ are two functions of x, we obtain

$$(uv)' = u'v + uv'.$$

In this case, too, it would be interesting to relate its discovery. But here lies the line between history for its own sake and history for the sake of illuminating the development of mathematical thought. [...] About the product rule, however, there is nothing to bring to light. Hence the history of its discovery does not concern us. (Toeplitz, p. 99ff)

The derivative

$$(\cos x)' = -\sin x$$

is deduced from the relationship $\cos x = \sin\left(\frac{\pi}{2} - x\right)$ and the chain rule. In general, skills in analytical calculus improve with practice and through practical group discussion of various curves. The cognitive basis remains the detailed introduction to the derivative concept described above. All other concepts are useful extensions, discovered through the exercises, which can then be quickly handled as independent results.

The exponential function is the key to many applications in the natural sciences. What are the characteristic properties of the number e in this regard? This question should certainly handled in some depth. Following this, the formula

$$e = 1 + \frac{1}{1!} + \frac{1}{2!} + \frac{1}{3!} + \frac{1}{4!} + \cdots$$

is sure to meet with the pupils' approval.

Finally, equation solving as a whole can be reviewed and deepened where necessary (exponential and logarithmic equations, biquadratic equations, equations solved by substitution, higher-order equations, approximate solution using Newton's method).

This article was based on the observation that when it comes to understanding the principles of the infinitesimal calculus, pupils enjoy an approach where they experience a meaningful context and can work with numbers in a familiar way, as opposed to an approach where they are confronted with a purely mechanical set of rules. We do not fix or force, at the start, the mental picture of the tangent. In fact discovering it for themselves is one of the crown jewels of the differential calculus. The eye sees what thinking has already recognized as possible.

Discussing extreme values

UWE HANSEN

In dealing with extreme value problems, discussion of the result is specially important. This will be illustrated in two examples.

Example 1 (the well-known "athletic ground problem"):

Two semicircles are to be fitted to a rectangle with sides x and $2r$ (see Figure 1). The perimeter U is to be 400 m long and the inner rectangle is to have maximal area. The area is $A = x \cdot 2r$, and the constraining condition between the two variables is $U = 2x + 2\pi r$. Therefore

$$r = \frac{U - 2x}{2\pi} = \frac{200 - x}{\pi}.$$

It follows that

$$A = 2x \cdot \frac{200 - x}{\pi} = \frac{2}{\pi}\left(200x - x^2\right)$$

and hence

$$A' = \frac{2}{\pi}(200 - 2x).$$

So the area is maximal when $x = 100$ m. The perimeter of the whole figure is thus divided into four equal parts.

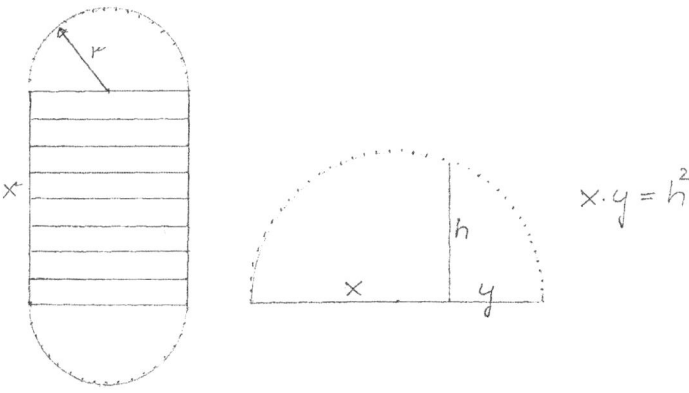

Figure 1   Figure 2

This result can be obtained directly without differentiating. Because from the theorem shown in Figure 2 (which can be deduced from the intersecting chord theorem, or from Pythagoras' theorem) it immediately follows that if the sum $x + y$ of two quantities x and y is constant, then their product $x \cdot y$ is greatest when $x = y$. The altitude h is of course greatest when it is in the circle's center. This law can be generalized as follows. If the two quantities x and y satisfy the condition that $kx + py$ is constant, then the product $x \cdot y$ is greatest when $kx = py$. Here k and p

are arbitrary positive coefficients. This follows because $kx \cdot py$ is maximal if and only if $x \cdot y$ is maximal. Setting $x_1 = kx$ and $y_1 = py$, the claim follows from $x_1 + y_1$ being constant and hence $x_1 \cdot y_1$ being maximal. Since in the above example $x + \pi r = \frac{1}{2} \cdot U$ and is therefore constant, $x \cdot 2r$ is maximal precisely when $x = \pi r$, so that x must be one quarter of the perimeter. This law is also applicable in the following cases.

If for example two equilateral triangles are fitted to the rectangle (Figure 3), then $A = x \cdot s$ and $U = 2x + 4s$, hence $x + 2s$ is constant. So the area must be maximal for $x = 2s$. So x is again 100 m, assuming the perimeter is 400 m long. One can also fit two half hexagons to the rectangle (Figure 4):

$$A = x \cdot 2r \quad \text{and} \quad U = 2x + 6r$$

In this case we must have $x = 3r$. The whole perimeter is thus again divided into four equal parts. If we choose two half-squares then

$$A = x \cdot a\sqrt{2} \quad \text{and} \quad U = 2x + 4a$$

In this case too x is a quarter of the whole perimeter U (see Figure 5). Note however that in these four cases the maximal area is different for the same whole perimeter.

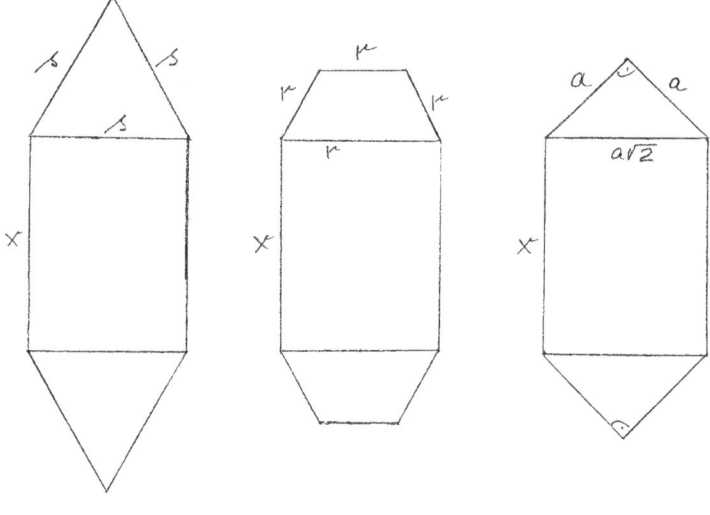

Figure 3   Figure 4   Figure 5

What was essential in these different variations on a problem was that the plane figures set on the rectangles maintained their form as the variable x changed, i.e. similar figures were attached. What happens when something is added on only one side of the rectangle? Even in this case x is equal to one quarter of the perimeter, as follows from the general rule given above.

But we get fundamentally different results if we require that not part but the whole of the figure should have maximal area. In the case of Figure 1 we then naturally get the value $x = 0$, i.e.

we get a circular area. In the cases shown in Figures 3 and 4 the results are $x = (2 - \sqrt{3})s$ and $x = \frac{3}{2}(2 - \sqrt{3})r$ respectively, which are both the same proportions of U.

The result is also fundamentally different in the so-called "tunnel problem". The tunnel is to have the cross-section drawn in Figure 6: a shape, in this case a semicircle, is only attached to one side of the rectangle. For a given perimeter, the cross-sectional area is maximal when the semicircle augmented to a full circle touches the lowest side of the rectangle. This solution is immediately plausible since with this form we arrive – under these conditions – at the form nearest to the circle.

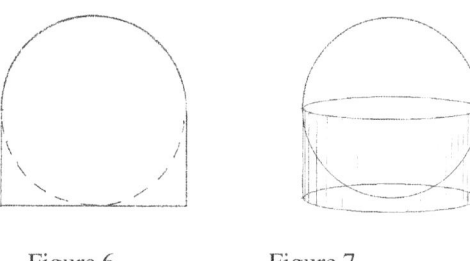

Figure 6   Figure 7

This problem has a spatial variant: suppose a hemisphere is set on a cylinder. In this case, for a given constant total surface area the volume is greatest when the hemisphere augmented to a full sphere touches the bottom of the cylinder (Figure 7).

Example 2:

We look at following problem. In a hemisphere is to be put a cylinder of maximal volume (Figure 8). The result obtained is $r = \sqrt{2} \cdot h$. Replacing the cylinder with a cone (Figure 9) gives the same result. These two problems can be translated into two dimensions, when they become ones of inscribing in a semicircle a rectangle and an isosceles triangle of maximal area respectively (Figure 10, Figure 11). For this problem we would clearly obtain $r = h$.

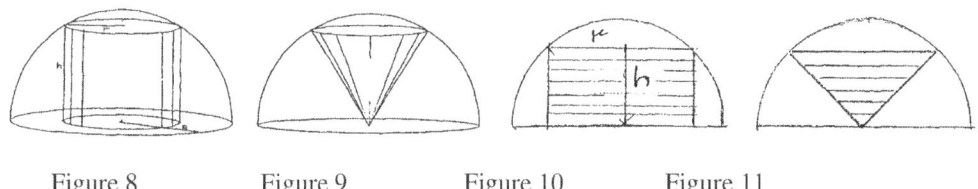

Figure 8   Figure 9   Figure 10   Figure 11

In the three-dimensional case it turns out that the radius r is greater than the height h, since a greater radius has an impact in two directions, while in the planar case radius and height are equal. In the case shown in Figure 10 we get a double square. This is evident inasmuch as the problem of inscribing a rectangle of maximal area in a complete circle naturally leads to a square. If the rectangle is replaced by an isosceles triangle (Figure 11), we necessarily arrive at the same result, since the triangle is half the rectangle.

The following problem can also be solved in this way. A rainwater gutter is to be built out of two identical planks to contain the greatest possible amount of water. For this the planks would have to be mounted at an angle of $2 \cdot 45° = 90°$. If three equal planks are used, for maximal volume one would need a half-hexagon as cross-section, assuming that a symmetric arrangement is required.

These two examples have further variants. Suppose a cylinder of maximal volume is to be put in a cone (Figure 12). As solution we obtain $r = \frac{2}{3} \cdot R$ and $h = \frac{1}{3} \cdot H$. If the problem is simplified to inscribing a rectangle in an isosceles triangle, we get the result $r = \frac{1}{2} \cdot R$ and $h = \frac{1}{2} \cdot H$ (Figure 13). Conversely one could consider the problem of circumscribing a given rectangle with a triangle of minimal area, or of circumscribing a given cylinder with a cone of minimal volume. With the latter problems we arrive at the same results as with the converse problems.

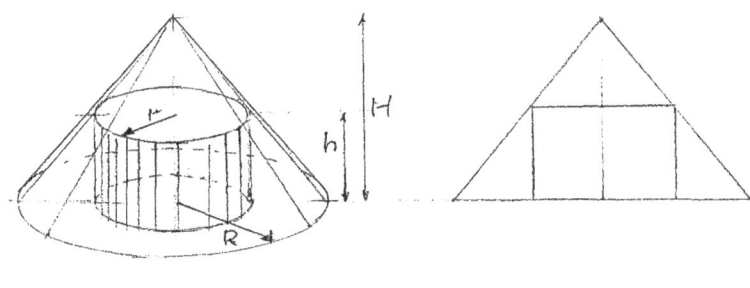

Figure 12   Figure 13

If in Figure 8 we replace the hemisphere with a full sphere, for reasons of symmetry the result does not change. The same goes for Figure 9, if the apex of the (double) cone remains in the center of the sphere. Whereas if the apex is located on the surface of the sphere, we get the greatest volume when $h = \sqrt{2} \cdot r$ (Figure 14). In the planar cases the results are a square and an equilateral triangle (Figure 15) respectively.

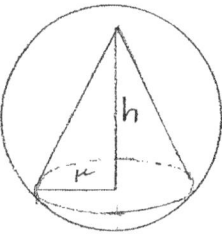 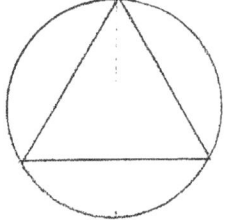

Figure 14   Figure 15

It is a source of satisfaction for the student to be able by discussing the extreme value problems to put the results in a greater context.

The integral as an expression of "$\infty \cdot 0$"

WALTER HUTTER

The themes discussed here constitute a compendium for the teacher. The various quotations included in the text refer to literature that goes further and draw attention, in a self-explanatory way, to historical connections.

The familiarity students may already have with functions and derivatives will directly help when introducing them to the concept of the integral. Their joy of discovery leads, often already in dealing with the derivative, to the question: What happens if we reverse the process of differentiation? Sections 1 to 3 explore this, free of any claim to pedagogical completeness. The lemniscate introduced in Section 7 should be seen as a theme for further development. Understanding how to transform Cartesian to polar coordinates is something students find absorbing and enjoyable. The simplicity of finding the area enclosed by a lemniscate is astonishing, and begins to show the real power of the integral calculus. Finally Section 8 addresses the question, What is a logarithm?

In the differential calculus, the expression "$\frac{0}{0}$" is given several meanings. When we speak of "nascent zeroes" (quantities *becoming* zero), $\frac{0}{0}$ makes sense only as a limiting process; it cannot be understood simply as a static numerical expression. In this article, attention is focused on phenomena of the form "$\infty \cdot 0$".

We begin with an obvious idea. A function can be differentiated. So given a derivative, shouldn't we be able to see to which function it belongs? Can we *anti-differentiate*?

The *integral calculus* is the reverse of the differential calculus in the following sense. In differentiating (finding the derivative) we produce from a given function (the *primitive*) the associated slope function (the *derivative*). In *integrating* ("anti-differentiating") on the other hand, the slope function is given and we seek an associated primitive function. From the rate of change of a function we should be able to find the function itself. If we take, say, the slope function

$$f(x) = 0.5x,$$

the primitive functions which result are:

$$F_c(x) = 0.25x^2 + c, \quad c \in \mathbb{R}$$

since $(0.25x^2 + c)' = 0.5x$. For a given slope function there are infinitely many primitives, which differ from each other by an additive constant. As a totality they are denoted by the symbol $\int f(x)\,dx$, and we call this the *indefinite integral* of f.

1 The direction field

The curves of the primitives become visible when we make a picture of the associated slopes. Suppose the slope function f is given by the equation

$$f(x) = \frac{3}{20}x^2 + 0.8x.$$

To each value of x is associated the slope $f(x)$. We imagine an arrow, whose slope is $f(x)$, positioned at each point with horizontal coordinate x and obtain the following direction field:

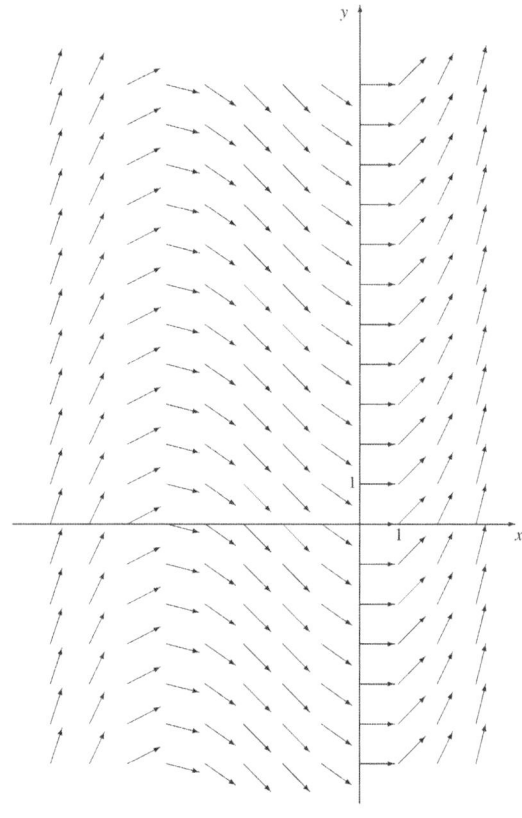

| $f(x)$ | 3,2 | 1,75 | 0,6 | −0,25 | −0,8 | −1,05 | −1 | −0,65 | 0 | 0,95 | 2,2 | 3,75 |

The integral curves (curves of the primitives) are those curves that can be fitted into the direction field in such a way that their direction at each point coincides with the direction of the field. The primitives' equations are

$$F_c(x) = \frac{1}{20}x^3 + 0.4x^2 + c, \ c \in \mathbb{R}$$

since $F_c'(x) = f(x)$. By specifying a point that should lie on the integral curve we determine a specific integral curve. If say $P(0,4)$ is required to be a curve point, then from the above equation

we have that
$$4 = \frac{1}{20} \cdot 0^3 + 0.4 \cdot 0^2 + c$$
$$c = 4$$

and the equation of the integral curve thus determined is
$$F_4(x) = \frac{1}{20}x^3 + 0.4x^2 + 4.$$

2 Standard integrals

The integral calculus is, in fact, much older than the differential calculus, because the computation of areas, surfaces, and volumes occupied the greatest mathematicians since antiquity: Archimedes, Kepler, Cavalieri, Viviani, Fermat, Gregory St. Vincent, Guldin, Gregory, Barrow. The decisive breakthrough came when Newton, Leibniz and Johann Bernoulli discovered independently that integration is the inverse operation of differentiation, thus reducing all efforts of the above researchers to a couple of differentiation rules. (E. Hairer and G. Wanner, *Analysis by its history*, Springer Verlag, New York-Berlin-Heidelberg, 1996, p 107)

Using well-known standard derivatives we can pause a moment and think through the following transitions.

$$\text{function } f \xrightarrow{\text{indefinite integration}} \text{primitives } F$$
$$\text{function } f \xleftarrow{\text{differentiation}} \text{primitives } F$$

$$f(x) = x^3 \;\Rightarrow\; F(x) = \frac{1}{4}x^4 + c, \text{ since } F'(x) = x^3$$
$$f(x) = x^2 \;\Rightarrow\; F(x) = \frac{1}{3}x^3 + c, \text{ since } F'(x) = x^2$$
$$f(x) = x^1 = x \;\Rightarrow\; F(x) = \frac{1}{2}x^2 + c, \text{ since } F'(x) = x$$
$$f(x) = x^0 = 1 \;\Rightarrow\; F(x) = \frac{1}{1}x + c, \text{ since } F'(x) = 1$$
$$f(x) = x^{-1} \;\Rightarrow\; ???$$
$$f(x) = x^{-2} \;\Rightarrow\; F(x) = \frac{1}{-1}x^{-1} + c, \text{ since } F'(x) = x^{-1}$$
$$f(x) = x^{-3} \;\Rightarrow\; F(x) = \frac{1}{-2}x^{-2} + c, \text{ since } F'(x) = x^{-3}$$

$$f(x) = x^n \implies F(x) = \frac{1}{n+1}x^{n+1} + c, \; c \in \mathbb{R}$$

Here n is any exponent except -1. This exception is, on the one hand, obvious due to the impossibility of the formula when $n = -1$; on the other hand, it a singular phenomenon arousing our wonder. We shall refer to this in Section 8.2.

> Fermat knew how to handle this problem, for he was at that time in possession of large parts of the differential calculus. Hence he could indeed prove that [the exponent becomes $k+1$] for all values of k, except of course for $k+1 = 0$ or $k = -1$. Strangely, he does not seem to have investigated this case, that is, the area under the curve $y = x^{-1} = \frac{1}{x}$. (Otto Toeplitz, *The calculus: a genetic approach*, edited G.Kothe, trans. L. Lange, University of Chicago Press, 2007, p 55.

The integration of the exponential function and the trigonometric functions is immediately understandable as the reverse of differentiation.

$$f(x) = e^x \implies F(x) = e^x + c, \text{ since } F'(x) = e^x$$
$$f(x) = \cos x \implies F(x) = \sin x + c, \text{ since } F'(x) = \cos x$$
$$f(x) = \sin x \implies F(x) = -\cos x + c, \text{ since } F'(x) = \sin x$$

Examples:

1. $f(x) = 3x^2 + x - 7 \implies F(x) = x^3 + \frac{1}{2}x^2 - 7x + c$
2. $f(x) = \sqrt{x} = x^{\frac{1}{2}} \implies F(x) = \frac{2}{3}x^{\frac{3}{2}} + c$
3. $f(x) = 5e^x + x^5 \implies F(x) = 5e^x + \frac{1}{6}x^6 + c$
4. $f(x) = -2\cos x + x^{-3} \implies F(x) = -2\sin x - \frac{1}{2}x^{-2} + c$

3 The definite integral

Newton and Leibniz worked out two distinct concepts of the integral. Newton's concept was based above all on the indefinite integral and defined integration as the reverse operation of differentiation. This point of view prevailed during the whole of the 19th century. Leibniz on the other hand had interpreted areas and volumes as sums of rectangles and cylinders respectively and arrived at the definite integral. Cauchy, who was the first to give a precise definition of the integral concept (1823), was an adherent of Leibniz's point of view. (Amy Dahan-Dalmedico and Jeanne

Peiffer, *Wege und Irrwege - Eine Geschichte der Mathematik*, Birkhäuser Verlag, Basel-Boston-Berlin, 1994, p 219)[1]

A more precise understanding of integral curves is enabled by the following starting point, conceptually independent of the differential calculus[2]. Suppose a function f is given. We imagine the direction field it produces, that is to say arrows in a coordinate system, arrows which have slope $f(x)$ at points with horizontal coordinate x. By specifying a point P_a positioned at $x = a$ we then have just one integral curve through the direction field. We determine the ordinate difference between it and a following curve point, positioned at $x = b$ say.

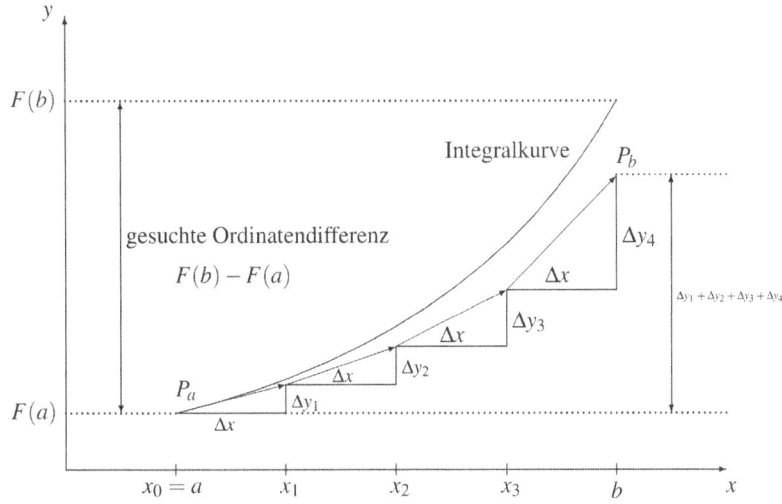

This is done approximately at first. Since $\frac{\Delta y_1}{\Delta x} = f(x_0)$ it follows that

$$\Delta y_1 = f(x_0) \cdot \Delta x$$

and similarly

$$\Delta y_2 = f(x_1) \cdot \Delta x, \quad \Delta y_3 = f(x_2) \cdot \Delta x, \quad \Delta y_4 = f(x_3) \cdot \Delta x.$$

Thus we have

$$\Delta y_1 + \Delta y_2 + \Delta y_3 + \Delta y_4 =$$

$$f(x_0) \cdot \Delta x + f(x_1) \cdot \Delta x + f(x_2) \cdot \Delta x + f(x_3) \cdot \Delta x.$$

We are thus dividing the interval from a to b into four equal subintervals Δx. Now we set out from P_a along the tangents with slopes $f(x_0)$, $f(x_1)$, $f(x_2)$ and $f(x_3)$ until we reach the point P_b in four steps. This point does not in general lie on the required curve. To obtain the total increase

---

[1] Translated as *History of mathematics: highways and byways*, Mathematical association of America, 2010.
[2] See Louis Locher-Ernst, *Differential- und Integralrechnung*, Birkhäuser Verlag, Basel, 1948, p 341ff.

(the ordinate difference between P_b and P_a) we must add together all the individual increases. A notation that suggests itself is

$$S_{a,4}^b f(x) \Delta x := f(x_0) \cdot \Delta x + f(x_1) \cdot \Delta x + f(x_2) \cdot \Delta x + f(x_3) \cdot \Delta x$$

(S for sum). The smaller we allow the steps on the x-axis to become, the better is P_b as an approximation to the actual position of the curve point at $x = b$. Thus $S_{a,10}^b f(x) \Delta x$ is a more precise approximation to the required ordinate difference, and $S_{a,100000}^b f(x) \Delta x$ is more precise still. The finer we make the subdivisions the smaller Δx becomes and the more increases must be added together. If we let Δx tend to zero and the number of steps increase, accordingly, unboundedly, then, after this transition to the limit, P_b will lie on the integral curve.

Causing the ordinate differences to become infinite in number and *to the same degree* infinitely small in size thus leads to the sought-for ordinate difference. We denote it with the symbol

$$\int_a^b f(x)\,dx := \lim_{n \to \infty} S_{a,n}^b f(x) \Delta x.$$

The expression on the left can be taken as the definition of $f(x)dx$.

The sign $\int$, which is a stylized S, was used for the first time by Gottfried Wilhelm Leibniz in 1686. It calls to mind the word "sum". From now on we shall speak of the *definite integral of f from a to b*.

> The integral sign is due to Leibniz (1686), the term *integral* is due to Johann Bernoulli and was published by his brother Jacob Bernoulli. (Hairer and Wanner, p 107)

> Jacob Bernoulli suggested the expression *integral* to Leibniz; the expression function dates from Leibniz as well but was first used by him in the last years of the 17th century. (Paul Tannery in Jules Tannery, *Elemente der Mathematik*, Teubner Verlag, Leipzig, 1921, p 338)

At this point we should mention that a definite integral of a given function does not necessarily always exist. To see this we must be prepared to go deeper into the mathematics. This is a crucial point in the integral calculus.

When is a function integrable, that is to say, when can it be treated in the way we've done? When in general does an integral exist in the sense of the procedure we've just described?[3]

After all, we are adding together more and more values, which are simultaneously becoming smaller and smaller, a situation almost impossible to imagine.

---

[3]The so-called Dirichlet function given by

$$d(x) = \begin{cases} 0 & \text{if } x \text{ is irrational} \\ 1 & \text{if } x \text{ is rational} \end{cases}$$

A sufficient condition for integrability is: The graph of the function must be able to be drawn continuously with one stroke from a to b inclusive (i. e., the function must be continuous over a compact interval). Then we find ourselvs again on firm ground.

If a primitive F of f is known, the definite integral can easily be calculated (see the previous diagram) as
$$\int_a^b f(x)\,dx = F(b) - F(a).$$

It should be noted that not every function has a primitive however[4].

Replacing the upper limit of integration b with the variable x, we have
$$\left(\int_a^x f(t)\,dt\right)' = (F(x) - F(a))' = f(x).$$

The derivative of the *integral function* of a continuous function f is thus the function f itself.

---

is not integrable on any interval $[a,b]$. d can be modified to produce the integrable function g where
$$g(x) = \begin{cases} 0 & \text{if } x \text{ is irrational or } x = 0 \\ \frac{1}{q} & \text{if } x \text{ is rational and } x = \frac{p}{q} \text{ as a fraction in its simplest form} \end{cases}$$

and the integral
$$\int_0^1 g(x)\,dx = 0$$

(Hairer and Wanner, p 224).

The Function f with formation rule
$$f(x) = \begin{cases} x\sqrt{x}\sin\left(\frac{1}{x}\right) & \text{for } x > 0 \\ 0 & \text{for } x = 0 \end{cases}$$

has derivative
$$f'(x) = \begin{cases} \frac{3}{2}\sqrt{x}\sin\left(\frac{1}{x}\right) - \frac{1}{\sqrt{x}}\cos\left(\frac{1}{x}\right) & \text{for } x > 0 \\ 0 & \text{for } x = 0. \end{cases}$$

Yet the derivative f' is not definitely integrable on any interval $[0,b]$ (f' is unbounded in a neighborhood of 0).

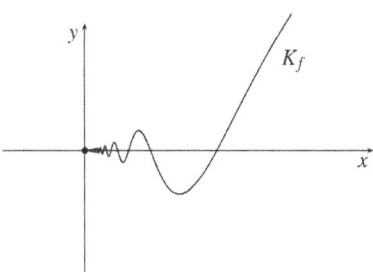

[4]The function r given by
$$r(x) = \begin{cases} 0 & \text{for } -1 \leqslant x < 0 \\ 1 & \text{for } 0 \leqslant x \leqslant 1 \end{cases}$$
is definitely integrable on the interval $[-1,1]$, but has no primitive there.

This so-called *Fundamental Theorem of Calculus* [5] shows in what sense integration and differentiation are complementary.

$$\text{function } f(x) \quad \xrightarrow{\text{definite integration}} \quad \int_a^x f(t)\,dt \quad \text{integral functions}$$

$$\xleftarrow{\text{differentiation}}$$

An integral is the result of forming a sequence of sums. The sums consist of ever more summands ($\to \infty$), which tend to zero ($\to 0$). In this sense we speak of the integral as an expression of "$\infty \cdot 0$".

4 The definite integral as area

In the last section we were concerned with the curve of a primitive function (integral curve) F. The initial function (slope function) can be represented not only as a direction field but also, like any other function, simply as a relation between two variables.

If we consider the graph K_f of the initial function f carefully, the expression

$$\int_a^b f(x)\,dx$$

can be interpreted geometrically. This expression arose as a result first of subdividing the interval $[a,b]$ into sections Δx, then of multiplying the function values at the dividing points by Δx and finally of adding everything together. Equipped with this picture, we then started a refinement process, we considered a limit value. We make a sketch to emphasize what's important:

---

[5] The Fundamental Theorem can be proved without starting from direction fields as follows:

$$\frac{\int_a^{x+h} f(t)\,dt - \int_a^x f(t)\,dt}{h} = \frac{\int_x^{x+h} f(t)\,dt}{h} = \frac{f(z)\cdot h}{h} = f(z)$$

for some z such that $x \leqslant z \leqslant x+h$. Therefore

$$\left(\int_a^x f(t)\,dt\right)' = \lim_{h\to 0} \frac{\int_a^{x+h} f(t)\,dt - \int_a^x f(t)\,dt}{h} = f(x).$$

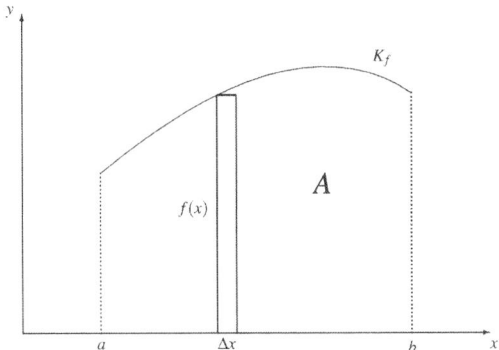

The strip between K_f and the x-axis shown has area $f(x)\Delta x$. The sums of all such strips beneath K_f between a and b thus bring us, as $\Delta x \to 0$, to $\int_a^b f(x)dx$. The area of the region A enclosed by K_f, the dotted lines and the x-axis must therefore be numerically identical to the definite integral from a to b.

$$A = \int_a^b f(x)\,dx = \Big[F(x)\Big]_a^b = F(b) - F(a)$$

5 Examples

The benefit is, that if such a calculus corresponds to the innermost being of situations that occur frequently, then everyone who has fully learnt it can, without having to rely on the unconscious and unpredictable inspirations of his genius, solve the problems associated with those situations, can even solve them "mechanically" in cases which are so complicated, that without such help even the genius is powerless. (Carl Friedrich Gauss in Harro Heuser, *Analysis I*, Teubner Verlag, Stuttgart, 1991, p 434)

Area between a curve and the x-axis

Suppose the function f is given by

$$f(x) = -\frac{1}{10}x^4 + x^3 - \frac{12}{5}x^2$$

We determine the area of the two regions A_1 and A_2.

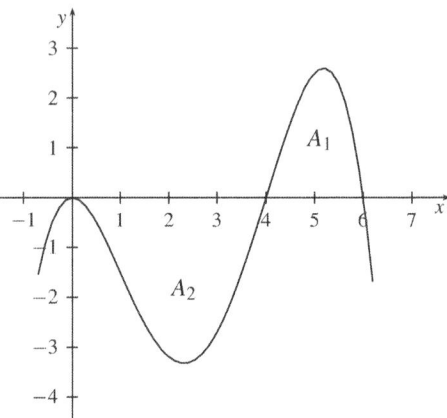

$$A_1 = \int_4^6 \left(-\frac{1}{10}x^4 + x^3 - \frac{12}{5}x^2\right) dx$$

$$= \left[-\frac{1}{50}x^5 + \frac{1}{4}x^4 - \frac{4}{5}x^3\right]_4^6$$

$$= \left(-\frac{1}{50}6^5 + \frac{1}{4}6^4 - \frac{4}{5}6^3\right) - \left(-\frac{1}{50}4^5 + \frac{1}{4}4^4 - \frac{4}{5}4^3\right) = 3.36$$

In calculating A_2 we take into consideration the fact that all function values are negative. To obtain a positive result we write a minus sign before the integral.

$$A_2 = -\int_0^4 \left(-\frac{1}{10}x^4 + x^3 - \frac{12}{5}x^2\right) dx$$

$$= -\left[-\frac{1}{50}x^5 + \frac{1}{4}x^4 - \frac{4}{5}x^3\right]_0^4$$

$$= -\left(-\frac{1}{50}4^5 + \frac{1}{4}4^4 - \frac{4}{5}4^3\right) + \left(-\frac{1}{50}0^5 + \frac{1}{4}0^4 - \frac{4}{5}0^3\right) = 7.68$$

The total area thus amounts to
$$A = A_1 + A_2 = 11.04.$$

Area between two curves

The equations
$$f(x) = x + 5 \quad \text{and} \quad g(x) = \frac{1}{2}x^2 + 1$$
represent two functions f and g which intersect at the points $x = -2$ and $x = 4$.

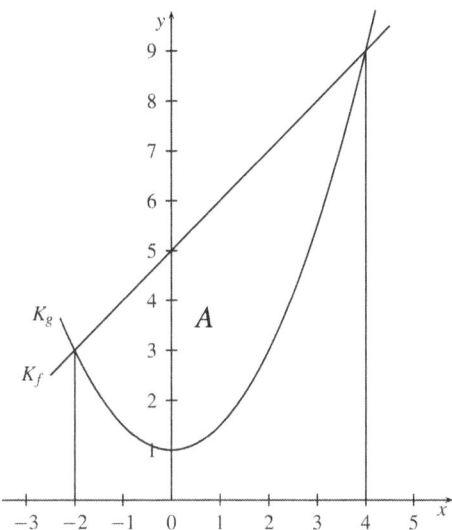

We subtract the lower area between the two vertical lines, the x-axis and the curve K_g, from the trapezoidal area bounded by the two vertical lines, the x-axis and the line K_f.

$$\begin{aligned} A &= \int_{-2}^{4} (f(x) - g(x))\, dx \\ &= \int_{-2}^{4} \left(x + 5 - \frac{1}{2}x^2 - 1\right) dx = \int_{-2}^{4} \left(x - \frac{1}{2}x^2 + 4\right) dx \\ &= \left[\frac{1}{2}x^2 - \frac{1}{6}x^3 + 4x\right]_{-2}^{4} = 18 \end{aligned}$$

The result is always positive as long as the upper curve is K_f and the lower curve is K_g and we integrate between the x-values a and b of the points of intersection.

$$\boxed{A = \int_a^b (f(x) - g(x))\, dx}$$

6 Volume of revolution

From the investigations Archimedes made about the sphere arose a series of observations about generalized solids of revolution. These solids, which he called conoids and spheroids, are created by rotating conic sections. To calculate their volumes he cut the solids into discs of equal thickness perpendicular to the axis of rotation. For each individual elemental disc, he now constructed and calculated the volume of both its inscribed and its circumscribed cylinder. Summing these series of cylinders gave an upper and a lower bound for the total volume required. The finer the slicing was done, the more closely did the bounds obtained approximate to the true volume. Here too it is the method of exhaustion which was Archimedes' means of achieving the goal, and which, precisely in these derivations, is found at the highest stage of classical development. [...] [They] have to be seen as an embryonic stage of the integral calculus as we know it. In this sense we can describe Archimedes as forerunner of a Newton or a Leibniz. The intuitions of Archimedes were succeeded by those of Johannes Kepler (1571–1630) and Bonaventura Cavalieri (1591?–1647, Bologna). (Johannes Tropfke, *Geschichte der Elementar-Mathematik*, Vol. 2, Verlag von Veit & Comp., Leipzig, 1903, pp 394, 396)

Archimedes himself thought about approximating the volume of a solid of revolution by means of thin cylindrical discs. This was suggested by the fact that sections perpendicular to the axis of rotation are circles. So the volume of the solid must be related to the area of a circle. Once again an "∞ · 0" phenomenon is apparent. Suppose the graph of the function f given by

$$f(x) = -\frac{1}{10}x^4 + x^3 - \frac{12}{5}x^2$$

rotates about the x-axis in the region $0 \leqslant x \leqslant 4$. The result is a spatial solid with the following cross-section:

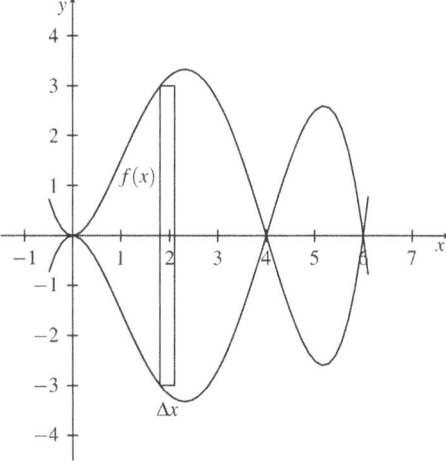

The thin cylindrical disc has radius $f(x)$ and height Δx. So the volume of the cylindrical disc is $\Delta V = \pi \{f(x)\}^2 \Delta x$. The sums of all such discs in the region $0 \leqslant x \leqslant 4$ bring us, as $\Delta x \to 0$, to the volume of the solid of revolution between $a = 0$ and $b = 4$.

$$\int_0^4 dV = \int_0^4 \pi \{f(x)\}^2 dx = \pi \int_0^4 \{f(x)\}^2 dx = \pi \int_0^4 \left(-\frac{1}{10}x^4 + x^3 - \frac{12}{5}x^2\right)^2 dx$$

We record the general formula for the volume

$$V = \pi \int_a^b \{f(x)\}^2 \, dx$$

and conclude by determining the precise numerical value:

$$\begin{aligned}
V &= \pi \int_0^4 \left(\frac{1}{100} x^8 - \frac{1}{5} x^7 + \frac{37}{25} x^6 - \frac{24}{5} x^5 + \frac{144}{25} x^4 \right) dx \\
&= \pi \left[\frac{1}{900} x^9 - \frac{1}{40} x^8 + \frac{37}{175} x^7 - \frac{24}{30} x^6 + \frac{144}{125} x^5 \right]_0^4 \approx 62.09
\end{aligned}$$

7 The lemniscate

An article in the June 1691 issue of the *Acta Eruditorum* dealt with the logarithmic spiral, and in the May 1692 issue Jacob came back to just this curve, which he called *spira mirabilis*, the miraculous spiral.[...] Another investigation of Jakob Bernoulli concerned the elastic curve. Shortly afterward he discovered the lemniscate. (Moritz Cantor, *Vorlesungen über Geschichte der Mathematik*, Vol. 3, 2nd edition, B.G. Teubner Verlagsgesellschaft, Stuttgart, 1965, p 220)

What joy to discern the minute in infinity!
The vast to perceive in the small, what divinity!

(Jacques Bernoulli in Eli Maor: *To Infinity and Beyond: A Cultural History of the Infinite*, Princeton University Press, 1991, p 25)

In this section we deal with a fourth phenomenon of the form "$\infty \cdot 0$". In the process we determine the area enclosed by a lemniscate. The equation of the lemniscate is

$$(x^2 + y^2)^2 - 2t^2(x^2 - y^2) = 0.$$

The number t is the eccentricity ($u \cdot v = t^2$, see the picture). The foci of the lemniscate are on the x-axis at $\pm t$.

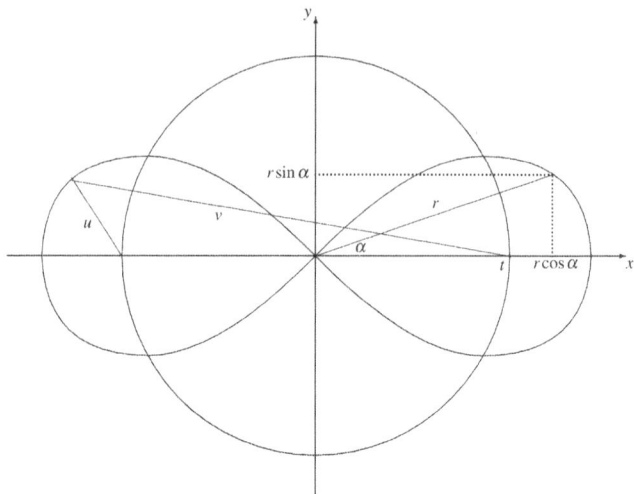

Setting $x = r\cos\alpha$ and $y = r\sin\alpha$ we obtain an equation for the lemniscate which is rather more intuitive:

$$r^4 - 2t^2(r^2\cos^2\alpha - r^2\sin^2\alpha) = 0$$

$$r^4 - 2t^2 r^2(2\cos^2\alpha - 1) = 0$$

$$r^4 - 2t^2 r^2 \cos(2\alpha) = 0$$

Dividing by $r^2 \neq 0$ we obtain the equation of the lemniscate in polar coordinates:

$$\boxed{r^2 = 2t^2 \cos(2\alpha)}$$

For the problem of finding the area of the lemniscate we need to reason from the formula

$$A_{2\pi} = \pi r^2 = \frac{1}{2} r^2 \cdot 2\pi$$

for the area of a circle to the area of a sector (pie slice) of a circle of radius r:

$$A_\alpha = \frac{1}{2} r^2 \alpha.$$

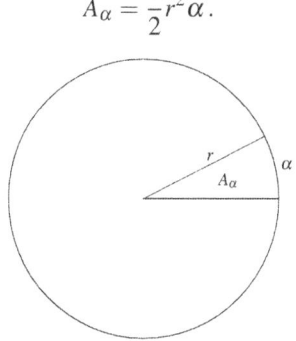

α is the angle, measured in radians, at the center of the circle. So for an change $\Delta\alpha$ in the angle α we have an change in area of

$$\Delta A_\alpha = \frac{1}{2} r^2 \Delta\alpha$$

and the circle's area can be thought of as the sum of infinitely many such changes in area (changes which are at the same time becoming infinitely slender).

$$A_\circ = 4 \int_0^{\frac{\pi}{2}} \frac{1}{2} r^2 d\alpha = 2r^2 [\alpha]_0^{\frac{\pi}{2}} = \pi r^2.$$

We have thus understood the circle's area as an integral. The particular ideas on which this depends we shall now transfer to the lemniscate.

In the following picture sectors A_α, where $\alpha \to 0$, are seen as as sectors of a circle with a variable radius. A sector near one of the mutually perpendicular tangent lines is much shorter than a sector lying near the horizontal axis.

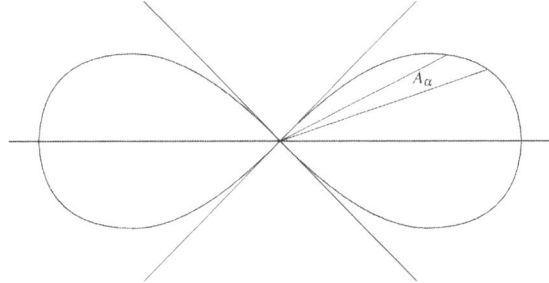

The total area consists of four parts each of which can be determined as a definite integral ("summation") from 0 to $\frac{\pi}{4}$.

$$\begin{aligned} A &= 4 \int_0^{\frac{\pi}{4}} dA_\alpha = 4 \int_0^{\frac{\pi}{4}} \frac{1}{2} r^2 d\alpha \\ &= 4 \int_0^{\frac{\pi}{4}} \frac{1}{2} \cdot 2t^2 \cos(2\alpha) \, d\alpha \\ &= 4t^2 \int_0^{\frac{\pi}{4}} \cos(2\alpha) \, d\alpha \\ &= 2t^2 [\sin(2\alpha)]_0^{\frac{\pi}{4}} = 2t^2. \end{aligned}$$

So the lemniscate with eccentricity t encloses an area of $2t^2$.

8 The logarithm

The word *logarithm* (λογος αριθμος, ratio number, numerus rationem exponens, numerum rationum compositarum) is a creation of John Napier's (1640).

(Tropfke, p 176)

The indefinite integral of the function $f(x) = x^{-1}$ surfaced in Section 2 as an unexplained exception among the power functions. As we shall see, it turns out that this exception can be removed with the help of a new function, the *logarithm* function. Furthermore, we go into the details of a paradox of the integral calculus. Sections 8.1 and 8.2 make the necessary preparations.

8.1 The natural logarithm

The term "natural logarithm" was first used by Mercator (1620–1687; London, Paris), actually for logarithms defined by means of the series

$$l(1+a) = a - \frac{a^2}{2} + \frac{a^3}{3} - \frac{a^4}{4} + \cdots$$

(Tropfke, p 176)

Suppose a number a is written as a power of the number e. The resulting exponent x is called the *logarithm* of a to the *base e*, or *natural logarithm* of a:

$$a = e^x \Leftrightarrow x = \ln a.$$

A consequence of this convention is that $e^{\ln a} = a$ and $\ln(e^x) = x$. We give two examples.

1. Exponential equations

$$e^{2x-5} = 30$$

Taking natural logarithms gives $\ln\left(e^{2x-5}\right) = \ln 30$

$$2x - 5 = \ln 30$$

$$x = \frac{5 + \ln 30}{2} \approx 4.20$$

2. Logarithmic equations

$$\ln(2x+7) = 3$$

Applying the exponential function gives $e^{\ln(2x+7)} = e^3$

$$2x + 7 = e^3$$

$$x = \frac{e^3 - 7}{2} \approx 6.54$$

8.2 The logarithmic function

If in the equation of the exponential function $y = e^x$ we exchange the variables x and y, the result is the equation of the so-called logarithmic function: $e^y = x$, which implies $\ln(e^y) = \ln x$ and therefore

$$y = \ln x.$$

The logarithmic function is obtained as the inverse of the exponential function. The graph of the logarithmic function arises from the graph of the exponential function by reflection in the line $x = y$.

From the symmetrical positioning of the slope triangles it's obvious that the slope of the logarithmic function at point x is equal to the reciprocal of the slope of the exponential function at the point $y = \ln x$. Therefore $(\ln x)' = \frac{1}{e^y} = \frac{1}{x}$ and we obtain the rule for differentiating the logarithmic function

$$(\ln x)' = \frac{1}{x}$$

as well as the following integral:

$$\int \frac{1}{x}\,dx = \ln|x| + c, \quad c \in \mathbb{R}$$

We saw in Section 2 that the integration of $f(x) = x^{-1}$ is an exception and now its full importance becomes visible.

8.3 A paradox

If we compare the definite integrals with an increasing upper limit of the function $f(x) = x^{-1}$ on the one hand, and its square, the function $f^2(x) = x^{-2}$, on the other, we find that the two integrals behave quite differently. Geometrically we have a situation which from the perspective of elementary geometry is a contradiction. We draw the function f given by $f(x) = x^{-1} = \frac{1}{x}$, $x > 0$; we also draw the curve's reflected image in the x-axis.

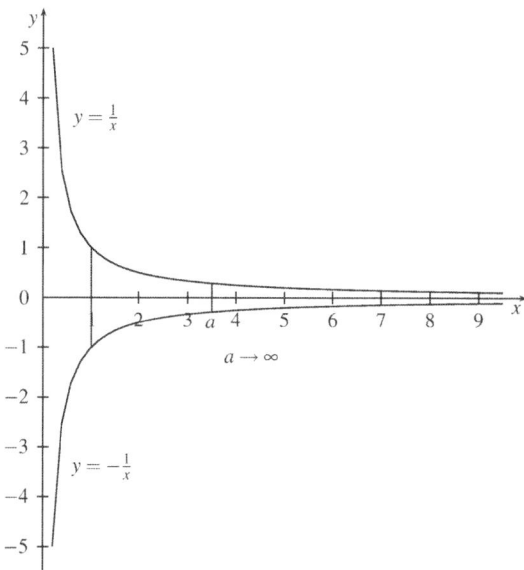

In the region $1 \leq x \leq a$ the area between the curve of f (a hyperbola) and its reflection in the x-axis is

$$A_a = 2 \int_1^a \frac{1}{x} dx = 2[\ln |x|]_1^a = 2\ln a.$$

As a tends to infinity this area becomes infinitely large.

$$A_a \to \infty \text{ as } a \to \infty$$

If we rotate the initial function about the x-axis, the result is a funnel open in both directions. Its volume in the region $1 \leq x \leq a$ amounts to

$$V_a = \pi \int_1^a \frac{1}{x^2} dx = \pi \left[-\frac{1}{x}\right]_1^a = \pi \left(1 - \frac{1}{a}\right).$$

As a tends to infinity the volume tends toward π.

$$V_a \to \pi \text{ as } a \to \infty$$

The volume of the infinitely long funnel is finite!

On the one hand, since the area between the curves is infinitely large, the surface area of the infinitely long funnel is infinitely great.[6] Yet on the other hand its holding capacity is finite. We could never paint the funnel right to the end, yet it could be filled to the brim.

> This paradox has no elementary "explanation"; it shows again that when the infinite is involved, our common sense may fail us. (Maor, p 85)

> We have no resolution of this paradox to offer. It is an illustration of the difficulties encountered when we try to use intuitive geometric ideas in connection with infinite regions of the plane or in three-dimensional space. (Philip Gillett, *Calculus and analytic geometry*, D.C. Heath and Company, Lexington-Massachusetts-Toronto, 1984, p 371)

9 Overview

> The two apparently unconnected limiting processes involved in the differentiation and integration of a function are intimately related. They are, in fact, inverse to one another, like the operations of addition and subtraction, or multiplication and division. There is no separate differential calculus and integral calculus, but only one *calculus*. (Richard Courant and Herbert Robbins, revised by Ian Stewart, *What is mathematics? An elementary approach to ideas and methods*, 2nd edition, Oxford University Press, 1996, p 436)

> Were we to understand the second part of the infinitesimal calculus, the integral calculus, merely as the reverse of the differential calculus, as the reversion of the differential quotient to the original function, then we could content ourselves with discussing the principles of the differential calculus. But the integral calculus has its own independent meaning owing to the definite integral. This appears as the sum of infinitely many summands, each of which is separately vanishing. The integral calculus considers what has come into being, while the differential calculus follows, all the way back to its origin, what is coming into being. (Prof. Dr. Paul Freyer, *Studien zur Metaphysik der Differentialrechnung*, commissioned by W. Weber in Berlin, 1883, p 5)

---

[6]The surface area of the funnel over the interval $[1,a]$ is

$$\begin{aligned} M_a &= 2\pi \int_1^a \frac{1}{x}\sqrt{1+\left(-\frac{1}{x^2}\right)^2}\,dx \\ &= 2\pi\left[\left(-\frac{1}{2a^2}\right)\sqrt{a^4+1}+\frac{1}{2}\cdot\ln\left(a^2+\sqrt{a^4+1}\right)\right]-2\pi\left[\left(-\frac{1}{2}\right)\sqrt{2}+\frac{1}{2}\cdot\ln\left(1+\sqrt{2}\right)\right]. \end{aligned}$$

On taking the limit we obtain

$$\lim_{a\to\infty} M_a = \infty.$$

The integral calculus can be applied to various types of function. *Linear substitution* can enable direct integration of a function with known primitive when the variable x is replaced by a linear expression $ax+b$. For functions whose primitive cannot be found easily or at all, Simpson's rule provides a quick way of calculating the integral approximately.

One application of the fundamental law of calculus is the mathematical description of supplies[7] and their rates of change. A supply can be be reconstructed by integrating its rate of change. On the other hand the rate of change can be seen as the derivative of the supply. The pivotal link embodied in this law enables the mathematical treatment of questions in physics about distance, velocity, acceleration and above all in the field of population dynamics and growth processes. In doing so the (idealized) assumptions of a system are summarized in an equation which establishes a relationship between rate of change (derivative) and state (function) at a particular time. Such an equation is called a *differential equation*.

To recapitulate: we first explained what integrating means. The synchonized confrontation of something becoming infinite (the number of subdivisions) with something vanishing (size of the subdivisions) led to the concept of the definite integral. This was applied to the analytic solution of the classical problem of calculating areas and volumes of revolution of regions bounded by curves.

> With the twelfth grade, we have a kind of conclusion, and we must draw conclusions everywhere. [...] Eighteen-year-olds need to understand the various historical periods in a living way, particularly regarding the "getting younger" of humanity. (Rudolf Steiner, *Faculty meetings with Rudolf Steiner*, 25.4.23, Vol. 2, GA 300b and c, Anthroposophic Press, 1998, p 608)

Here also we arrive at a kind of conclusion, in that the development of the whole of mathematics is reflected in the question of infinity. The historical beginnings of the differential calculus reach back to the geometry of antiquity, to Euclid, Archimedes and Apollonius. Leibniz knew the writings of Nicholas of Cusa (Nicolaus Cusanus) who saw the resolving of contradictions in the infinitely small as a picture of the relation of the world to the infinitely great, to God. For Cusanus the infinite was not merely an aim of knowledge but a means of knowledge, as well. A valuable pedagogic motive is hidden here! Standpoints related to the primal phenomena of the infinitesimal calculus exert an immediate fascination in the classroom and positively challenge the student's will to know. The student learns, to begin with, to become aware of his own thinking, then begins to handle models of reality and to evaluate them. She also sees – and experiences – especially clearly that the world is shaped by our thought-imbued actions. Our ideas become a part of reality. By cultivating what is sense-free, young people become conscious of themselves as responsible and free actors, giving form to their own future.

---

[7] The original German here is *Bestand*, which can mean supply, inventory, stock or population, none of which fit well in this context. We have chosen the what we consider the least misleading option.

A note about integration

UWE HANSEN

Using the integral $\int_0^t x\,dx$ we can calculate the area bounded by the x-axis, the graph of $f(x) = x$ and the ordinate at the point $x = t$ (see Figure 1). The result, which is $\frac{1}{2}t^2$, is immediately obvious, being the area of half of a square.

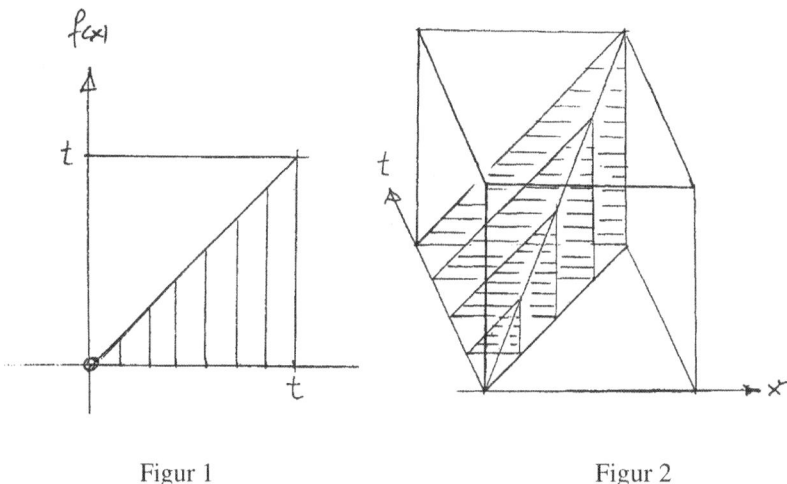

Figur 1   Figur 2

If we integrate this result a second time, we get

$$\int_0^p \frac{1}{2}t^2\,dt = \frac{1}{6}p^3.$$

How is this result related to the original function $f(x)$? How can we interpret the factor $\frac{1}{6}$? Since we are dealing with the double integral

$$\int_0^p \left(\int_0^t x\,dx \right) dt = \frac{1}{6}p^3,$$

that is to say with an infinite summation of areas, it is natural to interpret this double integral as the volume of a solid, so that the result $\frac{1}{6}p^3$ signifies one sixth of the volume p^3 of the cube. The areas summed – they are triangles – generate a tetrahedron, as shown in Figure 2. The volume of this tetrahedron is one sixth part of the volume of the cube in which it sits, because a tetrahedron is one half of a square pyramid and the volume of a pyramid is one third of the volume of the cube.

To elucidate this we compare the three graphs shown in Figure 3. First of all $y(1) = \frac{1}{6}$. This value of $\frac{1}{6}$ appears in the middle graph as an area. The area under the parabola is well known to be one third of the area of the rectangle shown with height $\frac{1}{2}$ and width 1. In the lowest graph the value

187

of $\frac{1}{6}$ is the volume of the tetrahedron that arises when the right-angled triangle recedes, the right hand boundary t running from $t = 0$ to $t = 1$ in the process – as was shown in Figure 2.

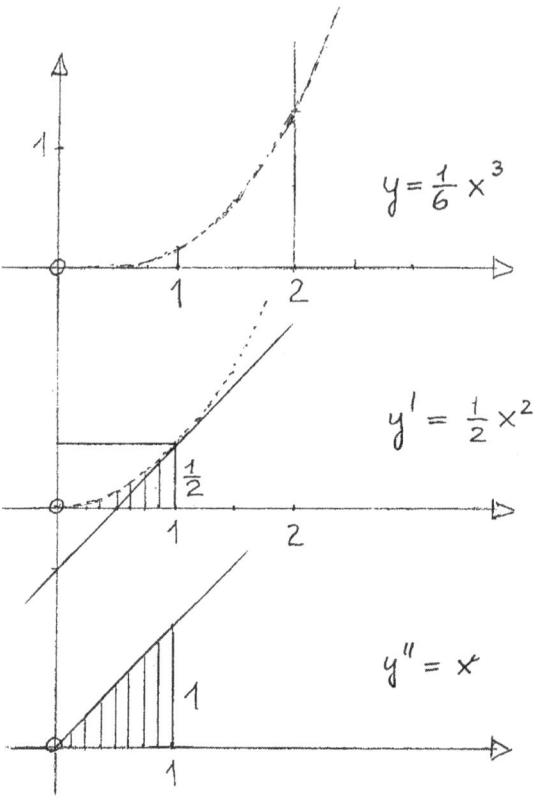

Figur 3

Thus double integration leads from a line-segment via an area to a volume. Figure 3 can also be considered in the opposite direction. Firstly $y''(1) = 1$. This value of 1 appears in the middle graph as the gradient of the tangent at the point 1. In the top graph this value of 1 means that at the point 1, $\frac{dy}{dx}$ varies at exactly the same rate as x. These relationships show once again the contrast between differentiation and integration. Whilst in integration we come more into the spatial element, in differentiation time plays an important role.

In our second example we start from the integral

$$\int_0^t x^2 dx = \frac{1}{3}t^3.$$

The result is integrated again:

$$\int_0^p \frac{1}{3}t^3 dt = \frac{1}{12}p^4.$$

This process of double integration is represented in Figure 4; the volume of the solid shown is one twelfth of the volume of the cuboid with sides p, p and p^2.

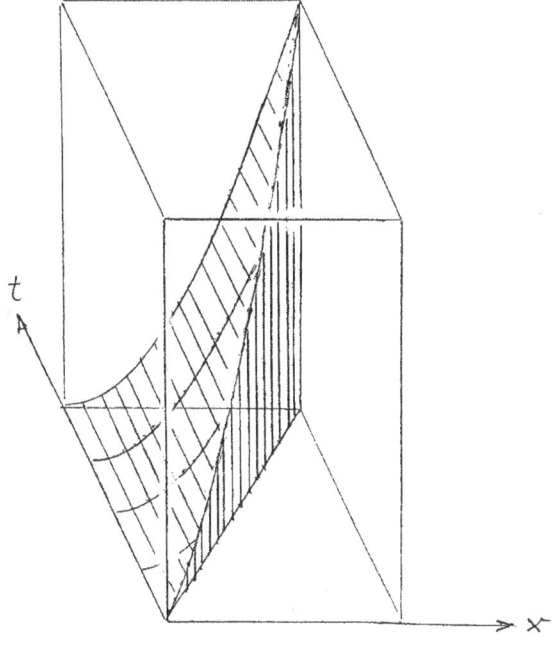

Figur 4

The area bounded by the parabola $y = x^2$, the x-axis and the ordinate at the point $x = t$ is shifted backwards with increasing t generating the solid shown. If we let $p = 1$, the volume of this solid is one half of that of the volume of the tetrahedron shown above. In this case the cuboid becomes a cube.

Index

actual infinity, 51
anthroposophy, 90
antiquity, 95
Appolonius of Perga, 105
archetype in mathematics, 153
Archimedes, 96
Aristotle, 54, 63

Bernhard, Arnold, 104
Bolshevism, 93
Brianchon, Charles Julien, 105

Cantor, Georg, 65
cardinal, 50
Cayley, Arthur, 104
complex numbers, 112
conclusion-judgment-concept, 13
consciousness soul, 95
continuous compounding, 150
continuous function, 140
continuum, 68, 139
correspondence, 64, 66, 67
countable, 53, 65

Danckwerts, Rainer, 100
definitely integrable, 173
Desargues, Gerard, 106
Descartes, R., 106
differentiability, 157
direction field, 168
discussion of curves, 102
dividing a segment, 66
duality, 105

ego-perception, 29
Einstein, Albert, 89

empiricism, 89
Ernst, Louis-Locher, 171
esoteric, 106
Euler's number, 151
exoteric, 106

Fermat, Pierre de, 106
formalism, 81
fundamental theorem of calculus, 174

Gauss, Carl Friedrich, 58, 63
genetic method of learning, 11
George Berkeley, 79
Goethe, Johann Wolfgang von, 103

Hegel, Georg Wilhelm Friedrich, 147
Hilbert, David, 60, 63
hyperbola, 184

incidence geometry, 104
infinite decimal, 139
inner perception, 89
instantaneous speed, 144
integral curves, 168
integral function, 173
irrational numbers, 68, 109

Kant, Immanuel, 103
Kepler, Johannes, 105

Laplace's demon, 80
laws of the circle, 91
Leibniz, G.W., 94
Leibniz, Gottfried Wilhelm, 106
lemniscate, 179
logarithm, 181
logarithmic function, 183

Index

mathematical schooling, 16
Mobius net, 105
moral action, 92

nascent zero, 79, 148
natural processes, 99
Newton, Isaac, 94
null sequence, 46, 111
number relationships, 91

occultism, 90
ordinal, 50

paradoxes, 61, 69
Pascal, Blaise, 105, 106
Philosophy of freedom, 96
Plato, 90
Platonism, 81
points at infinity, 105
Poncelet, Jean-Victor, 105
Popper, Karl, 89
potential infinite, 83
potential infinity, 51
power, 52
processual thinking, 96–98
projective geometry, 104

rate of change, 100
rational numbers, 108
real numbers, 109
rhythmical part, 15

sense of thinking, 96
sense-free thinking, 89
skills, 89
Snell, Karl, 79
speech-sense, 30
Stillwell, J., 106
subsidiary exercises, 18

tangent, 100
tangent problem, 111, 114, 156
tangents, 100
the imagination, 103
the number line, 66
the senses, 28
thought, 90
thought-forms, 93
threshold, 93, 96
threshold experiences, 89, 104
types of numbers, 64

Vogel, Dankwart, 100
volume of revolution, 177

Wagenschein, Martin, 107
Wallis, John, 106
Whitehead, Alfred North, 93
will process, 93
world of ideas free of sense-perception, 91

www.ingramcontent.com/pod-product-compliance
Lightning Source LLC
Chambersburg PA
CBHW080433230426
43662CB00015B/2262